The Archers Anarchists'
Ambridge Jubilee

The Archers Anarchists'
Ambridge Jubilee

Fifty Years of a Medieval Village

Ian Sanderson

First published 2001 by **Boxtree**
an imprint of **Pan Macmillan Ltd**
Pan Macmillan, 20 New Wharf Road, London N1 9RR
Basingstoke and Oxford
Associated companies throughout the world
www.panmacmillan.com

Parts of this book were originally published by Boxtree 1998 as
The Archers Anarchists' A–Z and 1999 as *The Archers Anarchists' Survival Guide*

ISBN 0 7522 2012 8

A CIP catalogue record for this book is available from the British Library.

Designed and Typeset by **Neal Townsend**
Printed by **Mackays of Chatham plc**

Dedication

This book is dedicated to Sammy the Cat (neglected by Peggoi, murdered by Wiwyerm) – Ambridge is less furry without you.

Disclaimer

Books often contain errors and inaccuracies. This one is no
exception and indeed boasts more than most.

Acknowledgements

We would like to thank the many millions of Archers
Anarchists who keep us fed with all the dirt on what really
happens in Ambridge. It would also be appropriate to thank the
cuckoo who stays on in Ambridge until October despite the
departure in July of all his wimpish colleagues to warmer climes.

Becoming an Archers Anarchist

It is just possible that you could be deemed suitable for membership of Archers Anarchists subject to rigorous security checks and the satisfactory completion of a series of initiation rites. For more information on our glorious movement please send a stamped addressed C5-size envelope to:

Archers Anarchists,
15 Hewgate Court,
Henley-on-Thames,
Oxon RG9 1BS.

Contents

Introduction
and Hello

Archers Anarchists appeared suddenly without warning in the summer of 1995, just as Lynda Snell was remembering that she suffers from hayfever and ought to start sneezing. The movement began as a spontaneous uprising against castism. For those unacquainted with what is fast becoming one of the greatest ills in society we should explain that castism is the promotion of impostors, known as 'actors or actresses' who claim to be characters from Ambridge.

We run regular 'Castism Awareness' courses during which people are encouraged to come to terms with their own innate castism. Most of us have a degree of castism in us. Who can honestly say that they have not at some time in their lives uttered phrases such as 'The actress who plays. . .' or words such as 'scriptwriter'? Archers Anarchists urge the nation to confront itself and banish the whole foul lexicon of castism forever.

The Ambridge Jubilee follows the phenomenal success of The *Archers Anarchists' A–Z* and *The Archers Anarchists' Survival Guide*, sales of which have been surpassed only by the Bible and Anthea Turner's autobiography. Due to the eternal nature of *The Archers*, any attempt to catalogue those weird creatures who inhabit Ambridge is constantly thwarted, yet we feel we have a duty at least to try to keep you up to date with the truth. The BBC only tells you what they want you to know whereas we will spare no effort in giving you the darker side of life in Ambridge.

This tome leaps aboard the bandwagon that sees fit in 2001 to mark the fiftieth anniversary of a village that cheerfully admits to being medieval in origin. To put this absurdity into context you might imagine how you would feel if a seventy-year-old threw a party to celebrate his eighth birthday. But if you read on, you will find that this is just par for a very peculiar course in Ambridge.

This book is a fully updated version of the *A–Z* and *The Survival Guide* with revised commentaries on many of the live characters and dozens of new entries. We offer no apologies if descriptions for some people such as Fat Man Forrest are largely the same as before, but you will surely accept that 'once a murderer, always a murderer.' We have dropped some of the previous entries in the interests of space, in so far as space is interesting. But we have retained the main players for the benefit of many people who missed out on the *A–Z* when it went out of print. Don't get eggy if you think we've missed people out – we've either forgotten them or they're too boring to contemplate.

In recent years, the whole discipline of Ambridge seems to have gone to pot. It used to be that you had your speakers and a select bunch of silent people who gradually earned our love and respect. The turnover would always be slow but dignified. Nowadays, however, you find that new silent people are mentioned almost daily, many of them banished from everyone's lips and thoughts within a few days. We have gone to some trouble to remind you of some of these fly-by-nights.

After more than six years of constant battle, not only against castism but against the cosy blandness that can pervade Ambridge for long periods of time, our resolve is as stiffened as Sammy the Cat and as undiluted as one of Lillian's gin and tonics. We wish you well with *The Ambridge Jubilee* and if you end up detesting Shulugh, Horrible Hayley *et al* half as much as we do, it will have been money well spent.

Glossary

Those who are unfamiliar with the affectionate names by which we know some of the characters might be confused. We have endeavoured to list below anyone who is generally known by another less appropriate name.

Angel of Death/Horrible Hayley	Hayley Jordan
Archers Anoraks	The 'official' fan club of *The Archers*
Damien Hebden-Blandvoice	Daniel Hebden
Deeevid Archer	David/Dayvid Archer
Dog Woman	Marjorie Antrobus
Dr Death	Richard Locke
Dr Dim	Tim Hathaway
Edweird	Edward Grundy
Fallen	Fallon Rogers
Foghorn	Jill Archer
Freebie	Phoebe Aldridge
Glucose	Lucas
Handbag Hebden	The late Mark Hebden

Hey Nonne No	Whatever the ridiculous name given to Kate's second child is meant to be. What's wrong with Keith?
Jailbird Carter	Susan Carter
Jaaarn	The late John Archer
Jeck	Jack Woolley
Lancastrian 'Trasher' Tommy	Tommy Archer
Loathsome Lizzie	Elizabeth Pargetter
Mrs High and Mighty	Jennifer Aldridge
Oilslick	Simon Gerrard
Oliver Foxbrush	Oliver Sterling
One-eyed Monster/Cyclops	Mike Tugger (Tucker)
Peeep	Pip
Peggoi	Peggy Woolley
Phallustair Blandvoice	Alastair Lloyd
Poll Doll	The late Polly Perks
Sheyawn Haveitaway	Siobhan Hathaway
Shulugh Hebden-Blandvoice	Shula Hebden-Lloyd
That Fisher Woman (TFW)	The Reverend Janet Fisher
The Village Bicycle	Caroline Pemberton
Wiwyerm	William Grundy
Mrs High and Mighty	Jennifer Aldridge

A SHOCK Every now and then AUNTIE SATIA attempts to get ST USHA fixed up with a 'nice Indian boy'. A Shock was one such suitor who swept her off her feet for all of two days before she moved on to someone with a larger wad.

ACCENTS We have long wondered what exactly constitutes a Borsetshire accent. Various characters in Ambridge, despite never apparently having set foot outside the village, have completely different accents from their brothers and sisters. Whereas HELEN Archer is a Sloane, her brother, when he erupted into speech at the tender age of fourteen, revealed a broad Lancashire accent. More recent speakers amongst the county's youth, such as JAILBIRD's daughter EMMER, DOREEN's daughter FALLEN and EDWEIRD Grundy have a strong West country burr positively dripping with clotted cream. These inconsistencies are by no means a new phenomenon. NELSON, the wastrel son of village idiot WALTER GABRIEL had a cut-glass accent for no apparent reason. The long since DISAPPEARED LUCY PERKS had an accent that was a mixture of posh and Dalek.

ADAM TRAVERS-MACY One of the things people have to realize about Ambridge is that it is the closest Britain gets to some South American state, run by a military junta. Pinochet's Chile was a bowl of roses compared with the number of DISAPPEARED in Ambridge. Adam is one such victim. Begat of Jennifer, then not so MRS HIGH AND MIGHTY Archer, and

Mr Paddy Redmond, an Irish farm labourer, Adam has had three fathers, been kidnapped and bitten by an adder, and has unaccountably vanished to unknown parts of the globe. It is extremely suspicious that the only references to him are postcards or birthday cards that he may or may not have sent. Without any known means of support he just spends his life 'travelling' – that is if he still has a life. Out of the blue, someone purporting to be Adam showed up at HEY NONNE's christening in South Africa. His excuse for his 20-year absence was that he'd been goat farming. Could you make it up? Was it a body double?

ADRIAN MANDERSON We don't go a bundle on Adrians in Ambridge but this one has yet to set foot in the village. He was the smarmball defence barrister at LANCASTRIAN 'TRASHER' TOMMY'S 'Trasher Trial' and rather keen to get inside ST USHA'S sari. So far as we know this relationship is proceeding apace. The difficulty is that if she were to shack up with him, it would almost certainly mean her leaving the village, as Blossom Hill Cottage doesn't have room to swing a ferret. To lose Usha would be. . . bearable.

ALICE ALDRIDGE The years roll by, yet as she approaches her fourteenth year, Alice shows no sign of speaking. But it is only a matter of time and the bookies are already doing steady business on the likely accent. You can get evens on 'OK ya', 2/1 on the standard issue Cornish, 5/1 Brum, whilst a few people are nibbling at an attractive 12/1 on Pakistani with a hint of Black Country. Her silence was duly rewarded at Christmas 2000 when she found a pony in her stocking. Anarchists were somewhat taken aback by this development as we had long wished for SHULUGH to wake up with a horse's head at the bottom of her bed. You can't rely on Santa's receptionist to take a proper message nowadays. Alice allegedly refuses food and seems set to become Ambridge's first anorexic – another triumph for the dysfunctional Aldridges.

ANDREW EAGLETON A philanthropic member of the Borchester Land Board who suffered a gross slander from BIG BRENDA. He owns a Jaguar dealership in London and was kind enough to give a Jaguar to a Borsetshire County Councillor, Stephen Charkham with whom he was seen having lunch. Andrew was doubtless as amazed as the rest of us to discover a councillor in this political desert. Daft Brenda was trying to allege that this had some connection with the excellent proposal to build much-needed houses in Ambridge. She said that the councillor was a 'leading member' of the Planning Committee. This shows the danger of letting a tea girl loose on a journalistic story. Firstly, everyone knows that County Councils don't have planning committees, planning being the responsibility of the District Council. And anyway, if generous Andrew wants to give his friend a wild animal as a present, who the hell is Big Brenda to stop him?

ARCHERS ADDICTS These are the sworn enemies of all decent Anarchists. They describe themselves as the 'official' fan club for *The Archers*, which means they are in the pockets of the establishment. Numbering several thousand conscripts, each wears a worn-out 1970s anorak with a bit of fake rat fur as its collar. Clearly positioned for the proletarian market, they run cruises on ocean-going liners at exorbitant rates. What narks us is that they exist to damage the whole creation that is the Home Service's *The Archers* by encouraging people to meet 'the faces behind the voices and by flogging tacky merchandise which misrepresents the pictures we all have of such hallowed institutions as THE BULL, GREY GABLES, or

BROOKFIELD. They even dare to publish something called the *Borchester Echo*. They exist solely as toadies to the BBC establishment and stand for nothing. Their members regularly desert them in favour of the noble path of Anarchy but we have to do a tremendous amount of deprogramming work on them as they tend to have been brainwashed into believing that there are such things as actors and scripts connected with Ambridge.

ARKWRIGHT HALL Only in Ambridge could they suddenly discover a large, fully built seventeenth-century country house in their village. Seasoned listeners will remember that Arkwright Hall used to be mentioned on a regular basis. It was turned into some kind of community centre and was the hub of the village for the local brat pack. But apparently it disappeared for a couple of decades in that endearing way that Ambridge edifices can, only to come roaring back in 2000 to the apparent amazement of many people who must have become well acquainted with it over the years. The Landmark Trust took it over but it is hard to imagine it proving attractive to holidaymakers. Ambridge has never been known as a great tourist resort and it also seems rather irresponsible of the Landmark Trust to take on a building that has such a propensity to disappear. When the renovations were complete, they invited people to nose around, leading FAT CLARRIE to ask whether 'open house' meant that anybody could go.

AUNTIE SATIA Memorably described by one Anarchist as 'Keith Vaz's Granny' Auntie Satia's role in life is to enforce DIWALI in Ambridge. Like all ethnic minorities in Borsetshire she is highly popular with everyone in the village. In fact the only person who ever demurs is ST USHA herself.

b

BADGER Stripy was the badger lovingly cared for by animal-loving WIWYERM GRUNDY. Unfortunately, with complete disregard for the law, DEEEVID murdered it and then buried it. Badgers are a protected species, and if CLIVE HORROBIN had been indulging in a bit of light badger baiting, the whole village would have gone ape. And was Deeevid completely let off? Is the Pope a Catholic?

BAGGYNSNATCH Never to be separated, these two mates of EDDIE are well hard. You don't mess with them, you don't see them, you don't hear them. But they are never far away if you need a car clocked or someone else's possessions to be liberated in their absence. Tough but fair. You couldn't ask for better friends.

BARKING Although most of the population of Ambridge are completely barking, you hear very little dog noise for a rural community. Admittedly, THE DOG WOMAN is generally heralded by a faint smattering of Afghan baying, but people seem to be able to barge into each other's farms with gay abandon. Anybody who has tried to go within a hundred yards of most farms will know that you have to run the serious risk of being torn limb from limb. Why are dogs so docile in Ambridge? It is a very localized phenomenon because when EDDIE AND NEIL went to construct a patio for MADDY WATKINS a few miles outside the village they were confronted by a whole collection of dogs of differing degrees of ferocity. And being used only to the silent nature of Ambridge hounds they were completely nonplussed and unable to cope.

BECKY (See HENRY)

BEDDY TUGGER This workhorse is in a permanent state of worry and is one of many Ambridge folk who spends her whole life shouting in a rather breathy way. To be fair, life isn't easy for the poor woman. For a start she is married to THE ONE-EYED MONSTER. A few years back it was suggested that Mike might be about to become violent and Beddy fled to THE BULL with the kids. She was on the verge of striking up a non-platonic liaison with SID PERKS, but sadly common sense prevailed.

Beddy was in the village shop on the fateful day that CLIVE HORROBIN and his friend called in to arrange an unsecured loan from the post office. Owing to a totally understandable mix-up, Clive ended up taking the money without asking first. DEBBIE ALDRIDGE and KATE were both in the shop at the time, and instead of saying 'Oh it's all a bit of fuss about nothing' they all raised a great hoo-ha about it and poor Clive became the Ambridge One for a while. Beddy was very un-Christian where poor Clive was concerned and was always resentful whenever he came in to the post office for a stamp or a packet of biscuits for his old mum – all this long after he'd done his time.

Money has been in perpetually short supply in the Tugger household since The One-eyed Monster will always blow any available wonga on a hare-brained 'get rich quick' scheme. It is uncertain how they survive. Beddy always does fairly low-paid menial work – although when she was a cleaner at Home Farm it seems highly likely that she was selling sexual favours to the lecherous BRIAN, and of course working in the post office she will be able to avoid paying for many stamps.

It was therefore rather surprising when Beddy suddenly revealed that she had amassed the princely sum of £2,500 in a maturing account with the Ambridge Friendly Society. Typically she blew it on the tacky wedding of HORRIBLE and

ROY when poor old Cyclops would have preferred a DVD and 'woide-screen' TV.

BERT FRY The most recent in a long and distinguished line of village idiots. Bert is the kind of person who simply doesn't exist, and therefore poses a great challenge to the Anarchist motto. Were a cast to exist, Bert would most certainly be part of it. Bert is essentially the type of person for whom adult literacy classes were intended – which makes it all the more daft that he writes poetry and had the gumption to become a pub quiz cheat. His main purpose is to indulge those of us who are essentially urban and assume that all people in the agricultural sector go 'oooh arrr' at thirty-second intervals. Where we can sympathize with him is in the misery he must endure having to work under DEEEVID and ROOOTH. He has suffered the constant humiliation of being blamed every time his sloppy employers balls up in any way. Who would not have shared his pain in April 2001 when he was kept prisoner in Brookfield for a month with nothing but quiz books to read? It doesn't really matter if and when Bert dies because he, like the other TOKEN OLD FARMING RETAINERS, will automatically be replaced by someone with an identical voice and character.

BEVERLEY Despite having a name that suggests she lives on Atora Suet, Beverley is the mainstay of Lower Loxley. She is silently efficient and manages the Conference Centre against all the odds. To be fair, the job is made easier by the fact that the Centre never seems to have any users apart from a steady stream of Trappist monks.

BIG BRENDA TUGGER Brenda has finally emerged from the depths of some Cornish tin mine and has immediately gone from silent to verbose. Born of pure Tugger stock she predictably has an IQ that reads like half a football score. Emerging from school with the usual worthless certificates in Pokémon Studies she was a happy beneficiary of the Ambridge Job Fairy. No one is unemployed for more than a nano-second in Ambridge before a hitherto unknown job becomes magically vacant. So whereas most people find they need an Oxbridge first before they can even get a job on their local paper reporting the erection of bus shelters, Big Bren waltzed straight into Radio Borsetshire where she instantly became their only reporter. She has the untrained journalist's nose for a good story, which is why we have been treated to riveting documentaries about her father's strawberry-growing disasters. Having a face like a bag of spanners, she has rarely been troubled by suitors,which explains her capitulation to the slime of SCOTT. Signs are that she'll come unstuck trying to mix it with the big boys. MATT CRAWFORD was justifiably livid that she was asking questions about 'matters that don't concern her' and asked BRIAN to put her right on things. Looks like Jack 'The Hat' McVitie might be having some company in the foundations of Crawford Villas.

BISHOP CYRIL The Bishop of Felpersham speaks approximately once every three or four years. He is only occasionally referred to although he is a mucker of JECK WOOLLEY's. For some reason he seemed to stick his crook into the business of ROBIN STOKES and THE VILLAGE BICYCLE when they were considering tying the knot. Being a wise and intuitive old geezer he presumably realized that it was hardly going to be a match made in heaven to splice together a holy joe with a prospective professional murderess (and an atheist to wit). Anarchist respect for Cyril went into sharp decline when he permitted the installation of the obvious fraudster THAT FISHER WOMAN as the vicarette at St Stephen's. He allowed himself to have the mitre pulled well and truly over his eyes and should have listened to PEGGOI who did her best to prevent the whole business. He has done nothing to redeem himself since by ignoring the antics of TFW as she did her best to seduce the appalling DR DIM. Even when he had her bang to rights, if that is not a slightly unfortunate phrase, he came out with a load of platitudinous God-bothering stuff, when what she needed was a taxi to Hollerton Junction and a one-way ticket.

BLACKBERRY LINE John Prescott's integrated transport system received a welcome boost at the end of 2000 when a steam railway suddenly appeared from nowhere. Thanks to the generous-hearted locals, it was soon made to feel at home and no one was tactless enough to question its sudden arrival. It must have been flattered that KATE should choose it as the ideal place to go into labour although it was probably commonplace for heavily pregnant women to decide to have a day out and a train ride on a gloomy December weekday. Lest it should feel insecure and unwanted, the Blackberry Line has since been mentioned every now and then with a regularity that contrasts sharply with the fifty years it took for anyone to notice it.

BORCHESTER FEED MILLS They must have a strange commission system since they were prepared to employ complete divots such as NEIL CARTER who has about as much sales acumen as a bag of pig nuts. On the other hand they also employed a silent bloke called Derek whose legendary sales abilities were forever being rammed down poor Neil's throat at one time. Neil was right to quit, because when a mute is beating you at sales you really have to accept you may not have found your true vocation. In 2001 the county's worst-kept secret was out, Borchester Mills had gone bust. Everyone had known this was on the cards except for dopey DEBBIE who lost a cool twenty grand of Daddy's dosh and a further seven thousand quid of MATT CRAWFORD's hard-earned cash. And then she expects to be trusted to run the farm.

BOONGALOW This strange edifice was constructed for the dreaded DEEEVID and ROOOTH, and all that ungrateful couple have done is moan about it since the day they moved in. Like many Ambridge structures, it has the capacity to shrink or expand so that at one moment all talk is dominated by its overcrowding that would make Calcutta seem like a walk in the park. Then when it suits them you will find Deeevid turning to Roooth, who has only been in another room, saying 'Ah, there you are, I've been looking for you for ages.'

BORING CHRISTINE Although part of our anarchic creed is to gainsay the existence of actors, we have to make an honourable exception in the case of Christine. Her whole being revolves around reading lines in such a manner as to sound as if she is permanently on stage in one of the loathed VILLAGE PRODUCTIONS. Whatever she says is uniformly without conviction. In her seventieth year, she has a deceptively young voice and has a couple of fine hours of note in her history. In the mid-1950s her horse was kindly contributing to a barbecue, presumably for some French people, when busybody GRACE ARCHER offered to take its place. Then in summer 1997, she was at the centre of the great vomit in the duck pond party at the village hall, throwing her weight around left, right and centre and carefully picking up bits of broken glass and diced carrot.

Newer listeners should bear in mind that she drove her first husband, businessman Paul Johnson, to a nervous breakdown. So tortured was he by the pressure exerted on him by the Archer mafia that he crashed his car on the German autobahn. Mystery surrounds the fate of their adopted son Peter. He is barely mentioned by Christine, never apparently visits, and no one ever asks her about him. Clearly another of THE DISAPPEARED.

Christine is only really interested in horses, which is just as well as horses are the only creatures likely to be interested in her. Her reaction when GEORGE was allegedly attacked a few years ago was, by any standard, bizarre. She exclaimed, 'Oh why did it have to happen on a Tuesday?' We all accept that Tuesday is a damned inconvenient time to have your husband beaten up, but surely it wouldn't be at the forefront of the mind of a truly loving wife. When Christine was a Johnson they lived at Wynfords Farm, which had to be sold to pay off debts. Who on earth bought it, because it's never been mentioned since? Perhaps the Americans bought it to put next to London Bridge in the Arizona Desert.

This one-dimensional figure becomes less of an Ambridge player each year. Her sole contribution nowadays is as a back-pain victim, which is of course constantly exacerbated by her propensity to try and leap on horses when she should be sitting in her bath chair eating fig rolls. Anarchists' hopes were suddenly raised when she and her equally boring husband contemplated getting out of Ambridge for good. Unfortunately the destiny of the most boring residents is to remain in the village and live to an offensively ripe old age.

BRIAN ALDRIDGE The village owes Brian a huge debt of gratitude as he is the only serious, job-creating entrepreneur in Ambridge. He has been plagued with problems over the years – being married to MRS HIGH AND MIGHTY, being seduced by THE VILLAGE BICYCLE, having the drippy, directionless DEBBIE perpetually moaning on about not being kept informed.

Brian has stoically fought his epilepsy and runs a thoroughly successful series of farming enterprises. He is forever having to fend off woolly environmentalists and do-gooders but he persists with the right attitudes. Brian knows that the best thing to do with a public footpath is plough over it and hope everyone forgets it was there. Hedgerows are for wooftahs and pesticides get rid of pests – although sadly not all of them.

Sad as we were when HARD-WORKING SIMON left us, we were delighted when Brian formed a consortium with Borchester Land and the excellent MATT CRAWFORD to buy the Estate.

Brian is all man and likes a bit of female variety in his life. He enjoyed his fling with The Village Bicycle and also took a great interest in the Pony Club, where he had another fling with one Mandy Beesborough. The best thing about Brian is that he has a first-class sarcastic sense of humour, a quality to be treasured in a dour village like Ambridge.

Sadly, Brian has shown worrying signs of becoming rather too cosy and verging on the pleasant. His reaction to the saintly GLUCOSE was ludicrously PC and he has even taken to consulting Debbie occasionally and going out for romantic dinners with his wife. Most distressing is his failure to be guided by Matt who is one of those people who always knows the right thing to do.

BSE ANDY An old college friend of ROOOTH'S for whom she clearly carried not only a torch but also a child. Andy's farming specialities were very much in the area of tallow, bulls' semen and other derivatives and he was therefore hit rather hard by the BSE fiasco. If he'd gone in for FLAX this would never have been a problem. Roooth and Andy met again at a reunion – not attended by DEEEVID – shortly after which she announced her pregnancy. Deeevid appears never to have noticed the coincidence of the dates, but when Josh suddenly metamorphoses into a hamburger at the age of 18 the dreadful secret will out.

BULL, THE At the heart of any English village is its local pub. SID PERKS has run down The Bull for nearly 30 years.

A few years ago its fortunes went downhill as villagers deserted it in favour of THE LATE PINK CAT. It was of course entirely in keeping with the liberal-minded nature of Ambridge folk that they preferred the local gay bar to a traditional English pub with boring real ale, darts and conversation. The main problem with The Bull was that KATHY PERKS had a pathological hatred of customers, pubs and cooking. When a landlady of a pub utters the immortal words 'I try and go in the bar as little as possible' you know there is a problem. In contrast Sid has always clung to the old-fashioned and outdated notion of giving good service, which is why he irritatingly says things like 'all part of the service' when someone just so much as thanks him for their change.

Things took a turn for the better when Kathy took off for a week in London. Doreen Rogers turned up and started to give the customers an eyeful of her ample bosom. Overnight, coach parties appeared from every corner of Britain and The Bull was buzzing. Although the pub went back on the critical list when Kathy returned, it underwent a full recovery when Sid called time on her and Doreen moved in.

It should be noted that ownership of The Bull now resides largely with THE VILLAGE BICYCLE but, always ready to make a quick buck, she is quite happy to see Doreen adding those little feminine touches to the place such as pool tables and lager. No need to worry, its future at last seems secure, even if its character has gone down the U-bend.

C

CAMERON FRASER A Scottish person who owned the estate before HARD-WORKING SIMON, he was a good warm-up act for Simon because he too was one of those people who actually wanted to run the whole thing like a business. Indeed he was so keen on business that he acquired various amounts of investment from the more gullible members of the village including THE VILLAGE BICYCLE (amusingly) and THE DOG WOMAN (sadly). The Village Bicycle was only too keen to justify her epithet with Mr Fraser until he became more interested in LOATHSOME LIZZIE. Cameron led daft Lizzie a merry dance, finally inflicting the cruelest punishment that anyone could imagine – leaving her at a motorway service station. It was no thanks to him that she was eventually rescued from a potential life sentence of over-priced, over-cooked food, and people with tattoos playing space invaders. People always tend to speak ill of entrepreneurs after they've gone (just look at the things they say about that nice Mr Maxwell), so you can take with a pinch of salt those who say Cameron Fraser was a crook. Given the lawless nature of Ambridge folk, it is very much a case of pots and kettles. We can only hope that one day he will return to clear his tarnished name.

CAPTAIN The late beloved dog of JECK WOOLLEY was found dead by GEORGE (ALCOPOP) BARFORD – by no means the first time the words 'dog' and 'dead' have followed in close proximity when George is around. No one seems to have tumbled to the coincidence. Captain is now buried in the family vault along with SAMMY THE CAT.

CAT, THE LATE PINK Before the teenage brat pack got hold of it, The Cat and Fiddle was the noble watering hole of such distinguished luminaries as BAGGYNSNATCH Foster, FAT PAUL *et al*, the Bloomsbury Set of Borsetshire. It was also the place where the layabout Grundys always seemed happiest in the days before they joined the establishment. Predominantly patronized by lager drinkers, The Cat was a haven where characters could escape from the establishment figures who were perpetual bar flies at THE BULL. It was run by a succession of ne'er-do-wells until the day that SEAN MYERSON and his partner Peter took it over and turned it into an incongruously trendy place. On a bad night you could almost hear the silly piece of lime sticking out of a bottle of San Miguel and going up some spotty teenager's nose.

At times we have wondered whether or not The Cat was actually a caravan since it seemed to move around considerably. Sometimes it was within earshot of SID's homophobic remarks, whilst other days it could be well on the way to Felpersham. The introduction of wide-screen television just about encapsulated the utter vulgarity of the place. But even bad things have to come to an end and in the perverse world that is Ambridge, it was the Pink Cat that closed down despite being far more popular than The Bull. We were never given any proper economic explanation for this and the Cat's departure is frequently held up by Ambridge's whingeing countryside mafia as an example of the decline in rural services. Far more likely, it just fancied a change of scene and rolled away in the middle of the night.

CELL COUNT This is a subject that has come up a few times in recent years, especially when ROOOTH said that the cell count in Brookfield's milk was falling because BERT kept shouting at the cows. Apparently she thought that you get the best milk by moaning quietly but interminably in a strong Geordie accent. Alas, eventually she had to admit defeat and turn to the obvious panacea for dried-up cows, the CONSULTANT. We were given a sudden insight into the possible cause of the Brookfield cow problem when Phil let drop an apparently dull, but strangely revealing statistic – that their average cell count was 520 with 7 cows over a million. Thanks to the numeracy of a particularly observant Anarchist, we realized that this meant that the size of the Brookfield herd must be in excess of 13,000 cows. It gave us a new respect for Bert, who was surely entitled to raise his voice occasionally, particularly towards the end of evening milking when he was sat on his three-legged stool gazing wearily up at the 12,999th set of udders.

CHANDLER Yet another boring bit of horseflesh, this one belonging to Alice. Rather wasted on her as she never leaves her room. Adhesive manufacturers are eyeing him up enviously.

CLIFFHANGER Not a character but a much lamented institution that Anarchists would like to see revived. More long-in-the-tooth listeners will remember that in the good old days each nightly episode would end with a little cliffhanger. It would be something of the ilk of WALTER GABRIEL calling out 'NELSON, Nelson', there being no reply, Walter exclaiming 'Oh no', and the signature tune cutting in. In those days we didn't have car radios so the next day we'd be double de-clutching like there was no tomorrow to get home on time to hear the outcome. In the event the 'Oh no' would have been because one of Walter's marrows had exploded, but it had us on tenterhooks overnight.

On a Friday, it was the real business with a mega cliffhanger to stop us ditching the Home Service over the weekend and deserting to The Light Programme. This would be the great Ambridge mail van robbery or something with a bit of meat in it. Nowadays there is no proper structure. Cataclysmic announcements are as likely to come in the middle of the programme on a Monday as at any other time. JAAARN's death, which must rank as one of the most harrowing events in the history of *The Archers*, happened on a Wednesday. We are forever treated to soppy endings like THAT FISHER WOMAN saying, 'Happy Easter to you all.' Where is the oomph?

CLIVE HORROBIN Clive has been dealt a real bum rap in many respects. First, he was unlucky in love. Despite his best efforts he was been unable to keep his relationship with SHARON together. He desperately misses his daughter KYLIE and should be given proper access to her. He was then unfortunately mixed up in an overblown incident in the village shop which was all a big fuss about nothing. He simply took some money without asking first, and waved a gun at BEDDY TUGGER in an amusing and playful little gesture. Normal people would have laughed it off but of course Beddy had to go and involve the police, as if they didn't have better things to do.

Clive had the good sense to keep away while he was on remand, and he was simply doing this because he realized how much taxpayers' money it costs to keep people in prison, so thought he would do everyone a favour by fending for himself. JAILBIRD was most ungracious when it came to giving her brother a helping hand, and he ended up back inside. Anarchists were delighted when in summer 1997, Clive returned to Ambridge having done his time and more than paying his debt to society. One or two people, notably THE ONE-EYED MONSTER made various threats against him, but LYNDA SNELL who recognizes that the establishment tend to have a downer on people for no good reason was very helpful in rehabilitating him.

Poor Clive was of course immediately under suspicion

whenever some dozy cow mislaid their purse, but being the good-natured chap that he is, he always took it on the chin. It would have been a heartless cur indeed who did not feel sympathy for Clive when he was fitted up for a minor assault on GEORGE (ALCOPOP) BARFORD – as if Clive would be interested in dead deer. Talk about circumstantial evidence, the establishment were desperate to pin this one on him and were relying on abstruse points of circumstantial nonsense such as George's watch turning up on Sharon's wrist. The treatment and lack of regard for Clive sits in sharp contrast with the acceptance of former armed robber NELSON GABRIEL or the adulation constantly heaped upon murderer FAT MAN FORREST over the years. If you go to prison as a result of an Ambridge crime you get banged up for a good stretch, irrespective of the deed. Most of the IRA have been in and out during the time that poor Clive has been detained. But we remain hopeful, Clive's day will come. We must have patience.

CONSULTANT Ambridge may sometimes be accused of being behind the times, but in its use of consultants it is streets ahead. Even FREDA FRY would think twice before submitting an entry to the flower and produce show unless she had run her preserves by a consultant. However, in Ambridge, consultant invariably means Alan. He is an expert on everything. Thus he was used by LOATHSOME LIZZIE to tell her how someone with no business acumen, education or common sense could run a conference centre. But he was also brought in to Brookfield when they had a problem with accidentally putting antibiotics in the milk and forgetting to test the cows for diseases. He really earned his money on this one, with key recommendations in his mammoth report being that they should remember to test the cows for diseases and make sure they stop letting antibiotics get into the milk. Amazingly he appears to fancy ROOOTH. This can be the only explanation for his suggestion that she, the cause of most of the cock-ups at Brookfield, should consider becoming a consultant.

COUNCIL HOUSES We don't know how many people live in the council houses nor even how many houses there are. We know SHARON and KYLIE lived in one. When they left it was then occupied by some people about whom we know only one thing: that they were annoyed when JAAARN went round to see if the errant SINGLE WICKET TROPHY was still lurking from the days when he used to live there. We can safely assume that the Horrobins live in one, but as far as we know the only other people who live in municipal housing are the elderly folk who live in MANORFIELD CLOSE.

CRAVEN There is nothing we can say of Craven to distinguish him from SPANNER. He seemed to have exactly the same attributes and shortcomings. Indeed they were probably Siamese twins.

CRICKET The village cricket team provides a constant story of acrimony and under-achievement. Rather like VILLAGE PRODUCTIONS, the desire of anyone to participate in the team perennially works in direct inverse proportions to their ability. Thus duffers like Eddie are always trying to get in the team, and the better players always fail to turn up to 'nets'. Captaincy of the team often falls into the hands of relative newcomers rather than established villagers. Thus the team has been led in recent years by SEAN MYERSON, HANDBAG HEBDEN, DR DEATH and PHALLUSTAIR BLANDVOICE. The annual grudge match is against neighbouring Darrington and this inevitably brings out the true spirit of village cricket – fraud, deception and bitter hatred. We never hear any discussion of test or even county matches and no one goes to watch their local county side.

CUCKOO A cuckoo used to arrive in Ambridge around April and be heard in every outdoor scene until July. In 1997 and 1998 it was not heard at all. This was doubtless due to excessive crop-spraying by non-organic farmers. Subsequently, it has shown itself prone to the most erratic and extraordinary behaviour, sometimes still hanging around in October or November. It put in a very early appearance at the beginning of April 2001. We are quite confident that if we could ever gain access to MRS POTTER's abode, we would find a cuckoo happily sitting on a perch in a small cage pecking at a piece of cuttlefish, while a couple of iguanas doze peacefully by the hearth.

DAMIEN Anyone who is familiar with the film *Omen* will realize that the child-creature begat of SHULUGH and a test tube is a child of the Devil. The sight of her, PHALLUSTAIR, DR DEATH, *et al.* desperately wondering what was wrong with him a few years back was pitiful indeed, yet we knew that the only real solution lay in a metal stake, a cross and a good supply of organic garlic from the farm shop. Rather belatedly, people in the village are beginning to comment on his weirdness with frequently used epithets such as 'strange'. One minute he speaks in clipped Oxford tones, the next he reverts to demonic sounds that are not of this world. He often demonstrates the attitude of a spoilt brat, but any old fool can see that he has something of the night about him. He is rapidly acquiring an unnatural interest in animals, particularly stag beetles, hedgehogs and miscellaneous rodents. Even TFW stopped short of agreeing to baptize his hamster when he demanded it. Not long ago he was caught drawing the Brookfield cows. He has developed an unnatural habit of answering all questions using full sentences. When his fangs are fully grown no one in the village will be safe. Already he has attempted to murder his grandmother FOGHORN by placing a toy on the stairs and causing her to break her leg. It is widely believed that as a cloven-hoofed beast, he may have been responsible for the introduction of foot and mouth into Borsetshire. Anarchists demanded the slaughter of his stick insects as a precaution. Listeners are strongly advised to douse their radio sets with holy water after his supernatural tones have desecrated the airwaves. You have been warned.

DAN ARCHER During his long life, Dan was the proud owner of no less than four radically different voices. He was a pioneer of Archer cosiness and he and his old bat of a wife DORIS spent their latter days clucking away in just the same self-congratulatory manner as FOGHORN and PHIL do today. Since the most unpleasant criminals are often the people you least expect, it must be odds on that Dan cunningly hid a very dubious side to his nature. It would not do to delve too deeply into the activities he got up to with Blossom and Boxer, nor should we ask too many questions about their demise. Dan had a vicious side to him – he was very unforgiving towards his younger brother Ben who had attempted to go the distance with young Doris and the poor bloke was banished to one of the colonies. Like many people in Ambridge, Dan was more or less murdered.

LOATHSOME LIZZIE was driving him when they spotted a sheep that needed a helping hand, as sheep so often do. Given a choice between the young healthy Elizabeth or frail ninety-year-old Dan, there was no contest as to who should go to the rescue. So good old Lizzie sat in the car painting her nails while Dan went twelve rounds with the sheep. Needless to say, the sheep won, and Elizabeth picked up a few quid in the will.

DAVE BARRY A policeman and an all-round good bloke. The problem is that everyone in Ambridge is suspicious of policemen, so Dave was only ever really liked by KATHY, who was particularly partial to his truncheon. Like JIM COVERDALE and various passing policemen since, Dave's crime was to try to turn in criminals, in his case NELSON and, as usual, EDDIE. Though he has never returned, we were given a joyous reminder of his dalliance with Kathy when SID pointed out some strong similarities between that event and his own rather more enduring romance with the LILY OF

LAYTON CROSS. Ambridge is a bit like the Maze Prison as far as law and order is concerned. Police are only allowed into the village when invited, and strictly on the condition that they turn a blind eye to any crime. They are never seen in Ambridge though crimes of all kinds, including a healthy number of murders, proliferate.

DEEEVID ARCHER (MURDERER) Listeners will all know that DEEEVID has a bit of a temper on him – and who wouldn't have, being married to the Geordie gorgon, ROOOTH. But newer listeners and those with defective memories may not realize that Deeevid should be locked up and the key thrown away. Back in the mid 1980s he was cutting down a TREE BRANCH with faithful retainer Jethro Larkin (a man who had never harmed anyone) when he allowed the branch to fall 'accidentally' on his head and kill him. Poor Jethro was a goner and this can only have been good news for Deeevid who often complained at the poor man for being a bit slow in his old age. Deeevid got off scot-free and of course there were no witnesses apart from a few million listeners. If there were any justice in the world, Deeevid would have been successfully prosecuted on a manslaughter charge. An effective establishment cover-up yet again, just like the BADGER. More recently Deeevid led a bloodthirsty spade attack on a family of innocent rats, commenting, 'It's years since I had a good rat hunt.' His blood lust is palpable.

Deeevid has no sense of humour. He never relaxes, and is one of those people who makes you feel guilty about enjoying yourself. He is always too busy to do anything except farming, an activity at which he is notably inept. And yet during the glorious Pemberton era he took on a whole chunk of Estate land without apparently increasing staff.

He has an irrational and violent dislike of being called Dave, the knowledge of which KEN TON put to good use in a memorable Brookfield showdown over the future of the farm. Like Roooth, Deeevid feels that he has a right to inherit Brookfield despite there being other family members with an equal claim and without regard to the fact that he and his wife have done their best to run the place into the ground. Phil, very sensibly was minded to leave the farm to his children jointly but on New Year's Eve 2000, Deeevid executed the most dastardly stunt of blackmail imaginable. He went and hid in a ditch under a cow all night, something that many of us would find preferable to standing in a circle holding hands and singing *Auld Lang Syne*. Phil, being essentially a nice bloke but a bit of a sucker, went out looking for him the next day, and was so relieved to find him that he immediately bequeathed the whole farm to him – no strings attached.

Ever since his wife's operation, Deeevid has become massively interested in sex and lewd innuendo between him and Roooth are drearily commonplace. Cynical observers have suggested this might be due to the typically PC attitude of Ambridge dwellers to all matters including disfiguring illnesses.

DEBBIE ALDRIDGE She has the distinction of being the only person in the village to have had four surnames (Travers-Macy, Macy, Aldridge) while only having married once. In fact, probably the only person in the world.

Debbie finds it impossible to strike up normal relationships with men and shows all the signs of having had a very disturbed childhood. She is a real drifter, the kind of person who if she was not bank-rolled by her parents would probably be sitting in a council house watching television game shows all day.

She went to Exeter University but blew that because of a relationship with OILSLICK GERRARD. She got involved with antiques for a while in a very dodgy partnership with crook

NELSON and since then has flitted around the farm working for Daddy. Debbie is constantly moaning about not being consulted on decision making, but then a hard-nosed businessman like BRIAN is hardly going to confide in some know-nothing who will start blabbing around if she doesn't agree with him. Brian realizes that the way to deal with his stepdaughter is to say 'of course I'll consult you' every now and then, but then just go off and do his own thing. She even went as far as claiming to have been offered some job in advertising in London. This was obviously a phantom offer because when Brian trotted out his usual line Debbie decided to stay at home after all.

Debbie had a fling with DR DEATH at one stage but then developed a liking for the Lady Chatterley role. She appeared to go the distance with Steve Oakley, a farm hand who later gave her the old heave-ho. Her liaison with HARD-WORKING SIMON gave her father some hope that he may at last get her off his hands. Sadly she got all upset about Simon's plan to introduce a bit of flax at Grange Farm and cut off sexual relations on the strength of it. This culminated in the unfortunate RIDING ACCIDENT.

The unexpected return of Oilslick to teach Canadian literature to the eager youth of Borsetshire created a bit of a stink at Home Farm. Unaccountably, Brian still finds it hard to accept that the perfect match for his stepdaughter is a serial sexual harrasser of students. Anarchists were very disappointed when Dopey Debbie and Oilslick managed to return from a honeymoon in Canada without encountering his existing wife, but presumably she'll show up at some stage. Though still financially dependent on Brian, Debbie has at last left home and lives with Oilslick in a newly discovered but ancient quarter of Borchester called The Woolmarket. As with ARKWRIGHT HALL, these places that suddenly appear are all very well, but you never know when they might up sticks and disappear. Anarchists have noticed that, increasingly, Dopey can be heard making disparaging remarks about Oilslick and confiding in DEEEVID. It would be terribly unfortunate if anything developed between those two. There would be queues in accident and emergency departments throughout the land as we all received repairs to our split sides.

DEMON DRINK Ambridge has had more than its fair share of inebriates over the years, which is a realistic characteristic much enjoyed by Anarchists. Grade-one boozers would have to include Jack Archer who died of it and GEORGE (ALCOPOP) BARFORD and his former live-in lover Nora Macauley who were both forced to sign the pledge. JOAN PARGETTER could put it away until she went on the wagon with unlikely ease. LILLIAN approaches the sherbets and booze with quite some style and pizzazz. Serious drinkers who don't mess around include the Grundys, THE ONE-EYED MONSTER, TONY ARCHER and LANCASTRIAN 'TRASHER' TOMMY.

DEREK FLETCHER This man is a hero as, along with PEGGOI, he is the only person to maintain his principled stand against TFW. He believes that the woman's place is at the sink rather than the font and is prepared to trundle all the way to All Saints in order to get a proper macho matins. He is the only resident of Glebelands licensed to have an opinion or an identity, but as all applications for a voice box have been peremptorily rejected he tends to need others to fire the bullets for him.

DISAPPEARED, THE There are essentially two categories of disappeared – those who are mentioned but never appear and those whose names never pass anyone's lips. THE

TREGORRANS seem to have left behind no friends in Ambridge though they did silently return to attend FOGHORN's 70th Birthday party. We never hear of Harry and Marilyn Booker. They allegedly live in Penny Hassett yet no one ever bumps into them in Borchester. PAT never mentions, or visits, her Uncle Haydn in Wales although he lived in the village long before she turned up and would presumably like to come and see old friends. Most children of Ambridge residents never come to visit their parents, nor do their parents visit them. Another sinister aspect to the whole business is that newcomers to the village generally have no past, and no relations. We can only conclude that they are someone else's disappeared. The key question is whether Ambridge's disappeared ever left the village. The answer is almost certainly that they didn't – there has to be some explanation for TONY and Pat's rich organic soil. And indeed we recently heard Boring GEORGE comment that the garden at Glebe Cottage has some of the best topsoil in Ambridge. Makes you think.

DIWALI This is an ancient Borsetshire festival, revived by SHIFFON GUPTA, which annually cheers up the whole village in a way that boring old Guy Fawkes night could never do. Each year it becomes a bigger event and nowadays eclipses the Village Fête. A few glasses of carrot juice and a vegetable samosa and everyone is well away.

DR DEATH (MURDERER) There are relatively few intruders from the outside world, and when they enter Ambridge it is as if they are joining a closed order. Richard Locke appeared to have no relations. Indeed he may not even have been a real doctor. Dr Death was without question a murderer. He clearly gave old MRS BARRACLOUGH a little helping hand, and few of us were surprised to learn that she had 'remembered' him in her will. Locke was pretty quiet about just how much he was left or what he did with it, but he was certainly given a fright when MR BARRACLOUGH rightly got the GMC on the case. It transpired that the 'Dr' had failed to keep proper notes. Before shacking up with ST USHA, Locke first set his stethoscope at DEBBIE but rapidly moved on. It was noticeable that he used to make a huge number of house calls, almost always to women. He did this with an enthusiasm quite unparalleled in his profession, members of which usually feel that the only reasonable grounds on which they should be expected to visit a patient's house is to issue a death certificate. Before finally departing for Manchester, Dr Death rogered the dreaded SHULUGH, not without excessive encouragement, we all remember her 'I want you now!' scene that did little to deter him. His unhealthy interest in her while DAMIEN was waiting for his first attempted exorcism had led rapidly to an uncontrolled snog. Despite her saintliness, Usha did not feel inclined to accept Death back given that he had done the business with her best friend. Unfortunately, he had rather burnt his boats because Shulugh did not find the offer of an immediate move to urban Manchester very attractive given that she had a nice little local business, murdering her friends and relations. Even by Ambridge standards his position had become untenable and with Shulugh's propensity to blackmail he was effectively driven from the village. We have never heard sight nor sound of him again.

DR DIM (Thick Person) Dr Dim arrived from Islington, which means he is probably a designer Arsenal supporter who never knows who they are playing next. His background was in the Army so he must be able to strangle someone with his bare hands, always an asset in Ambridge. Doctors in Ambridge are all too often ridiculously nice to their patients and Dim has continued the tradition, making house calls to people who have merely been overheard clearing their throats. In recent years Ambridge doctors have given the medical profession a bad name and Dr Dim has similarly contrived to maintain this low reputation. He turned up in Ambridge with his appalling wife SHEYAWN and set about desecrating the honeysuckle at Honeysuckle Cottage (now renamed Crawford View). It did not take too long before he decided to set his cap at the Vicarette, a mission for which he was given plenty of encouragement. This all got rather exciting at Christmas 2000 when Dim manoeuvred TFW under some mistletoe that was strategically placed in his surgery. Before you could say Consistory Court, TFW found his tongue down her throat. Dim had warmed up for this great moment by thoughtfully giving her a present of a green scarf that he had already given to and had rejected by his wife. Like many husbands he had completely failed to realize that the colour he had chosen was his wife's least favourite. Sheyawn discovered his liaison with TFW by the usual official channels of information in Ambridge, JAILBIRD CARTER. When confronted, Dim consoled his wife by explaining that it had not progressed beyond a snog but that he wished it had. Unfortunately the Dim/TFW relationship seems to have been put on at least temporary hold which is extremely disappointing. We would hope with a bit of luck that TFW could be in the family way before too long, Dim's stethoscope proving irresistible.

DOG WOMAN, THE We like Marjorie Antrobus because she has the ability to be free of malice yet remain unsanctimonious. She is a lonely lady who has done a lot for the village – not least in offering 'no strings attached' cooking and accommodation to some of the dullest menfolk in Borsetshire. If she didn't surround herself with smelly Afghans, she would be a true saint.

Marjorie brings the spirit of the Raj to our multicultural village. You can almost hear the sound of her late husband Teddy's rifle as another tiger bites the dust. She is a true toff and yet she does not despise the riffraff. During her years in the village, The Dog Woman has had a number of platonic relationships with gentlemen of the old school – Colonel Freddie Danby and Rev. Gerry Buckle come to mind. She's always quite keen on vicars and if we have one quarrel with her, it is for tolerating THAT FISHER WOMAN with whom she is often known to demolish a bottle or two of sherry.

Alas, the world's nice people tend to be taken advantage of, and in her twilight years Mrs A has come under the evil spell of HORRIBLE HAYLEY and the neanderthal Racist ROY TUGGER. They have taken up residence in her home on a peppercorn rent and gradually preyed upon her good nature to extort large sums of cash on the pretext that they are hard up. You rarely hear a conversation between them and Mrs A that doesn't involve the need for some more dosh and, nice old bat that she is, she goes tottering off to the pawnbrokers to offload one of her few remaining tiger skins.

At the age of 78, Mrs Antrobus played a leading role in Dopey DEBBIE's hen night and attempted to seduce a whole vanload of rugby players. That's the kind of spirit we like to see in our old folk.

DON AND DOUG These two gentlemen put in a silent appearance at Racist ROY's stag party. Their sole contribution seems to have been removing Tugger's trousers. Everyone can be famous for 15 seconds. It is only to be expected that Tugger should have friends with such a devastating sense of humour.

DOORS CLOSING All doors in Ambridge sound exactly the same (even the FOGHORN's Aga ones) when they close. Now how could that be?

DORIS ARCHER We know what you're thinking – 'Doris Archer was a goddess, Ambridge's Queen Mum. No one, but no one can have a word to say against her, surely?' We're almost scared to comment in case some of the sadder listeners send us poison-pen letters or set fire to our HQ. The truth is that Doris was as boring as hell. She was all jam and cooking and recipes and giving milk to obstinate little lambs that couldn't be bothered to find their mums, and dishing out pseudo 'wise' words. Why is it that when people become old they are described as 'wise'? What generally happens is that we go gaga, and Doris was just the same. By far the worst thing she did was to bequeath her home, Glebe Cottage, to SHULUGH of all people. Just how divisive can you get? She had seven grandchildren plus BORING CHRISTINE's Peter but she still left her house to the dreaded Shulugh. And we'll give you one guess as to who 'found' her dead in an armchair – yep, you've got it, Shulugh.

DROSS You can stick Beethoven, Bach and that lot of posers where the sun don't shine. Real music is that provided by Ambridge's premier and only band – Dross. It consists of EDWEIRD on lead guitar, singer-songwriter FALLEN, the excellent Jazza on drums and maybe someone else. There's nothing like it.

DUCKS Once in a while it is remembered that Ambridge has a VILLAGE POND, and therefore ducks. Small children such as FREEBIE and BSE Josh allegedly feed them. And of course LANCASTRIAN 'TRASHER' TOMMY thoughtfully fed them in 1997. But otherwise they go months, sometimes years without a mention. Now that the village is so cosmopolitan, it's only a matter of time before a Chinese family moves in, and then it will be curtains for the ducks.

e

ECCLES Sid's silent peacock is now a long-term resident at THE BULL and played a major part in the upbringing of JAMIE TEALEAF-PERKS to whom he has been like an elder brother.

EDDIE GRUNDY Some years ago there was a fine and worthy organization called 'The Eddie Grundy Fan Club'. It owed its success to the fact that the Grundys in general and Eddie in particular were reviled by the cosy establishment figures, notably the Archer clan.

There are two clear explanations for the demise of that august body. First, it was an overtly CASTIST organization and used to delight in parading absurd people who claimed to be characters from *The Archers* at its 'Eddie ups'. Second, Eddie has gradually become an accepted bastion of the slightly disestablished establishment. If an equivalent organization were to be formed today it would have to centre on CLIVE HORROBIN, FAT PAUL, FALLEN or someone of that ilk.

Anarchists have long since ceased regarding Eddie as the rebel we would like him to be. Gone are the days when he sought to improve the tone of the piano in THE BULL with the injection of a large quantity of diced carrot, though it is comforting to know at least that he keeps a photo of Dolly Treadgold, his former betrothed, in his guitar case .

For years, Eddie has described himself as a farmer and lovingly reared an endless supply of scrap metal at Grunge Farm. His bankruptcy and eviction from the farm were a just reward for a life of idleness and criminality. Typically he and his family were housed in a luxurious apartment block, Meadow Rise, in

Borchester – the kind of place that could happily have provided shelter to a few hundred asylum-seekers. But there was no gratitude and their return to Ambridge was a retrograde step for mankind. Above all, anyone who pronounces Christmas as 'Crissmerse' is simply beyond contempt.

EDWEIRD GRUNDY We first heard the sound of Edweird when he sang 'Once in Royal David's City' at the Ambridge carol service in 1995 with a voice that made King's College choristers sound decidedly second rate. He then lapsed into silence for a few years until suddenly bursting forth with a peculiar sort of gravelly lout's voice that comes from no recognizable area of the United Kingdom. Edweird is quite a lad and a hot-blooded male of whom we have great hopes. If he has not got FALLEN in the family way by the time you are reading this, he will have failed in his duty. And ideally we would expect EMMER Bedwetter-Carter to be another of his conquests. He has a creditable fondness for the finer things of life, like lager, and comes from a family where lard is the staple diet. Unlike his appallingly goody-two-shoes brother he knows what he wants and he goes for it without bothering anyone else. Thus he helped himself to some of THE VILLAGE BICYCLE's small change without wasting her time in unnecessary prior negotiation in order to fund a culturally enriching visit to Blackpool. He knows his father is an idler so is always reluctant to work for him and he has great musical talent. The generous amount of his free time that he allocates to helping OLIVER FOXBRUSH is very impressive. He could be the first Grundy since Alf to make something of himself.

EMMER CARTER One of the many Ambridge children who ought to have been of interest to the social services. Poor girl used to wet the bed when she was worried about having a

JAILBIRD for a mother. She also began taking things from the village shop without asking first, specializing in sanitary towels. And why shouldn't she? It was only something she picked up from her uncle. Several years back she was being bullied at school by Karen. Typically of the PC Archers, instead of expelling Karen or giving her six of the best, they had a policy of being nice to her and before we knew it Emmer was a guest at Karen's house being plied with hot doughnuts. Perhaps we should have tried this tack with Adolf Hitler – we might have averted a world war.

Emmer, now 17, is developing the more admirable traits of the Horrobins – lying, cheating and educational subnormality. Having dropped out of school, she is now enslaved at LOWER LOXLEY where she works an 18 hour day at half the minimum wage and eats out of a dog bowl. She counts amongst her friends such luminaries as FALLEN and EDWEIRD.

FALLEN The beautiful creature begat of Doreen Rogers and Mr Wayne Tucson is one of those breaths of fresh air that occasionally burst upon the Ambridge scene. Borsetshire born and bred, it goes without saying that she boasts a fine Cornish accent. She is very much following in her mother's distinguished footsteps as a singer-songwriter and slapper and has large quantities of attitude. She carries a torch for LANCASTRIAN 'TRASHER' TOMMY but to date he has not reciprocated so she will probably use it to set fire to his pig arcs. Her position as lead singer in DROSS, the band formed with EDWEIRD and some silent musicians, serves to confirm that punk has finally arrived in Ambridge. Our only slight disappointment to date was at hearing the news that she was working hard for her GCSEs.

FAT CLARRIE In the good old days before political correctness took its stranglehold, there used to be readings on *Listen with Mother* about 'Big Fat Rosie'. The voice used to portray the character was exactly the same as that of Clarrie. She has to wander around Ambridge sounding like some halfwit. It is quite obvious that she is a lump of lard, and why EDDIE settled for her when he could have had THE LILY OF LAYTON CROSS is baffling. She is a beast of great burden and manages to hold down about 15 menial jobs at any given time. It would be hard to find anyone more feckless than Clarrieluv and when you hear complaints about the Government giving people vouchers instead of money, it is because they are thinking of her. Who else, fresh from bankruptcy, would buy a lottery ticket, win 300 pounds and spend it on a guitar? When the local council generously housed her and her family in a pleasant Borchester apartment we heard nothing but moans and she had the cheek to call her poor old father-in-law a 'stupid, selfish old man'. This led directly to him going on the rampage and assassinating three of the nicest, most lovable ferrets you could ever care to meet. Clarrie has undoubtedly got their blood on her podgy hands. But, unlike JAILBIRD, She has accepted her rightful place at the bottom of the pile and for that we thank her.

FAT MAN FORREST (MURDERER) The thing that many people forget about the late dear old Uncle Tom is that he was a murderer. Some years ago he shot and killed Bob Larkin who was allegedly poaching. More to the point, and for some unaccountable reason, Bob had his eye on PRU (this was before Tom and Pru were married), and it was highly coincidental that Tom should 'accidentally' kill him. Unsurprisingly the village establishment closed ranks and backed Tom. He was acquitted in a court case redolent of the justice system of some banana republic.

In 1996, evidence came to light to suggest he may be a war criminal. A German bomber was dug up in the village with the pilot still in it. Tom seemed to know about the crash so why didn't he rescue the poor hun?

Fat Man Forrest has often been one of the stomach-churningly cosy characters, always poking his nose into other people's business, always ready with a disapproving view on things, and boring beyond measure. His tendency to sing *The Village Pump* and other boring old folk songs was to be deplored. Towards the end he became quite gaga. But in Ambridge, all gaga people suffer from 'Saundersism' – a rare condition that renders the sufferer completely incapable one minute, and like a contestant on *Round Britain Quiz* just a few moments later.

Like his wife, Tom was dragged kicking and screaming to

THE LAURELS, but still emerged to hold thoroughly lucid conversations, with barely a discernible 'um' or 'er'. Fat Man Forrest had the distinction of being one of those few characters who moved from being detested by Anarchists to being quietly respected by us. This is mainly due to the fact that he went from being nauseatingly cosy to being a cantankerous old bar steward. He was crotchety, unreasonable and negative about everything. But at the end of the day he was a murderer and should have be treated as such.

As you sow, so shall ye reap and Fat Man was himself murdered amid a frenzied barrage of scones from FOGHORN. A double murder, including PRU, it was followed by a typical Ambridge cover-up. No one even asked about the cause of death, though we have no doubt that both were on the wrong end of a batch of poisoned scones in order to hasten the time when Foghorn could inherit moi Pru's recipe book.

FAT PAUL There is a whole bunch of people in society who eschew the services of our high street banks on the grounds that they charge heavily for lending wonga. This is understandable, but what is less easy to follow is why they look instead to the fattest slob they can find in the most seedy of pubs where they instead enter into an agreement to borrow money on generous compound interest terms of 50 per cent per day. Mr Fat Paul is just such a person, though he is more of a broker. For it was he who fixed the lazy and inefficient Grundys up with a backbreaking loan through a friend of his. Fat, is yet another of these metaphysical characters who only exist when you need them. Despite his size, he is never bumped into by anybody and never generally comes up in conversation.

FEATHERS, THE A posh pub out of the village where some of the nobs go when they want to get their ends away. Whilst the place gets no mention for years on end, if a character ever does go there, they inevitably meet someone else from Ambridge whom they are wanting to avoid, but then that also applies to any eating or drinking establishment outside the village.

FERGIE, THE Considering it was only a tractor, The Fergie really did play a starring role over a period of time. It was falsely accused of murdering poor JAAARN, yet we all know that it was not really to blame. Earlier it had been accused of nearly causing TONY to get involved in a little extracurricular activity with a weird girl called Sandy who had a particularly unhealthy interest in old tractors. After Jaaarn's death, Tony exiled it to some Fergie museum, which we can assume is the tractorial equivalent of THE LAURELS. It is ironic that the dreaded Archers Anoraks calendar showed Tony lovingly tending his Fergie in June 1998, some months after he had disposed of it.

FIFTEEN MINUTES This is the standard answer to the question 'How long is a daily episode of *The Archers*?' It is also completely untrue. It has to share the space with the news, adverts for other radio (and even television) programmes and blatant commercials for the dreaded Archers Addicts. The programme is now some meaningless and variable length.

FLOWER AND PRODUCE SHOW, THE This is a good event that always manages to create genuine acrimony and adds nicely to the sum of human misery. There is generally some rivalry over the quality of jam on show or the size of marrows. Unfortunately some of the great protagonists are now themselves part of the fertilizer – WALTER, FAT MAN FORREST, PRU, MARTHA.

A village has to have a super-cook, someone who enters every class at the show and expects to win as if it is their birthright. Nowadays this is the silent FREDA FRY. Having a husband with such an absurd voice is obviously something of a deterrent to having a voice herself so she throws her weight into produce manufacturing. There are the inevitable bit-part players such as FOGHORN who drearily enter their Victoria sponges – indeed the year 2000 saw her romp home with 2nd prize for runner beans. A new entry appeared in the same year from ST USHA: lemon curd – rather surprising for a woman who appears to live on take-aways, but then we suspect she had just relabelled a jar she'd bought from UNDERWOODS. The judges used to be people of stature, but now it's as likely as not to be TFW. How times have changed.

FOGHORN Where would we be without Jill? A darn site happier. At least it would be easier to keep our evening meal down. Not to put too fine a point on it – she sucks. She is the epitome of cosiness. Jill is to the fore in those dreadful episodes where the 12 minutes have elapsed but nothing has happened. It's been 12 minutes of Jill saying, 'Aren't we lucky Phil?' and 'If only your mother could have seen little Daniel', and 'I'm worried about SHULUGH, she didn't have a third cup of tea this morning when she called round', and 'Do you know it's our 300th wedding anniversary and it only seems like yesterday. Come over here and give me a kiss', and 'I've made plenty of supper if another six million people would like to come round into our warm cosy. . .' Urgh, urgh, urgh. Please pass the sick bucket.

FOGHORN. . .AGAIN We had to break off the last entry to get a pint of milk of magnesia but there is more to be said about Jill. Early in 1998 she suddenly 'came out' as a business expert. After years of saying 'yes sir, no sir, three bags full sir' to her dreary beloved husband, she temporarily took on a mind of her own and supported DEEEVID and ROOOTH in their plans to expand the cow herd. PHIL was needless to say gutted, and refused to speak to her for three days on account of her gross insubordination. Sadly they kissed and made up in the cosy way that only these two paragons could, and we were back to normal. Her judgment was of course impeccable and Deeevid and Roooth have long since shown to be incapable of looking after animals properly.

There were times in the past when the Foghorn was muffled. In one of few mentions of the word LAVATORY she memorably collapsed in one. She also had a kind of nervous breakdown at one time. This was clearly induced by having to re-enact the feeding of the five thousand on an hourly basis.

Notwithstanding any health problems in the past, Foghorn has become super-human and the older she gets the more she takes on her shoulders. She keeps bees and chickens, runs a bed-and-breakfast business, does child-minding for all and sundry, takes part in VILLAGE PRODUCTIONS, serves on any committee that is formed, and her cooking activities are ridiculous.

In her twilight years Foghorn seems finally on the verge of being prised out of Brookfield and out to grass. Yet she becomes ever cosier and shouts more by the day. Foghorn will only be shaken out of her perpetual state of cosiness when Deeevid eventually mistakes Phil for a rat and attacks him with a spade and when it is conclusively confirmed that DAMIEN is indeed the son of Beelzebub.

FOOT AND MOUTH Brookfield first suffered foot and mouth disease in 1956, but predictably in 2001 news of the latest outbreak was slow to reach them. It did not become a topic of interest for a couple of days after the rest of Britain's rural communities had already been gripped by fear. It clearly posed a great dilemma for the people of Ambridge who, to a man (or woman) regardless of racial origin or sexual orientation, were desperate to do the right thing by New Labour. The situation was 'under control' and therefore no one in THE BULL was allowed to venture otherwise. But in order not to appear too cavalier, DEEEVID AND ROOOTH suddenly bought six litres of disinfectant and barricaded themselves and a few other hostages inside Brookfield. Of course the village was still very much 'open for business', so in stark contrast people on the other farms constantly visited each other, held parties like EDDIE and TONY's 50th birthday celebrations, went to restaurants and generally did their best to spread the disease. And in order to prove that it was perfectly in order to proceed with election campaigns, all the do gooders who wanted to keep Loxley Barrat School open went round delivering leaflets to all the farms who were only too pleased to see them. We were only surprised that the general Borsetshire public did not heed the words of the Government more enthusiastically, as we expected to see coachloads of people arriving in the village to purchase things from the village shop and walk on the delightful tarmac roads that were still perfectly accessible to ramblers. The moment there was a hint that the outbreaks were reducing and Deeevid had received his call from Alastair Campbell, the gates of Brookfield were immediately flung open and it was all hunky-dory.

FOOTBALL Our national sport, yet it is barely mentioned in Ambridge apart from the occasional haphazard kick around in the village. A few years back EDDIE took his boys to see Aston Villa, but that's it. No one at the THE BULL ever chats about the weekend results. The regularly poor form of Aston Villa generally goes unnoticed and no one was the slightest bit interested when Birmingham reached the League Cup Final in 2001. DR DEATH used to allude to being 'mad on football' yet neither he nor anyone else commented on the results of key games in the 1998 World Cup. ROY TUGGER is said to be 'crazy about Aston Villa' which could lead us to wonder why he manages to last years at a time without mentioning them. Once in a while it is said of someone 'oh, he's watching the football' but it is noticeable that no alleged football watcher ever emerges after the game to comment on the result.

FRANK BANNERMAN By no means unique in the chronicles of Borsetshire history, poor Frank Bannerman was pronounced dead in his middle age without apparently ever having lived. Given the number of Ambridge folk we would just love to see sent on their way, it is a tragic waste of death for Frank to have suffered such a fate. He left behind a silent wife, Elaine, and a quantity of farm machinery. Eddie, to his credit immediately went to work giving Elaine the full service and even managed to come away with a tractor for his pains. How it was that these great mates of Eddie had never been round for a lard supper with him and Fat Clarrie or even so much as a half of Shires at the Bull, or even had their names uttered by the Grundys, we cannot explain.

FREDA FRY At any given time there has to be a jam and home produce fascist who seeks to achieve village domination as the supreme producer of pickles, jams, cakes and vegetables. This role was filled for many years by moi PRU, with the occasional pretender to the title such as the late MARTHA WOODFORD. It seems that the baton has now passed to Freda. Since she is the microwave operative at THE BULL, she obviously has a flair for these things. Unencumbered by the burden of speech, Freda is able to devote all her energies to producing the most phallic marrows. Being married to BERT must be a miserable experience, having to listen to the old git's ramblings and poetry. The arrival of THE LILY OF LAYTON CROSS to replace customer-hating KATHY in 2000 caused Freda reportedly to express the view that Doreen was 'no better than she ought to be.' Anarchists have sat for many hours with wet towels over our heads trying to ponder this statement, but eventually we have to hold our hands up and admit we can't.

FREEBIE Some of the less reasonable listeners may have thought that KATE was wrong to take a little holiday without her child, but the real horror was how this nice upper middle-class West Indian child degenerated into Tugger riff-raff in such a short time. The child of a liaison with eco-warrior Luther, Freebie was wrongly decreed to be Roy Tugger's child despite having dreadlocks and an innate sense of rhythm. At a very formative time she learned to speak with no consonants and developed a taste for the less fine things of life. By the time poor Kate returned she had acquired the working-class epithet 'Feebs', was hearing BEDDY TUGGER referred to as 'Nanna' and was well down the road to Kyledom. Like many Ambridge children she preceded her enforced silent period with a short spell of manic gurgling at an age when most children can't stop talking. The poor child has been brainwashed by HORRIBLE HAYLEY so that she is often upset and confused when she meets her real mother. There seems no reason why she shouldn't be in jolly Jo'burg with HEY NONNE and her real family.

g

GAY PRIDE Many national events go unnoticed in Ambridge but one that certainly did not was the annual Gay Pride March. This event, in which homosexuals get together in London, was the talk of the village in 1997 for about ten days before it occurred. Obviously the reason for its prominence was that SEAN completely abandoned the CRICKET team of which he was captain in order to go to this great festival. With the exception of SID PERKS, the whole village was entirely understanding and supportive. The likes of THE DOG WOMAN were to be heard saying, 'He's going to Pride you know' as if it was a meeting of the over-60s. The late but highly heterosexual JAAARN took it in his stride as if he expected the whole village to take a coach to Hyde Park. Apart from DIWALI it is now the most important date in the calendar of rural Borsetshire.

GEORGE (ALCOPOP) BARFORD George is Yorkshire's answer to THE ONE-EYED MONSTER. He is forever whingeing about something or other and has a chip on his shoulder that would take a baking potato to fashion. His main claim to fame, apart from liking the odd glass or 20, is that he murdered Patch, the beloved mutt of the now departed and forgotten ROBIN STOKES, who was once the unpaid vicar of Ambridge. Needless to say he was never reported for laying poison traps using prohibited chemicals.

George plays the cornet and chairs the parish Politburo. In 1997 he was assaulted for trying to impede the progress of some honest country folk who were, on a totally voluntary basis,

culling some of JECK WOOLLEY's deer. He made something of
a palaver over this event, took absolutely ages off work and, in
order to assist his malingering, developed some sort of designer
form of agoraphobia.

Now married to BORING CHRISTINE, Barford (a former
policeman) deserted his Yorkshire wife Ellen and their two
children, Terry and Karen, with the result that Terry went off the
rails and turned to crime. He has basically taken over the role
previously given to WALTER GABRIEL of making a rather silly
and disapproving 'doh' noise every other sentence.

When the time came for Barford to hang up his gun we were
given an insight into his deceitful nature. He calmly received a
long-service award for gamekeeping without volunteering the
fact that the time span seemed to cover a period of time when he
was actually in the police force. He is the holder of a particularly
absurd office, namely the Ambridge Tree Warden, the purpose of
which baffles all of us.

Unfortunately, since his retirement, he has become more
benign and thus boring, perfectly complementing his wife. But
life with the Barfords is not always dull and there are few
Anarchists who will ever forget the riveting episode in March
2001 when the two of them struggled to get a duvet into its cover.

GINGER SPICE The calf lovingly reared by arsonist
WIWYERM GRUNDY until it was manslaughtered by layabout
father EDDIE who failed to clear up a whole host of ring pulls and
other scrap metal from his fields. Cows are pretty stupid and
don't seem to be able to taste the difference between a succulent
mouthful of grass and half a drink can – until it's too late. THE
VILLAGE BICYCLE kindly replaced Ginger Spice with Posh
Spice: a Jersey heifer. Since it is apparently still alive, we can only
presume Posh Spice is more partial to a ring pull pasty. The idea
that you might get David Beckham turning up and leaving the

gate open is enough to make you think seriously about turning the beast into quality leather goods at the earliest opportunity.

GLUCOSE The only positive contribution that KATE's husband made to Ambridge life was being in possession of a return ticket to Cape Town. He is the nicest, kindest, most syrupy, thoughtful, wonderful, even-tempered, considerate, understanding human being that ever trod the Earth. For all this we detest him. Obviously forewarned by Kate that Ambridge is the most liberal-minded village in Britain, he was embarrassed to be a Boer and made strenuous efforts to pretend to be black. Armed with a fake Afro-sounding name – Madagascar – he found that everywhere he went in the village he was known and welcomed like an old friend. Even BRIAN took to him. And his disguise paid off handsomely with no one being heard to say 'Who's that white South African guy who's suddenly turned up in the village?' or 'Fancy Kate knocking around with a white bloke.' This man is just a saint, a Cadbury's Cream Egg incarnate.

GRACE ARCHER One of the establishment icons, Grace was a silly empty-headed woman who, had she lived, would have condemned herself to a life of jam making and servile subjugation to good old reliable PHIL. Made of poor-quality flammable material in an era prior to EU directives on such matters, Grace went up in smoke, which was highly inconsiderate since she was supposed to be at a dinner party at the time. The real tragedy about her demise back in the 1950s was that a load of sad listeners sent flowers to the BBC. These people now have several worthy alternative activities available, such as anorak wearing, joining the dreaded Archers Addicts, or queuing overnight for the January sales. Phil used to comment on the anniversary of her death and even the

FOGHORN would respectfully lower the decibel level of her voice to deafening. But we don't seem to observe the occasion nowadays.

GRAHAM RYDER We are clearly not intended to like Graham. He was brought in by HARD-WORKING SIMON to manage the Estate when it became clear that the dreadful SHULUGH was making such a Horlicks of it, acting in a thoroughly unprofessional manner and letting her personal feelings get in the way of work. Graham, on the other hand, is cheerful and efficient.

At the Estate office Christmas party in 1996, while SHULUGH was looking like a wet weekend, Graham was the life and soul with a string of tasteless jokes. This went down well with Hard-working Simon who likes to let his hair down on these occasions. The fact that the Estate has been sold and partially broken up does not seem to bother Graham who still seems to be managing it. He continues as one of BRIAN ALDRIDGE's henchman and plays a kind of Goebbels role. Graham at one time seemed very keen to get on the business side of THE VILLAGE BICYCLE's aristocratic knickers, but one does begin to wonder about the bloke when he persuades a very reluctant Bicycle to go to a posh eight-star hotel in the Lake District, only to tell her when they get there how he doesn't fancy her. Graham is obviously completely screwed up and doesn't know whether he's best going for her, her horse or just maintaining a casual relationship with a flock of sheep. A great friend of PHALLUSTAIR BLANDVOICE, this relationship is presumably maintained, in large measure, to ensure a constant supply of animals.

GREG TURNER The keeper employed by BRIAN ALDRIDGE arrived in what was, for Ambridge, a most unusual manner. He was recruited for the job, his impending arrival was heralded and when he turned up he was introduced to people and spoke. This must have caused a whole host of petty jealousies in the village amongst those who thought he should have served his time before being allowed to speak. It seems *de rigueur* for keepers to be miserable sods with major attitude problems and Greg certainly fits the bill. He also fits in well with the essential role of any employee at Home Farm which is to resent DEBBIE and more or less ignore anything she asks to be done.

On his first day, Greg was accosted by poacher's son and arsonist WIWYERM GRUNDY who had been sent by FAT CLARRIE to 'introduce' himself. Dense Debbie failed to understand that Greg wanted to settle in and that welcoming Wiwyerm was about as sensible as inviting a fox to a hen-house. Greg made a great start by going to Brian for 'arbitration' the very first time he was asked by Debbie to do something with which he disagreed, and good old Brian backed up his professional keeper over the university drop-out. Greg obviously carries more baggage than Posh Spice. As with most incomers, he has no past, relations or visitors – just loads of attitude. There is little doubt that he is a murderer, but we just have to be patient and wait for him to strike.

GREY GABLES There are some very sinister aspects to Grey Gables, which tends to emulate the Bates Motel rather than a large country house hotel, with country park, health club and golf course. One mystery is that it has virtually no staff although this is rarely a problem since it never really seems to have any guests either – even when it is full. It is rare for an unknown face to venture into the village shop but you might expect a fair number of guests to pop by. Occasionally even the riffraff of the village save up their euros and go for a meal at Grey Gables, but as with all other such establishments they only ever bump into other villagers. None of the locals ever plays golf, leading us to believe some of the bunkers have probably been constructed to incorporate generous numbers of THE DISAPPEARED. JECK and PEGGOI are not getting any younger and it will be interesting to see what happens to the place in due course. Anarchists would love to see the return of HARD-WORKING SIMON as proprietor – just imagine THE VILLAGE BICYCLE's reaction! But a more likely bet would be for MATT CRAWFORD to get hold of it – the country park and golf course should be good for several thousand houses.

GUY PEMBERTON He was one of a whole string of fat cats to buy the Estate, taking up where CAMERON FRASER had left off. Quite a nice bloke, he was unquestionably a kindly soul but Anarchists always took the view that he was too boring to live. THE VILLAGE BICYCLE was very quickly interested in the copious amounts of wonga he had about him. This was the beginning of his downfall. As a businessman, Guy instinctively realized that he ought to let his son, HARD-WORKING SIMON, make the decisions regarding the Estate, but sadly he let his dick do the talking.

Once they were married, The Bicycle immediately established a regime of non-stop nagging, consistently trying to get the poor bloke to haul Simon over the coals. The final denouement came when she was bawling out Guy over the phone in order to make him poke his nose into the HARRIET WILLIAMS business. He finally croaked it with a massive heart attack. Had Ambridge had a proper doctor instead of DR DEATH, this would have been put down as manslaughter, and Caroline would have gone the way of JAILBIRD CARTER for a while. Instead she pocketed the Dower House and half a pub with a 'thank you very much', clearing the way for the arrival of the next businessman to the village.

h

HANDBAG HEBDEN The only party political politician ever to have appeared in the village, Handbag Hebden was universally acknowledged as one of the most boring characters ever to run into a horse. Even SHULUGH (and this really is saying something) almost gave him the elbow because he was such a drip. Only his fat cat lawyer's salary made her see monetary sense. Anyone else but Shulugh would have seen the danger signs: a bloke who was a councillor for the SDP and had a mother called BUNTY was bound to be pretty dire. As memory of him fast fades, there is little to recall of him: he liked CRICKET, he brought the first ethnic minority into the village (ST USHA), and he left a test tube of sperm with which to enable the construction of DAMIEN.

HARD-WORKING SIMON Several Anarchists threatened to stop listening the day Hard-working Simon Pemberton was finally driven from the village. Never in the history of Ambridge has a man been so wronged. Already running a thriving business in Leamington, with his insatiable capacity for hard work he thought nothing of taking on the running of the Estate. It was inevitable that Simon's efficiency would cause problems for him, given that the Estate had been run by SHULUGH as a kind of family social club. Simon was keen to change the atmosphere in the Estate office so that it ceased to be a drop-in centre for JAILBIRD CARTER and SHULUGH's endless number of friends and relations.

Simon had tried to befriend Shulugh, but we know how she

reacted in the SLAP incident. His father, the goody-goody but harmless GUY PEMBERTON, had never given him the support he deserved, and once poor Guy fell into the avaricious clutches of THE VILLAGE BICYCLE, Simon was never going to succeed in Ambridge. The whole establishment turned against him when he tried to change the role of Grange Farm from scrap metal yard to that of a proper working farm with a decent crop of flax. The hypocrisy of the villagers was such that all the people who had spent years moaning about the Grundys were lining up to defend them when Simon tried to do something about them.

Shrewd businessman though he was, Simon made the mistake of giving some of the farming to DEEEVID and the ramshackle Brookfield operation. This caused him nothing but hassle and he was all set to take the work away from him. The big problem that he found was that none of the people he tried to do business with could separate their business lives from their personal lives. The straw that broke the camel's back was when DEBBIE ALDRIDGE, who had happily been playing hide the sausage with him, suddenly tried to blame him when she had a RIDING ACCIDENT. His defence lawyers attributed the whole business to OVERENTHUSIASM.

Always prepared to take the rap, Simon was a complete gentleman in court and Debbie was not even forced to give her perjured evidence. He did permit himself a well-deserved smile as he left the court, because he knew he was now off to Saudi Arabia for a good long time. We like to think he went off with HARRIET WILLIAMS, the only woman who really cared for him.

HARRIET WILLIAMS One of the most influential characters never to speak, Harriet was an old flame of **HARD-WORKING**. When her marriage hit a rocky patch, Simon kindly paid his respects to her. As far as we know, this did not include any OVERENTHUSIASM. A slight problem arose when Harriet kept phoning him at the Estate office and it transpired that this liaison was running concurrently with his rather misguided wooing of the dreaded SHULUGH.

THE VILLAGE BICYCLE blabbed to both Shulugh and GUY and indeed used her knowledge of this little matter to murder Guy in due course. For no apparent reason, calls from Harriet ceased soon after that SLAP – which was rather odd since the way should have been clear for her with Shulugh out of the picture. Harriet turned up at Guy's funeral following his murder, and of course this went down like Gerry Adams at an Orange Lodge with Shulugh and The Bicycle. It would be nice to think that she and Simon managed to get together in Saudi where Simon was heading after his minor court appearance. Hopefully she was able to give him the love and affection which had eluded him for so long and eventually they can live happily ever after in Leamington.

HAY FEVER Despite the increase in asthma and pollen-related allergies often induced by modern crops such as rape, Ambridge has only managed to increase the number of sufferers in its midst from none to one. LYNDA SNELL, because she is an outsider from Sunningdale, dutifully suffers in true Forsterian fashion during the season, whenever she can remember. This doesn't seem to stop her from keeping a large number of pet animals. Happily she often seems to forget her allergy and it is quite normal to hear her uncongested tones at the height of the hay fever season. In 1998 it was suddenly mentioned that she was having hay fever injections, the total success of which will come as a great surprise to most people who have resorted to the same remedy. But since then it seems to have returned with a vengeance. The poor woman often seems to get it worst when other sufferers are perfectly fine. She can be heard sniffing and sneezing away while the rest of us are witnessing unprecedented wet weather.

HAZEL WOOLLEY Why, oh why can we not have a return to Ambridge for the lovely Hazel? She always caused mayhem whenever she came to the village – particularly upsetting THE VILLAGE BICYCLE, which can't be a bad thing. Hazel would really get up PEGGOI's nose, and although she is only the stepdaughter of JECK, it is rather odd that she never turns up now. So far as we know Jeck is about the only family she has, as her mother Valerie Woolley is now pushing up the daisies. Peggoi phoned her in 1999 to invite her to Jeck's eightieth birthday party. When she answered the phone she was delighted to hear from her because she assumed Peggoi was ringing with the good news that Jeck had snuffed it. When she realized that it was to attend one of Peggoi's enforced enjoyment sessions, she sensibly stayed away but did send a delightfully large card hoping that Jeck would 'have a ball'. You can't get much nicer than that. To many listeners, Hazel is just a name, but to the diehards she is the thinking man's SHARON.

HENRY (See BECKY)

HEY NONNE NO Named after an English Madrigal, the Child of KATE and GLUCOSE was born in December 2000. Literally translated, the name is Africaans for 'snotty little brat who is going to be pampered with unnecessary fripperies by her snobby Grandma'. It is the most beautiful baby in the world bar none.

HEYDON BERROW This is another of the places that people are often 'over at/in' – just like MARNEYS or LAKEY HILL. We envisage it as the local rubbish tip, maybe boasting a little shelter that smells of urine, a place where the methane is building nicely towards a spectacular display of pyrotechnics on the day of Armageddon.

HIGGS JECK WOOLLEY's chauffeur and chrysanthemum grower. John Higgs is one of those characters who people will often claim have never spoken. This is not true, as he has uttered several words from time to time, and has emitted some particularly fine grunts over the years. On one occasion he was drunk as a skunk and was highly audible. Apart from LYNDA, THE VILLAGE BICYCLE, ROY of the racists and JEAN-PAUL, no one at GREY GABLES has much to say, so he is only par for the golf course.

HORNY HUGH A 'business friend' of LOATHSOME LIZZIE's who was/is hung like a horse. Elizabeth was disappearing for weeks on end to run 'courses' for him, leaving drippy NIGEL to hold the fort at LOWER LOXLEY. We were in no doubt that this was cover for the fact that hide the sausage was being played in a big way. The biggest give away was that Elizabeth had only been in business at Lower Loxley for five minutes and was clearly struggling to market her own enterprise. On the basis that 'those who can't, teach', it may have been just about plausible but we all sympathized when Nigel objected to her absences. Nigel may be stupid, but even he smelt a rat when, one weekend, Elizabeth announced that Horny Hugh had turned up unexpectedly in the area and that she would therefore have to entertain him. After all we are talking about a bloke from London who is a mere 90 miles or so from home, not an American tourist. Horny was putting good money her way, but everyone realized that this was the launch of her career as a hooker rather than as a John Harvey-Jonesette. Horny is the father of LILYNFREDDY.

HORRIBLE HAYLEY Those who have listened for a few years will remember that a girl called Julie worked at THE BULL for a while in the early 1980s. The similarities between her and Horrible are quite striking. Both were tarty Birmingham girls with Brum accents. Both reacted initially to life in Ambridge as if they had landed on the Moon. Both made a beeline for pig farmers, (Julie for NEIL, Hayley for JAAARN) and then proceeded to moan that they were only interested in their pigs and that pigs smelt etc. And both entered into totally unsuitable arrangements with their chosen blokes.

One of the most distasteful features of Horrible in this PC world is that she is overtly sexist and treated Jaaarn as a sex object. She was forever referring to 'his cute little bum' (when children might be listening – no wonder young people are in the state they are), and making sexual innuendo. It was quite understandable that he sought solace in the true love of SHARON – someone who wanted him for his wallet as well as his body.

Horrible is as tactful as an atomic bomb and is frequently putting her foot in it – a particularly memorable occasion being when she 'inadvertently' told ROY TUGGER about KATE's first pregnancy. The night before Jaaarn went FERGIE racing, he took Horrible to THE MONT BLANC where he proposed to her. She turned him down flat, and of course the moment he turned up his toes she was sobbing all over the shop and telling everyone how much she loved him.

The irrationality with which Hayley decided that she wanted to take over Jaaarn's pig business, despite living with her mum in Birmingham and not having had any agricultural training, indicates that she really should have been sectioned under the Mental Health Act. Her antics have since grown ever more insidious, and are reported in detail in their own chapter later in this book.

HOWARD FRIEND Howard was an interesting character whose allegedly malign influence has disappeared without trace or comment. He came on the scene to oppose TONY and PAT's attempts to enlarge their farm shop. On the face of it this was due to environmental reasons but Tony's millimetre-long fuse soon blew when it transpired that the bloke was intending to open his own organic shop. Tony is the Wall Street of the organic vegetable retailing world and when he sneezes THE ONE-EYED MONSTER catches a cold. In a small area it would have been reasonable to assume that a second organic retail outlet would pose a threat to Tony and then Mike, but for a long time we heard no more about it until LANCASTRIAN 'TRASHER' TOMMY suddenly remembered that he was just round the corner and started selling him sausages like there was no tomorrow.

HUNTING AND THE COUNTRYSIDE It has to be remembered that people in Ambridge would rather go to GAY PRIDE than a countryside march and as horny-handed sons of Blair they are very shy to admit to any real interest in hunting or rural pursuits. Some of them do go hunting, notably SHULUGH and PHALLUSTAIR, Dopey DEBBIE and of course THE VILLAGE BICYCLE and OLIVER FOXBRUSH, but they do it very quietly and apologetically. There are no hunting horns and the dogs are all muzzled so that you don't hear them. You do get a bit of shootin' going on at Home Farm and GREY GABLES but very little fishin'. DAN and FATMAN used to fish in the Am and PHIL has been known occasionally to dip his rod. Come the next countryside rally, you'll probably find there's a spare seat in the two-seater of the one person who bothers to go.

ILLNESS Ambridge is generally a very healthy place. Until recently it was extremely rare for someone to have a serious illness that hospitalized them and this could probably be explained by the excellent standard of healthcare in the village where the GP would pay a house call before you even had so much as a symptom. Then, shortly after we had pointed out this phenomenon, we suddenly had a whole crowd of people queuing up for treatment. To be fair you never have to queue in Borsetshire, except for the DOG WOMAN. Poor Mrs Antrobus was told she would have to wait eight months for a cataract operation, but in that true socialist spirit that made the Raj what it was, she was immensely grateful 'Oh I thought it would be much longer.' Another house-point to Blair and his boys. Mrs A was followed by a whole procession including FOGHORN with her leg, ROOTH and LOATHSOME. Each received spectacular service all apparently in a nurse-free environment. They are allowed to switch hospitals and change appointments at will. Thus ROOOTH was able to go up to Northumberland to visit her mum and have her chemotherapy sessions there and when Loathsome did not really fancy going in for her major heart operation she just cancelled it for a while. They have a very innovative maternity system as we witnessed when KATE gave birth to HEY NONNE NO. You just turn up with your mates, find a bed and have the baby without being bothered by any staff.

INTERNET Surprisingly Ambridge knows about the Net but references to it are rather uncomfortable and fit into PC stereotypes. ROBERT SNELL was naturally the first person to succumb because for many years he was the only person in the Village to own a computer. Now we all know that children learn about computers before they learn manners, spelling or wiping lavatory seats nowadays, but in Ambridge they crawl straight from the womb and begin surfing. All the brats like PEEEP and DAMIEN could give Bill Gates a run for his money. But of course we have to acknowledge the increase in 'silver surfers'. In the rest of the world there is a vague correlation between being a silver surfer and not being thick as a brick, so the idea that JOE GRUNDY would now be able to find his way to www.sadgit.com almost defies credibility. Similarly, the notion that Peeep could teach BERT the delights of a cyber world is also difficult to grasp.

IPPY The Shergar of Ambridge. He was THE VILLAGE BICYCLE's horse that completely DISAPPEARED and was never found. The facts are that she neglected him, and he got fed up standing in a field waiting to be turned into Copydex, so one day he leapt the fence and found somewhere better to live. Who can honestly blame him?

JAAARN ARCHER The unexpected demise of Jaaarn rocked the nation in February 1998. Anarchists genuinely regretted his death, principally because if anyone was to be crushed to death by a tractor there were plenty of eminently more deserving candidates. In contrast to his cousin DEEEVID, Jaaarn had an enviable degree of hedonism about him. He was hardly out of short trousers before he was bringing credence to the wise old saying 'Never come a knockin' when the caravan's a rockin'. When the lovely SHARON was staying in a grace and favour caravan on his parents' farm, we were delighted to see them strike up such an ideal partnership. It got up PAT's nose considerably since she is a hypocrite of the worst order. Jaaarn lavished fatherly concern on KYLIE and when Sharon managed to get a council house in the village, Jaaarn moved in with her. When she dumped him he was understandably a bit miffed but quickly recovered and established himself as the local stud, putting it about left right and centre.

By setting himself up in the disco business he had wisely twigged that DJs tend to have more groupies than pig farmers, something that NEIL CARTER has never really understood. He was quite money orientated, and why not? Thanks to numerous successful entrepreneurial ventures he had amassed plenty of chick-pulling dosh, which certainly came in handy while he was bankrolling Sharon and Kylie during their sojourn in the village. The coupling between Jaaarn and the HORRIBLE HAYLEY has always been somewhat irritating and it was fitting that it should be Sharon who managed to end it.

Jaaarn died amid a deluge of castism where the BBC and

Archers Anoraks really excelled themselves in trying to destroy our vivid picture of Ambridge life. Pictures of some spotty actor mysteriously appeared in newspapers throughout the land, always attached to some ridiculous story about poor old Jaaarn. A former and repeated winner of the SINGLE WICKET TROPHY, Jaaarn's memory will live on through his pork.

JAILBIRD CARTER Susan is desperate to climb out of her underclass. Born into the noble family of Horrobin, she was wooed by NEIL CARTER and a shotgun wedding ensued. Her big class-climbing break came when she was given a job in the Estate office. Working under the slack and sloppy supervision of the appalling SHULUGH, life there was one long holiday. She was forever on the phone to her mates, at the Estate's expense, and HARD-WORKING SIMON in particular found it highly irritating when people would call in to the office willy nilly to discuss WI and other non-work-related matters. When Jailbird was finally given the heave-ho from the Estate, they must have noticed an immediate reduction in the photocopying bill as she was constantly stealing large runs to produce leaflets for the dreaded VILLAGE PRODUCTIONS, and the endless number of do-gooding meetings she attends.

A delightful episode occurred when her ambitious brother CLIVE, a credit to the Horrobin name, decided to visit her and give himself a little break from prison – all part of the gradual rehabilitation programme so necessary if he was to play his full part in the community. Jailbird perverted the course of justice by sheltering him in a kack-handed and obvious way. She was rightly sent to prison, and showed just what a recidivist she is by absconding to attend the funeral of old HANDBAG HEBDEN. The typical hypocrisy of the village came into its own at this point. On the one hand there was Clive who had left prison without permission, and everyone was saying that 'hanging would be too good for him, throw away the key', etc. But when Jailbird did precisely the same thing, the whole village was up in arms about how unfair it was that she should be given an extra ten days for her rank disobedience.

Like many Ambridge mothers, Jailbird has a rather dubious parental record. Her daughter EMMER was a serial bedwetter, largely on account of having a mother whose idea of fashion was a trouser suit with an attractive arrow pattern on it. When Christopher was born, she turned against him simply because he looked like the elephant man and had 666 tattooed on his trunk. It simply didn't fit into her plan to have a child that could not be used as a model for Mothercare.

Jailbird has always been something of a Vicar of Bray, and was changing sides more times than a 78 record over the Pemberton v Grundy issue. At first, when it looked as if Pemberton would win hands down, and her so-called 'mates' the Grundys would be living in cardboard boxes, she was careful to keep quiet about his plans to evict them. FAT CLARRIE refused to speak to her when she realized that Jailbird had temporarily acted like a loyal employee and remained stum over the flax plans. But when it was quite obvious that everyone had deserted poor HARD-WORKING SIMON, she was all too ready to stab him in the back along with everyone else by betraying his confidence and sending information to the tribunal. Amusingly, with Simon gone, and the business units underway, Jailbird thought that she would be made the manager. After all, she had photocopied a few sheets of paper relating to the plans and she therefore regarded herself as an expert. Anarchists went wild with joy when BRIAN summoned her to tell her that he was indeed able to offer her a new job – as cleaner. Typically she went round saying how he could stick his job, and then proceeded to accept it.

When Neil chucked in his job, Jailbird was typically

unsympathetic – so determined was she that he should be a sales rep, regardless of how miserable it made him. She still berates the poor man on a regular basis if he is not toiling in the fields 24 hours a day earning half the minimum wage.

Another class-climbing opportunity presented itself early in 1998 when she signed up as receptionist to DR DEATH. At the surgery she is in her element, throwing her weight about and trying to prevent deserving patients from visiting the quack. When DR DIM took over, Jailbird developed a good line in breaking patient confidentiality, telling all and sundry about SHEYAWN's miscarriage and more recently spreading the good news of the sizzling affair between Dim and TFW.

To give credit where it's due she has made the spreading of malicious gossip something of an art and for that we are very grateful. She can be relied upon to open private letters and then broadcast the contents and her role in increasing the sum of human acrimony is to be welcomed.

As we know, there is never a job shortage in Ambridge so the lower orders always have several jobs to keep them above the poverty line. In Jailbird's case her second job is as part-time assistant at the post office, an ideal little number for a convicted criminal.

JAMIE PEACOCK-TEALEAF-PERKS Ambridge's most recent kleptomaniac, we have devoted a separate chapter to the village's greatest hope for the future.

JASON It's unlikely that the new housing estate will ever be built as the only builder in Borsetshire is Jason. He's a typical 'ten sugars please luv' builder with his buttocks hanging out of his trousers. His delightful Birmingham twang reminds us why opera tends to be in German or Italian. But his propensity to finish the jobs he undertakes is always slightly disturbing.

JEAN HARVEY In her heyday Jean had a fine pair of tonsils but something happened to traumatize her into total silence. She recently retired from the Parish Council after 21 silent years service. She lives at Bull Farm with her silent husband. Now when did you last hear that place mentioned?

JEAN-PAUL An entirely incredible character, he is nothing more than a French voice with a camp, prima donna-ish dose of stereotyping. We all realize that it is impossible to cook properly unless you are French, but he really is too ridiculous a character to exist outside a pantomime. Despite the fact that GREY GABLES sometimes seems quite large, there is never any mention of any other cooking staff or relief chefs, so Jean-Paul must work damn hard. We go a long time without hearing him, presumably because he's always in the kitchen and we're not. The only time he ventures out is when he has the opportunity to enhance his stereotype, such as one of SID's boules evenings. Otherwise he is condemned to an existence of arranging microscopic amounts of brightly coloured food on huge plates.

JECK WOOLLEY A star amongst men. Jeck Woolley, born in Stirchley, is a typical self-made man. He has no subtlety but his trademark pomposity has greatly subsided with age. Jeck really has undergone a fair degree of repackaging over the years and we can only assume that a top advertising agency has got hold of him. At one time, he wanted to be guest of honour at every event, chairman of every committee, etc. But now he is more like Uriah Heep in his general humility.

Jeck is not short of a bob or two and owns GREY GABLES country park, the *Borchester Echo* and the village shop. We have greatly enjoyed his tendency to interfere with the management of his enterprises, such as his insistence on introducing the 'Pleasant Valley' products into the shop. Even at his great age,

Jeck was keen to introduce an equal opportunities policy when he needed a part-time assistant. This was presumably in case ST USHA or SEAN were a bit short of the readies.

The most interesting feature of Jeck is the strange noises he makes when he hears some bad news or his feelings are hurt. When he speaks he has some amazing inflexions. It would seem that when the good Lord was dishing out adenoids, Jeck was occupying the first three places in the queue, which goes a long way to explaining why he calls THE VILLAGE BICYCLE 'Carolide'. For anyone with a dodgy ticker, Jeck is something of an icon as he seemed to have his first heart attack aged about two, and to have survived on a diet of lard ever since. He's now in his 80s and has that endearing habit of telling you the same story he has told you a few minutes earlier and dribbling over plates of custard creams. But he is one of the few people who, when he pops his clogs, will be mourned by Anarchists throughout the land.

JED The proprietor of Aladdin's Cave in Borchester. This gentleman will provide you with the finest knock-off goods at keenly inflated prices.

JIGGINS FIELD Ambridge is an amazing place so it came as little surprise when a brand new field descended on Brookfield in the early autumn of the year 2000 without even a by your leave. And the nice thing about the Brookfield lot is that they immediately accepted it as part of the landscape, cheerfully referring to it as if it had at some stage in the last 50 years been mentioned.

JIM COVERDALE Something that people have to realize about the PC village of Ambridge is that all police nowadays are fascists. This was not always the case. Some years back PC

Colin Drury was quite popular with the likes of DAN, but probably because he turned a blind eye to Dan's more dubious activities. Since then it's been downhill all the way. Coverdale was detested as the local bobby, and he then went off and married the Aldridge *au pair*, Eva Lenz, into whose knickers quite a large number of the village populace had sought to get (notably NEIL CARTER). Many years later, Coverdale returned for no apparent reason as a Detective Inspector. Laudably he was trying to get EDDIE banged up for duffing up GEORGE (ALCOPOP) BARFORD, but even Jim was no match for the Ambridge mafia. The strange thing is that, apart from Eddie, no one seemed at all surprised at Coverdale's return, nor showed any interest in it. Not one person asked after Eva who had been quite a well-known figure in the village. Not even one of the Aldridges remarked on the subject.

JOAN PARGETTER If you are going to change your name, you might as well make it a substantial change like, for example, from Tracy to Heavenly Hirani Tiger Lily. NIGEL's mum changed hers from Joan to Julia, yet the revelation that she had done this still shook the village to its roots. Joan is an easy person to be, as she is an actress. She sounds like an actress and is generally quite an incredible character. She has been dealt a very poor deal by both her son and daughter-in-law. If you think that LOWER LOXLEY was her marital home for years, it is quite outrageous that they should have kicked her out and, on the rare occasions that she is allowed there, should make it so unpleasant for her. Hardly surprising then that she sought solace in the bottle.

Joan is no fool and detested ELIZABETH whom she rightly regarded as a common farmer's daughter and well below the station of her Nigel. Joan enjoyed a rather curious friendship with NELSON over a number of years, and it was rather sad that as she sought comfort and refuge from her unfriendly family, the best she could do was an old queen with a background of armed robbery and antiques fraud. She was understandably a bit upset when Nelson suddenly went to visit Ronald Biggs but then struck up some kind of relationship with the highly peculiar STRANGE LEWIS. She is now apparently locked away for much of the time, though she is occasionally allowed out to look after the dreaded twins.

JOE GRUNDY Anarchists respect Joe. He knows that the cosy establishment will never offer him the genuine hand of friendship and he retains a healthy outlook on life in Ambridge. As he sees it, the whole village is run for the benefit of the Archer clan. If anyone else has a problem, it will only be solved if it is also a problem for an Archer. The lazy git that he is, Joe has traded on chronic farmer's lung, though it is more likely to be farmer's liver as he regularly gets boozed up, preferably at someone else's expense. Over the years, the establishment has become more accepting of the Grundys, which tends to make us feel less empathy with them. He has an extremely unlikely tendency to seek to defraud his own family, including his grandchildren. If he lived in London's East End he would have been the recipient of a concrete overcoat long ago. As time marches on, Joe has fallen victim to Saundersism, splitting the atom one moment, forgetting his own name the next. Thanks to FAT CLARRIE's constant nagging he has rather lost the plot and his Wacko-style disposal of the ferrets was a prime example. In recent times he has taken to breaking into people's houses, making himself a cup of tea and watching TV. Ambridge folk being as they are, most people find this perfectly understandable behaviour. Alas, the Laurels cannot be far away, along with the day he is finally reunited with Moi Soozan.

JOLYON GIBSON This public school-educated junkie shacked up with KATE, bonked her contemporaneously with her relationship with ROY and introduced a fine crop of cannabis plants to the village. Sadly he was arrested for his green-fingered endeavours and we have never heard of him since. An all-round good guy. But good guys never last in Ambridge.

JOSE HORRIBLE HAYLEY earned her living since invading Ambridge essentially by looking after Jose's children. Jose is always described as 'a working woman' though the nature of her work is never defined. Anarchists have since discovered that she works daily shifts in the Borchester Massage Parlour. She has been irritatingly tolerant of her paid childminder's constant demands to be allowed to look after all the other brats in Ambridge and therefore subsidizes the care of JAMIE TEALEAF-PERKS and of course FREEBIE. Jose's sudden realization that Horrible has been taking her for a ride and is as much use as a chocolate fireguard meant that she was only too pleased when she left to work in the Lower Loxley Kindergarten.

JULIAN GOODACRE (BAGPIPEMAKER) An Anarchist icon, one of the earliest members of our movement, one of the finest makers of bagpipes in the land and a keen detestor of SHULUGH. Anarchists attending the 2000 Castfree Convention were lucky enough to see him in the flesh, where he performed vigorously on the Leicestershire Smallpipes One of those attending was so moved by the occasion he asked 'when are these f***ing bagpipes going to stop?' You don't get much higher praise than that. If you have bagpipes to buy, then buy them from this man.

KARL SWIFT It was a case of an all too quick 'hello and goodbye' to Karl Swift, the silent phallus. No sooner had he been engaged as gamekeeper a few years ago by JECK 'Impeccable Judgement' Woolley, to work in tandem with the most boring and miserable man ever to play the cornet, than we knew we were in for trouble. Karl was never around long enough to earn a voice but he set about the silent GREY GABLES staff with heterosexual abandon.

Not content with rogering everyone in sight, he ultimately met his Waterloo when he committed the cardinal sin of greeting PEGGOI as 'Peg'. And you don't do that and live to tell the tale. Karl's departure was abrupt and involved him running off with someone we'd never heard of who was married to someone else we'd never heard of. It's a jungle out there.

KATE MADAGASCAR VAN DER VELD Anarchists feel massively betrayed by Kate. She is the one person with the capacity to wipe the smug smile from the face of HORRIBLE HAYLEY and she completely bottled it.

Kate was MRS HIGH AND MIGHTY's third child by as many blokes. Like mother like daughter, she has continued the tradition, though with the added feature of creating her own multicultural family with children from every continent.

In her early years Kate was rather obnoxious. Her obsession with being alternative and green follows in the same well-sandalled footprints as LUCY PERKS and LOATHSOME LIZZIE. Like her sister Dopey DEBBIE, she has had money, accommodation and clothes lavished upon her with no real requirement to do anything in return and her environmental considerations have quite understandably never come between her and her need for home comforts and life's luxuries.

But we have to give Kate her due. She became pregnant by a man who would not be regarded by her own parents as a 'good catch'. Luther, a Caribbean Swampy, was a bit much for Ambridge under the mildest of circumstances, but as a possible inheritor of Home Farm, he was not quite in BRIAN ALDRIDGE's marketing plan.

Ambridge is colour-blind, a paradigm of the PC world for which we all strive, and so the fact that FREEBIE was born with dreadlocks, gurgling 'no woman no cry' was something they all readily took in their stride. Not one to rush into things without a deal of thought, Kate did not choose the name Freebie for several months, during which the child was known by the charming epithet of 'baby'. But poor Kate reckoned without the intervention of trainee village idiot Racist ROY TUGGER. Undaunted by Freebie's obvious empathy with the late Emperor of Ethiopia, Tugger took out an injunction against Kate when she was attempting to take Freebie for a short holiday in the sun. Then, with the help of the crooked DR DEATH, ST USHA and the Ambridge mafia, he succeeded in rigging a paternity test that decreed him to be the father.

Naturally, Kate needed a bit of a holiday to get over the whole grotesque situation of having her right-on Rastafarian child randomly allocated to one of Ambridge's most obvious divots, so she went off, leaving Freebie in the gruesomely proletarian hands of Tugger and Horrible. She made every effort to keep in touch with Freebie despite the huge cost of international telephone calls and we were all delighted when she returned just before Christmas 2000, entering into the true spirit of the festivities by being great with child.

The birth of HEY NONNE NO was rather nauseating to

any true Anarchist, but presented Kate with the ideal opportunity to create a modern and successful single-parent family. The obvious solution was to tip off the immigration authorities about the revolting GLUCOSE and head off to Australia with Freebie and Hey Nonne with a view to producing a nice little Aborigine child. To our absolute disgust she gave in to Horrible and High and Mighty and disappeared back to South Africa. There was a glimmer of hope when news came through that she had married Glucose and demanded Freebie's presence at Hey Nonne's christening. Would she refuse to let her return to England or would she play the white man? Alas it was a long shot.

KATHY PERKS One of Ambridge's most irritating whingers, and that really is saying something. We first heard of her when she was called Miss Holland and was LUCY PERKS' domestic science teacher at school. It later emerged that she was a fraud on two counts. First, she was still married at the time, and should therefore have been *Mrs*. Second, one might have been forgiven for thinking that a domestic science teacher should be an able and willing cook if they expect to have a career telling other people how to do it. The opportunity to own and run a restaurant should therefore have been welcomed with open arms. Yet this woman, as soon as she married SID PERKS, had to be dragged kicking and screaming into the kitchen.

Kathy got together with Sid when he rented her Rose Cottage – a little bolt hole he had bought for himself and his first wife, the late POLL DOLL. Eventually, after a fair bit of playing hard to get, and some two-timing with the then local bobby DAVE BARRY, Kathy married Sid and proceeded to make his life a misery thence forward. What Sid had always needed to make THE BULL a success was to be in a proper partnership, but the dreaded Kathy kept going on about wanting her own career, space, all the usual stuff. Kathy finally gave up her teaching job, but instead of helping Sid she went off to GREY GABLES and effectively worked in competition with him, just as former Bull cook, THE VILLAGE BICYCLE, had done before her. In order to mess up Sid's life even further, she went AWOL with DS Barry. Sid had the good sense to show her the door but the rather less good sense to un-show it somewhat later.

Things never really improved. They had the sprog JAMIE TEALEAF-PERKS, a child about whom we should clearly have been concerned due to his constant neglect. But Kathy just continued moaning endlessly about her role in life. She was all keen about setting up the restaurant venture when they eventually bought the pub from PEGGOI WOOLLEY with dear old GUY PEMBERTON but seemed to think it could run itself without her getting her hands dirty. Kathy often talked as if she was the great intellectual force behind the business, and clearly felt that cooking was beneath her. Yet the marketing and creative side of The Bull appeared to be the very thing that was letting it down.

Christmas 1997 was really the last straw; after a disastrous year for The Bull in which all the heterophobic villagers preferred going to THE PINK CAT which isn't even in the village, Sid finally thought he had scored one over on The Cat when he had a completely full restaurant on Christmas Day. But was Kathy pleased? No, she spent the day saying how it had completely ruined Jamie's Christmas, and how she was never going to cook on Christmas Day again. She might reflect that if she'd opted for DS Barry, or an ambulance man, water board official, vicar, or even farmer, Jamie would have found a similarly disrupted Christmas, but would doubtless have survived.

By the dawn of the millennium, Sid had finally seen the light and when Kathy brought shame on the village by being the only person in Borsetshire to visit the Dome, he realized it was time to trade her in for THE LILY. Kathy took her sunny disposition to Willow Farm where she insisted on spending five hours in the bathroom every day, to the great inconvenience of all those in the household who were trying to do a proper job. PAT and HELEN showed their combined business acumen by readily employing this proven retailing albatross to work in their organic shop where she immediately started behaving like the manageress rather than hired hand. But before she could do any more damage, the Ambridge Job Fairy appeared with yet another unsuitable employment opportunity for her. This was the biggest farce of all as Loopy NIGEL proceeded to examine and be impressed by her totally irrelevant and fraudulent cv without asking her a single question about why The Bull had all but gone into receivership while she was the landlady there. Hold your breath for bankruptcy at Lower Loxley. And as she is now the latest occupant of the jinxed April Cottage we can only hope for worse to come.

KEN TON ARCHER An odious smarmball of the worst order. As the twin of the dreaded SHULUGH what can one expect? Ken Ton is a crook and a waster. The mystery is how he has come by any money at all since he is transparently stupid despite his endless posing. He is a kind of middle-class ONE-EYED MONSTER in that nothing he throws himself into seems to succeed for long. The good thing is that he disappears to Australia for long periods of time, and we don't have to hear him. He is usually on the 'apologies for absence' spot at family gatherings, but Christmas 1997 saw a particularly indigestible dose of him. He managed to get under the skin of ROOOTH and DEEEVID by showering large presents on the awful PEEEP. In fact, it was hard to see what their problem was with this since they bestow precious little attention on Peeep and her brother BSE Josh themselves.

Anarchists have long been of the opinion that Ken Ton may

be something of a SEAN, though he did go on about someone called Mel back in Oz who was apparently 25 and had long blonde hair. Had he realized how homosexual Ambridge now is, he could have brought rent-boy Melvin with him. Ken Ton managed to persuade SHULUGH that they should both celebrate their impending 40th birthdays at New Year 1998.

There then followed the most absurd situation imaginable where the venue was NELSON's wine bar, and where LOATHSOME LIZZIE had quite amazingly handed over complete control of the place to Ken ton. This despite her having been entrusted by Nelson to run the bar in his absence. Ken Ton didn't bother with proper invitations and allowed all the normal customers at the wine bar to enjoy free drinks all night. During his visit, it emerged that he was actually married to this Mel person – for reasons of tax. Most parents would have been quite taken aback by this news and, to give him his due, PHIL was not exactly dancing for joy. FOGHORN reacted with the immortal words, 'Better get that pie out of the oven.' If we were to believe Ken Ton (and why on earth should we?) he was in big trouble this time with the tax man. He will never learn his lesson of course because dopey Phil promptly shelled out a few grand to keep him going whilst sanctimonious Shulugh paid all his Ambridge debts for him.

In recent times we have begun to feel a little sympathy for him. His partner was apparently due to be the first male on earth to give birth, yet no one in Ambridge seemed particularly interested. Added to that was the news that Foghorn and Phil had decided to cut him out of their will on the spurious basis that 'the measly 50K' they had given him to get him out of a hole was deemed to be equivalent to a quarter of Brookfield. When he turned up to instigate the great Brookfield 'Dave' row, we developed a great respect for him as he repeatedly referred to Deeevid as 'Dave' and read them all their tea leaves.

After a gestation period of nearly two years, Mel was described as 'the size of a house' and in May 2001, the first male to give birth finally achieved his record, producing the delightful MERRYHILL, weighing in at a healthy 28 lb 9 oz.

KEVIN DUNN As with any village, it is not really the done thing to find yourself with too many Kevins, and Ambridge has followed this rule assiduously. Indeed it has remained virtually a Kevin-free zone for all but fifty years. Unfortunately where there's milk, there's Kevins. Long in the tooth listeners will recall that the milk tanker used to be driven by a Kevin, if not an indigenous one. He was no ordinary Kevin because he did some pretty nifty work on poor old POLL DOLL. At last, to mark fifty years, Ambridge was granted its own temporary Kevin. Again, this was not your bog standard Kevin; this was 'Supermilker' Kevin. After whacking out huge consultancy fees, the dim shower who run Brookfield were advised that all their problems could be solved by bringing in some know-all to milk their cows. DAN ARCHER would have turned in his grave at the notion that farming standards had fallen so low at Brookfield that there was no longer anyone there capable of milking a cow. How he would have wept as he saw the poor beasts drying up under a constant barrage of Geordiness. So, enter Kevin, who from day one had such an amazing milking ability that the cows were soon producing gold top milk, pasteurized, bottled and ready for clogging up your arteries. The trouble with Kevin was that he could not help but poke his nose into other people's business. Hence, when there was a first-class opportunity for a bull to teach Precocious PEEEP a memorable lesson, he waded in and asked the bull to desist. Prior to the barricading of Brookfield against foot and mouth, Kevin just disappeared. As usual, nobody commented on it but it was quite obvious he wasn't there anymore. He'd just melted away.

KIRSTY Another Borsetshire northerner, Kirsty is LANCASTRIAN 'TRASHER' TOMMY's woman. She has an irritating whining voice and a record as an anti-GM agitator. To be fair, Trasher has treated her like a doormat, but she has been prepared to put up with it. Luckily we have never seen him in the shower, but he must have something going for him. She now works as an assistant in PAT's organic shop, the Ambridge Job Fairy coming into play yet again. No need for the 'New Deal' in Ambridge. Kirtsty is intensely jealous if Trasher so much as glances at another woman. She's probably right to be as the poor bloke could do better than some one who sounds as if she gargles with Domestos.

KYLIE RICHARDS The beautiful damsel begat of CLIVE and his good lady SHARON. Her name betrays the prejudices of those who think that Sharon is thick and that only thick people name their children after people in Australian soaps. Kylie was one of many non-speaking stalwarts in the village and one might have thought she would be a tearaway and delinquent when she reached her teens.

Despite being a young girl, she was always referred to as if she was a toddler. Some years back, Kylie beat ALICE in a vicious fancy-dress competition, much to the chagrin of MRS HIGH AND MIGHTY. Just before JAAARN turfed her and her mother out of his cottage, Kylie suddenly spoke, and revealed herself to be a thoroughly pleasant, articulate girl. Needless to say her accent was completely unlike her mother's and it is quite clear that Clive has funded her with a private education or perhaps a governess, not to mention regular elocution lessons. Though she went with her mother to Leeds, which won't have done much for her accent, we look forward to the day she returns to break the hearts of any of the remaining heterosexuals amongst the male population of Ambridge.

LA STRADA Long overdue, the MONT BLANC has been the only restaurant for nobs as long as we can remember, but La Strada is going to give it a run for its money. A good place to go where you can be sure you won't bump into anyone of lower class than THE VILLAGE BICYCLE or old FOXBRUSH. No danger of finding FAT CLARRIE trying to dig the olives out of her ciabatta with a toothpick, this is strictly toffs only.

LAKEY HILL A cross between Mount Olympus and Hampstead Heath, this is a place where people go when they are feeling down. Given the number of people who are perennially down in Ambridge it must be like Piccadilly Circus. No doubt littered with used condoms and syringes, it is also where SHULUGH and many others have been for a bit of Midlands nookie. The correct placing of these locations can be a bit tricky and can lead to some manifestations of the most crass castism. If you care to read *The Book of The Archers*, you will see a description of Lakey Hill as being 'to the north east of Ambridge'. No problem there, but the inside cover has one of those ghastly castist creations – a map. And where is Lakey Hill shown? Slap bang in the south east. Something about arses and elbows comes to mind. But it does go to show that castists never prosper.

LANCASTRIAN 'TRASHER' TOMMY Strangely, despite being the progeny of Welsh PAT and Ambridge-born TONY, and not withstanding the fact that he had spent his entire mute childhood in the village, Tommy is a Lancastrian with a broad accent to prove it. He didn't find it necessary to speak until his GCSE results appeared in 1997. He then went from silent shrinking violet to ringleader of the most debauched and inebriate party ever seen beneath the hallowed beams of the village hall. Much to BORING CHRISTINE's chagrin, not only did he cause damage and excessive mess to the hall, but he treated the DUCKS on the VILLAGE POND to an unexpected supper of diced carrot. But that's the traditional Lancastrian way of letting your hair down.

Like his brother before him, Tommy had the hots for SHARON when she reappeared on the scene, but just as when JAAARN was interested in her at the same tender age, the love went unrequited. He's only got to wait a few years and perhaps she'll be back for him. PAT would just love it. Since the sad death of Jaaarn, Lancastrian 'Trasher' Tommy has, in many ways, taken up where he left off. He has developed an avaricious capitalist streak, carried on with the pigs and developed a difficult and cantankerous attitude. Quite rightly he will never forgive Jaaarn for messing up his birthday. There was Tommy dressed up to the nines and ready to party while Jaaarn, wallowing in self-pity, was more interested in doing wheelies on his FERGIE. His failure to win the SINGLE WICKET in the year of his brother's death brought shame on the Archer name and the whole of Lancashire. A couple of years later, all the other participants in the competition played blindfold in order that this petulant upstart could win.

At some indeterminate point in time, an amazing transition came over Tommy, he lost his 'my' and became plain Tom, without any explanation whatsoever. This perhaps coincided with his degeneration into vandal and thug, details of which are well chronicled elsewhere.

Thomas has become extremely un-PC in his old age and

runs the risk of becoming the pariah of Ambridge. For a start, he has an unhealthy interest in girls, particularly those with shoe sizes that outstrip their IQ. Lord knows what the rest of the villagers must think of him with his outdated notion of going out with girls to discos and clubs. He was pathetically grateful to be chosen as Tugger's best man for the sick-bucket wedding of the year and immediately reeled off a load of offensively sexist jokes, none of which seemed to have punchlines. But he's not all bad, at least he didn't let the side down by suggesting that GLUCOSE could be black.

LAURELS, THE This is a secure establishment that used to house FAT MAN FORREST, PRU and no one else. There is no evidence that it is a private home so we assume it is run by the council – which makes it extremely unlikely that it is the paradise we have been led to believe it is. We don't know its location but we have numerous candidates to send there when we find out.

LAUREN Over the years we have become accustomed to the temporary billeting in Ambridge of young women with reality-defying voices. Lauren has such a voice, sounding as if she has recently swallowed a live baby hyena. She bestowed sexual favours upon Trasher 'The Donkey' Tommy who seems to attract the county's slapettes with a kind of magnetism. Trasher two-timed her with the whingeing KIRSTY, including one memorable evening when he went to two different parties with both of them on the same evening. Lauren would have made an excellent wife for Trasher as their two single-figure IQs would have formed an unstoppable intellectual battering ram. As it turned out, she could sing like a bird (an owl), which came in quite handy for the appalling *Mikado*, the ongoing VILLAGE PRODUCTION at the time. She seems to have gone off with a bloke called Martin who has a sizeable wad.

LIBBY PURVES A fallen icon for Anarchists since she declared that she no longer wanted to listen to *The Archers* because there were too many 'fictional characters'. In her most glorious moment she once dared to write that, 'someone had to SLAP SHULUGH.' On these grounds she was made a lifelong honorary member of our august body. The loss of Libby Purves is tragic to the cause of anarchy, for even in her valedictory statement she described severing her ties with Ambridge as akin to a bereavement, an experience she 'wouldn't wish on anyone except perhaps Shulugh'. But she then tumbled into the abyss, declaring 'there is no Shulugh'. If only it were true. You can't be an ostrich Libby.

LILLIAN BELLAMY We used to like Lillian. She was one of those people who knew how to carry her wealth. Lillian oozed class. Unlike her sister MRS HIGH AND MIGHTY who is just rich, Lillian is absolutely rolling in the stuff. She lives in Guernsey, partly for tax reasons but mainly to get well away from her whingeing family. This is hardly surprising since when she does appear there is almost immediate speculation about how long she is staying and whether she's 'up to something'. If you remember that she inherited the Berrow Estate from her husband Ralph before the likes of CAMERON FRASER and HARD-WORKING SIMON had got into breaking it up, you will realize just how seriously rich she is.

Lillian really enjoys a drink and when she comes to the village, an all too rare occasion, the profits of THE BULL go into orbit. Her son James is one of THE DISAPPEARED which must be sad for her. She must have had a nasty moment early in 2001 when the boring Barfords were suddenly contemplating the idea of inflicting their vapid personas upon her island. We could almost hear her scanning the property pages of the *Mustique Mercury* in case she needed to move up-market in a hurry. Considering that it can't be a matter of saving up for the air fare her visits to Ambridge are rare indeed. But then, faced with the choice of a pint of SHIRES at The BULL or a few glasses of champers with Bergerac, there's really no contest. Anarchists were aghast when Lillian turned up for Nelson's funeral because it was immediately apparent that she had undergone a complete voice transplant. For some reason she had exchanged the voice of a youthful 50-something for that of an 80 year-old. Not only that, but she had obviously been to the Nigel Kennedy College of Elocution where they specialise in turning posh people into Barbara Windsor. With it she had acquired a complementary personality suddenly becoming common as muck and sex mad. She could not see a member of the opposite sex without making lascivious remarks about him, which is unthinkable when discussing the likes of ROY TUGGER. The villagers were particularly scathing when her true love SCOTT turned up at GREY GABLES. It was as if they'd never seen an actor before.

LILYNFREDDIE Probably Siamese twins, but in other respects they are typical Ambridge children. They make virtually no sound, never wake at night and have no character. These are very pampered children, coming as they do from Lower Loxley. We live in hope that one day, on a visit to their Grandma FOGHORN, they will disappear, only to re-emerge at the flower and produce show as a jar of pickle ignominiously bedecked with a third prize sticker.

LILY OF LAYTON CROSS, Doreen Rogers, had shown a lot of promise and at one time EDDIE had been all set to walk up the aisle with her. She was another Borsetshire bicycle but without THE VILLAGE BICYCLE's class.

A wearer of fine leather and possessor of a voice like a

nightingale's, Doreen has pursued a country-and-western career which has been just marginally less unsuccessful than Eddie's. Sadly her relationship with Eddie never quite flourished and she went off with the unlikely named Mr Wayne Tucson, a fellow country-and-western artiste. This did not endure and there was a good opportunity for her to put a bit of lead back into Eddie's pencil when she returned to the scene a few years ago. But Doreen seemed to have undergone a temporary moral transformation and was heard to tell FAT CLARRIE that she had nothing to fear. More's the pity, Eddie is much more entertaining when he is up to no good, and it is always fun to hear Clarrie imitating an exploding monkfish.

Fortunately Doreen reverted to type and soon rescued SID from the appalling KATHY. In 2000 we were treated to the most gratuitously inoffensive shower scene ever broadcast on radio. This featured Doreen allegedly scrubbing Sid's back. Angry listeners' letters poured in to protest at such filth.

Doreen has completely turned around the fortunes of the formerly ailing BULL. They now come in charabancs from all corners of the globe just to gaze upon her ample bosom and generally brassy demeanour. She is vulgarity incarnate and we love her.

LIME KILN COPSE It really is getting beyond a joke. In recent years there have been so many new fields, woodlands, villages and long-established residents suddenly cropping up out of the blue that we lose count. This is just another one.

LINE DANCING A sad pastime which in most parts of the country tends to take place on a Wednesday afternoon, and so presumably is patronized largely by librarians. In Ambridge, THE LILY OF LAYTON CROSS introduced it as a night-time event at THE BULL and it went down a storm with all the village anoraks. Inevitably SID and KATHY managed to lose it to THE PINK CAT on the basis that any form of dancing so gormless that it just requires you to stand in a line holding hands was going to appeal to SEAN MYERSON's clientele. With the Lily's arrival at The Bull coinciding with the death of The Cat, line dancing unfortunately came as part of the package. There is no shortage of people with the necessary intellectual rigour to partake, but the leading lights seem to be the senior TUGGERS and some generally silent villagers who have obviously been given special dispensation to make ridiculous 'eee ha' noises. You might have thought that morris dancing would be more appropriate in a rural English village, but that just wouldn't be PC enough for Ambridge.

LITTLE CROXLEY It's pretty bad luck when a long-forgotten village suddenly reappears in a county and the first thing that happens to it is that it acquires the status of Anthrax Island. For this is where the first outbreak of FOOT AND MOUTH occurred, caused when some farmer with no name gave the remains of his kebab to his hapless cows. The people of Ambridge have an unerring capacity to be unshockable, so it was quite natural that THE BULL did not resound to the sound of 'Where the f*** has Lower Croxley been for the last 50 years?' or 'We've really got to do something about these villages that keep turning up overnight.' Cynics have disbelieved the Anarchists when we have pointed out that buildings and whole villages can move around, yet in the case of Little Croxley we have cast-iron evidence. Scholars have studied maps of Ambridge and discovered Little Croxley in two completely different locations while on a third map it fails to appear anywhere at all. ROOOTH finally gave the game away when she said to DEEEVID 'There's no need to look at the map, Little Croxley is still where it was yesterday.' Any sane person will accept that this would be a nonsensical statement to make unless Little Croxley was known to have tendencies to mobility.

LOATHSOME LIZZIE One of the Archer brats, now in her 30s. If you want to know what she used to be like you need look no further than KATE. She too was all veggie and lefty in her youth. She failed any significant educational challenges that came her way and took up a career of picking up SHULUGH's discarded boyfriends, sandwiched between a whole series of unsuitable blokes on the way. On a slight deviation from this path, she took one of THE VILLAGE BICYCLE's boyfriends, CAMERON FRASER, and he managed to get her up the duff before abandoning her at a motorway service station and doing a runner off the face of the earth. Unlike Kate, Elizabeth decided she did not want to bring up a sprog, and ended the pregnancy. This, of course, went down like a pork pie at a bar mitzvah with Shulugh who is absolutely nuts about children and seemed to think that her sister should have gone into the surrogacy business for her.

When Elizabeth decided to marry, she chose another of Shulugh's discards, the loopy ex-ice-cream and swimming-pool salesman NIGEL PARGETTER. Nigel has only ever really fancied Shulugh and still does, but he has obviously regarded Elizabeth as the nearest he is going to get, whilst still keeping a foot in the door. Elizabeth has never really been head over heels for Nigel but saw an opportunity to get some unearned wonga by grasping hold of LOWER LOXLEY, Nigel's ancestral home.

Elizabeth's treatment of her mother-in-law has been nothing short of scandalous. From the day she married Nigel she has sought to edge poor JOAN ever further into oblivion, making her feel like an unwelcome guest in her own home.

One of the mysteries for a while was how Elizabeth was apparently earning large fees for lecturing in courses on public relations. As far as we could see, her only experience in this field was management of a struggling third-rate conference centre, where all the work was done by Nigel and a silent staff anyway. We soon realized that she was actually earning fees as a high-class hooker to satisfy the near insatiable appetite of HORNY HUGH. Of course she denied it, but you would wouldn't you?

After a lot of fuss, Loathsome produced two sprogs, LILYNFREDDIE and even had the insensitivity to give Freddie the second name of 'Hugo' after his real father. No one seriously believed that Loopy Nigel would be capable of fathering children. The children have proved very useful as a bargaining tool in the Battle for Brookfield. Quite reasonably, Loathsome feels that bequeathing them a mere stately home would hardly be any guarantee of security and she has been determined to get her rightful share of Brookfield. She has an excellent attitude towards her sanctimonious sister and was highly robust in pointing out that Shulugh's declaration that all she wanted to be left by FOGHORN and PHIL was 'an old plant pot' was made in the comfort of having been given a free house by her Grandmother and a massive payout on the death of HANDBAG HEBDEN.

In recent times it has suddenly been remembered that Loathsome has a heart condition and that she should therefore do the decent thing and collapse on a regular basis. Phil had a good wheeze that he would go and discuss his plans to leave her sweet FA in his will at a time when she was waiting for an operation. This served the purpose and she obligingly had an on-the-spot heart attack that would have seen off any normal being. But, real though they may be, Ambridge people are anything but normal. Loathsome had a major operation and was out and about before you could say Alan Milburn.

To our great disappointment, she seemed to have been given an overdose of emolience in hospital because she has started being chummy with ROOOTH and DEEEVID and wanting bygones to be called bygones, a particularly poor use for them. We can only hope that she sees sense, joins forces with KEN TON once again and really goes all out for her rightful share of Brookfield.

LOONY LARRY LOVELL This weird man suddenly appeared without warning as the self-appointed director of one of the dreaded VILLAGE PRODUCTIONS. His taste in women spans several generations as he has been pursuing both FOGHORN and THE VILLAGE BICYCLE. He drifts in and out of the village but only appears to exist when there is a play looming. Larry has clearly been planted by the BBC to make us think that *The Archers* is a soap opera with parts played by actors. They should hang their heads in shame – it's all part of the dumbing-down process.

LOWER LOXLEY The Pargetters turned loopy NIGEL's ancestral home into a two-bit conference centre. It has caused constant friction between Nigel and LOATHSOME since Nigel appears (against the odds for a complete idiot) to do most of the work, while, for a great deal of the time they were meant to be establishing the place, Elizabeth was giving HORNY HUGH one. It appears to be run in a chaotic fashion, as a kind of Fawlty Towers. It is unknown where the money came from to turn it into a business because Nigel was always stony broke, and it is hard to imagine him convincing a bank manager to let him open an account, let alone borrow money.

There was a very nasty dose of quasi VILLAGE PRODUCTION in 1996 when Lower Loxley was used as a film set. All sorts of people from the village got involved as 'extras' and the whole nightly episode was dominated by a complete summer pantomime for weeks on end. In recent years, Lower

Loxley has been filled with animals, restaurants and trashy shops in order to turn it into a tourist attraction. It was typical that, when they had a grand opening, they suddenly realized they hadn't got any food, a situation that can always cast a bit of a damper on a new eaterie. The solution saw one of the most disgraceful episodes ever witnessed as FOGHORN put all the members of the WI into a chain gang and forced them to manufacture scones and Victoria sponges for 48 hours until their wooden spoons were reduced to splinters. The arrangement was that Loathsome was only asked to pay for the ingredients, a flagrant abuse of the charitable services of the WI. Lower Loxley is staffed by a kind of *Dad's Army* of weirdoes – including MRS PUGSLEY, BEVERLEY, STRANGE LEWIS, EMMER CARTER and customer-hating KATHY. Visitors must think they've arrived on the set of *The Shining*. Allegedly, silent people come from far and wide, yet whenever we are allowed to eavesdrop we only seem to catch Ambridge residents there. Funny that.

LUCY PERKS One of the many useless features of this book is the completely gratuitous and mind-bendingly uninteresting bits of information we give you. Did you know that the very first words that Lucy ever uttered were, 'My name is Lucy Perks, THE BULL, Ambridge'? If you think about it, it is a trifle unusual to attach your address to your name, especially when you have never spoken before. The good thing about Lucy was that she didn't like KATHY. She saw through her right from the start, and realized that she was no substitute for her mother, POLL DOLL.

Like most of the teenage girls in the village she became a green-tinged lefty, sabotaging Brookfield's milking parlour and jumping aboard the animal welfare bandwagon. She also helped out a ne'er-do-well centre in Borchester. Just the sort of thing that TFW would encourage nowadays. Lucy also twigged pretty quickly when Kathy was carrying on with DAVE BARRY. She had a very peculiar automaton's intonation when she first spoke, but then developed a very clear voice without the trace of a local accent despite her rural upbringing, and her father's Brum brogue. As soon as Lucy finished at university she went off to New Zealand and got married. She is now one of Ambridge's DISAPPEARED, although SID has been known to talk to a phone that allegedly has her at the other end of it.

LYNDA SNELL Anarchists like Lynda because most of the village establishment sneer at her behind her back, and sometimes to her face. If they don't like her, she must be a good thing. For older listeners, Lynda is a replacement for Aunt Laura in that she is wheeled out whenever any issue requires a campaign. It must be very frustrating for her that the PARISH COUNCIL is run by deadbeats such as GEORGE (ALCOPOP) BARFORD. The campaigns Lynda has led are too numerous and uninteresting to mention, but some of them have been very successful. For example, you never hear any TRAFFIC in the village since people lost interest in her campaign against it.

Ambridge has never lived up to the standards Lynda had come to expect from having lived in the civilized southern enclave of Sunningdale, and the shabby way she has been treated speaks volumes for the insular and unwelcoming nature of the village. It has been suggested that Lynda could be in league with the Devil – her propensity to keep goats does little to dispel this notion. We quite understand how humiliating it must be for her to have to work as a receptionist at GREY GABLES when her boss TRUDY PORTER never speaks to her, and THE VILLAGE BICYCLE treats her as if she is a naughty adolescent schoolgirl. The one thing we do hate about Lynda is her insatiable desire for VILLAGE PRODUCTIONS. If another one were never to be staged for a million years that would be too soon.

Lynda is into middle-class alternative things like feng shui and other oriental foods. Her interest in aromatherapy has encouraged her to run an informal brothel where regulars include JOE GRUNDY and no one else. She's rather too keen on birds, trees and suchlike for our liking. No one can so much as remove a blade of grass without her making a fuss. She ought to take a look at the Sahara, they do OK without all that green nonsense.

LYNX Some years ago, an innocent lynx was roaming around the country park under the misapprehension that that is what country parks are there for, when JECK WOOLLEY, in a show of bravado, shot it dead. He then stuffed it, and put it in a glass case in GREY GABLES where it gazes down to this day. It used to be mentioned occasionally but nowadays only long in the tooth Anarchists are aware of its existence. If you remember the lynx, you'll want to take a look at SWEARING.

MADDY WATKINS In her own silent way, Maddy is a bit of a ground-breaker. She is a friend of LYNDA from outside the village. Now when does Lynda ever go outside the village? How does she come to have a friend? Maddy is the owner of a jerry-built patio, thrown together by the inadequate workmanship of NEIL and EDDIE. She also has some very fierce dogs that are amongst the only ones in the county ever known to bark. In fact, the fuss that Eddie and Neil made about what you would expect to be a daily occurrence bears out our observations on BARKING.

MANORFIELD CLOSE Ambridge's answer to Porton Down, a collection of homes for people who are born old but rather grotesquely never die. The main characteristic of the inhabitants is that they never speak and they are only referred to in terms of their incapacities: MR PULLEN (waterworks), MRS POTTER (walking frame), MRS BARRACLOUGH (cancer and then murdered). If you listen carefully, you might just occasionally catch the sound of manic cackling from behind the steel fences.

MARK WHITTINGHAM To be honest, in order to do justice to this man, we could do with a little more biographical detail. What we do know is that he had a large amount of manure to dispose of, duly taken off his hands, or at least his property, by EDDIE. He sounds the sort of chap you'd like to marry your daughter.

MARNEYS Whenever you go to Brookfield to visit any of the farming folk, they are always 'over in Marneys'. We are left to conjecture what this means, although it seems to be a code for 'not in'. Whilst the establishment would like you to believe it is an ancient name for a field over yonder, unkind folk have suggested it is a shed containing a stack of tins of SHIRES and a large pile of dirty magazines.

MARTHA WOODFORD People have already forgotten about Martha. She was the village postmistress, cleaner of the telephone box and feeder of bread to the DUCKS. Martha was also a great gossip, and often spread stories that were largely untrue. For that we loved her.

People have always had problems with becoming senile in Ambridge, FAT MAN FORREST and JECK being good examples. Martha was a fine example of Saundersism: she went from being completely scatty to turning up at the PARISH COUNCIL and questioning technical points of planning law. Her demise was rather sad because, as so often happens in this self-centred village, everyone completely forgot about her, failed to visit her, or even to mention her, and then just announced she had died. There is nothing so 'ex' as an ex-*Archers'* resident. But we'll always remember you Martha.

MATT CRAWFORD One of the main players in Borchester Land, Matt Crawford is a man who has the Midlands countryside coursing through his cockney veins. He is to the Ramblers Association what a beefburger is to a vegetarian. But he understands business and he likes to see profits. If he could turn Ambridge into a version of his beloved Old Kent Road he'd be in his seventh heaven and who are we to stop him?

Busy, he may be but Matt still finds time to eye up the girls and we fondly remember one day when he must have been wearing the wrong spectacles and tried to give Dopey DEBBIE the once over. It falls to Matt to put the lead into BRIAN's ever diminishing pencil and he works doggedly to ensure that Brian does not become soft in his old age. It was typical that while the goody-two-shoes busybodies of the village were going around spreading foot and mouth delivering bleeding heart leaflets to all and sundry about the school closure, it was Matt who quietly came up with the solution to the problem. The plan to build a massive housing estate in Ambridge is long overdue and Anarchists have been calling for this for years. It's just what we need to remove the smugness and SHEYAWN and co. can wrap their green belt round their middle-class necks.

MEMBER OF PARLIAMENT Although PAT claimed that they were writing to their MP about the school closure she seemed to have overlooked the fact that they have never had one. Indeed the political structure in Borsetshire is clearly different from the rest of England. They were also writing to their district councillor about the school despite the fact that this would be a matter for the County (there being no evidence that Borchester is a unitary authority). And when SHULUGH and PHALLUSTAIR wanted to get married in church and were experiencing slight difficulties on account of Phallustair being a bigamist, they lobbied boring GEORGE as Chairman of the Parish Council, rather than the PCC. Although there are occasional acknowledgements of the existence of elections, about once every ten years, no MP ever visits the village. It could be that the local MP is a Conservative but dare not show his face in a village where they are all card-carrying members of 'New' Labour.

MEN'S PROBLEMS It is an unfair world, and men would have it no other way. But it should be mentioned that Ambridge is even less fair. Whereas 'women's things' do get the odd airing we hear very little of anything in the men's department. The only exception is that there was a strong inference that ROBIN STOKES suffered from being stuck at half-past six when he had to perform with THE VILLAGE BICYCLE. Otherwise, nothing to report, and the idea that an Ambridge man should require a prostate operation is clearly preposterous.

MERRY HILL When push comes to shove, KEN TON is a nostalgic softie, so when his boyfriend Mel gave birth, it came as no surprise that the child should be named after a Midlands shopping centre. Given the silence of Ambridge children, we can't expect too much gurgling from an Oz-based sprog but at least Ken Ton will have an added incentive to renew his quest for a decent slice of the Brookfield cake.

MILK TANKER Under the careful stewardship of Kevin, it drove into a car containing PAT and POLL DOLL (the late Mrs Perks). Sadly it got the wrong person which meant not only that Pat is still with us but that SID ended up marrying the awful KATHY. In the days when the milk tanker was mentioned, good old Kevin often got a mention alongside it. Strangely no one ever stopped to ask what effect the whole dreadful business had on him. It is typical of Ambridge folk never to look beyond their own village.

MILLENNIUM Like many villages, Ambridge did its unnecessary bit for this arbitrary festival – planting a load of trees. Wow, that's so exciting, you can just feel THE ONE-EYED MONSTER's logger beginning to twitch. Predictably the tree-planting project was presided over by the usual sanctimonious suspects, THAT FISHER WOMAN and SHULUGH are never far away from such action. It was christened 'The Aldridge Millennium Wood' though we would have preferred 'Crawford Copse'. When the Millennium dawned and Mr Blair had finally released the Queen from an armlock, we were on the look-out for an example of incongruous Mandelsonian PRODUCT PLACEMENT. It had been revealed that the Government was desperate to promote the dreary Dome by encouraging the organization of coach parties from Ambridge, Coronation Street, Brookside Close, and other well-known locations, to visit it. In the event, it was beyond comprehension that the citizens of Ambridge who barely noticed the death of Princess Diana would have been aware enough to toddle down to Greenwich. KATHY and JAMIE the tealeaf did however put in a token appearance, and KATHY came back with a prepared eulogy written for her by Lord Falconer.

MO TRAVIS A delightful lady who, while NEIL's JAILBIRD of a wife was doing her time, took a shine to Neil and tried to get a look at his weaners. Being as wet as he is, Neil refused to go the distance, and when Jailbird came out there was a big scene after which Mo DISAPPEARED. This is most unrealistic, and we waited in vain to find a simmering rabbit in the Carter kitchen. Mo is a local woman whose children go/went to the same school as the Carters'. So where is she? Why does no one ever bump in to her? Why is she not anyone else's friend?

MOBILE PHONE (HANDBAG HEBDEN'S) One of the unsung icons of Ambridge. Hebden's mobile phone heroically distracted him while he was driving so that he missed seeing ROGER TRAVERS-MACY heading for him and drove into a tree and a horse. Anarchists celebrated long into the night, and had the mobile phone been present, it wouldn't have had to buy a battery all evening.

MOBILE PHONE (JAAARN'S) Very useful because it enabled him to give a number for sultry SHARON to use without having to identify his love nest with HORRIBLE HAYLEY. The fact that it would ring at an inconvenient moment never seemed to have occurred to him, but then we all know it never seems to occur to anyone.

MOBILE PHONE (MRS HIGH AND MIGHTY'S) Was ubiquitous at the time of her fling with her former husband, ROGER TRAVERS-MACY but has never been heard since. Maybe she was shocked by Hebden's experience and cast it into the Am.

MOBILE PHONE (EDDIE'S) After a period of borrowing other people's phones and notwithstanding his position as undischarged bankrupt without a penny to his name, he soon acquired his own mobile.

MOBILE PHONE (EDWEIRD'S) For a bloke who can hardly string two sentences together, this seems a rather superfluous piece of kit. Laudably he too obtained this gadget without any apparent means of financing it and it is good to see the noble tradition of Grundy larceny upheld with such aplomb.

MOBILE PHONES (GENERAL) Obviously they have not caught on in Ambridge at the same rate as everywhere else and we are not sure if the button A and B phone has ever been replaced in the village phone box. But there are more mobiles about than there used to be, and the one lesson that the people of Ambridge could teach the rest of the world is how to keep them largely silent. It would also be much appreciated if no one seeks to initiate them into the moronic art of text messaging. At the time of writing this plague has mercifully escaped Ambridge.

MONT BLANC, THE A top-class knocking shop outside the village. People go there for special occasions and, as with THE FEATHERS, invariably find it full of other people from Ambridge. Very expensive, you won't find yer Grundys, Tuggers or Carters there, although JAAARN went there for his last 'hurrah' before meeting his end. SHULUGH and THE VILLAGE BICYCLE go there when they can persuade some upper-class chinless wonder to take them and indeed BRIAN used to go there when he was having his notorious fling with The Bicycle and returned there more recently with his wife, of all people. Since we know that most people from the village go there rarely, at other times it must either be closed or perhaps choc-a-block with the silent conversations of people from Glebelands, Hollowtree Flats, and other nearby localities.

MORWENA THE WICKED WITCH This was a very alternative person of the kind found at craft fairs and folk festivals. She wore clothes made from the type of material where you can't tell where the shoulder bag, which looks as if it contains horse fodder, stops and the shapeless dress begins. She had a sinister hold over KATE and kept taking her away in untaxed vans with a load of hippies and gypsies. She claimed to be a qualified midwife but was desperately keen for Kate to give birth in a load of mud, not a practice recognized by the profession in general. BRIAN saw her for what she was but of course MRS HIGH AND MIGHTY insisted on trying to find her good points. She failed to find the needle in that particular haystack. She seems to have moved on to Benefit Offices new.

MOUNTAINEERING TEDDY A generous and thoughtful gift from HARD-WORKING SIMON to DAMIEN. It was given after a weekend away when Simon had been giving HARRIET WILLIAMS a good old-fashioned seeing to but pretended to have been rock climbing. Mountaineering Teddy was referred to in loving tones until that SLAP but since then seems to have become an un-bear. Damien has replaced it in his affections with a bunch of stick insects.

MRS BARRACLOUGH A delightful old lady who was murdered by DR DEATH in 1996. Locke tried to claim that she had died of cancer, but we all know that no one in Ambridge has ever died of cancer. Her death was widely mourned by a whole bunch of village establishment figures who had never hitherto been heard to utter her name, let alone talk to her. Typically, THAT FISHER WOMAN couldn't be bothered to visit her during her hour of need. She kept going on about, 'I must get round to see her.' But of course she was too busy practising witchcraft, whilst spouting PC nonsense, to have time for real vicarly business like visiting the sick.

MR BARRACLOUGH Devoted son of the above, who was devastated by her murder and fought an honourable battle to get DR DEATH struck off. Memorable scenes include the CRICKET Club dinner at GREY GABLES when Mr B accused Dr D of murder in full view of his fawning team mates. Death had to be restrained from hitting him. Yet it's to be noted that at no time did Mr Barraclough make any attempt to become physical himself. Dr Death made all kinds of smears against Mr Barraclough, suggesting that he didn't take much interest in his mother when she was actually alive. This is an allegation that could have been levelled at the whole of Ambridge, but poor Mr B was working a long way from the village and doubtless no one had bothered to inform him of his mother's plight. It is a source of great regret that we never hear of him nowadays.

MRS HIGH AND MIGHTY Jennifer has tended to spend a lot of her life going around with a mattress on her back, albeit a fairly expensive mattress since she married BRIAN. Her first child ADAM was begat of a liaison with Paddy Redmond, a lowly farm hand at Brookfield. She then married and had DEBBIE by ROGER TRAVERS-MACY, a hero for his role in ridding us of that troublesome HANDBAG HEBDEN. Poor old Roger was soon given the heave-ho when she caught sight of Brian Aldridge's wad. Since then she has been a complete stuck-up cow.

She managed to have a dalliance with posh John TREGORRAN, and then another with the jolly Roger. The biggest laugh was when Mrs High and Mighty started making a play for Saint SEAN MYERSON only to be told he batted the other way. Jennifer is unquestionably Ambridge's biggest snob but she does at least have a soft spot for her children. Rather too soft a spot in retrospect as they are all completely dysfunctional, a point conceded by Brian. At one time she used to fancy herself as a writer, quite a remarkable feat in a village where educational standards have always been so consistently low that it is doubted whether most people can read. Mrs High and Mighty in common with all Ambridge inhabitants, has taken the multi-ethnic nature of her grandchildren well into her stride. It is obviously galling for her to have to stand by while FREEBIE is denied access to a proper Rastafarian upbringing and the poor woman is mortified at the inculcation of Brumness that is going to set her back in life's great tussle. Life is best when Mrs High and Mighty is miserable, like when LILLIAN described her as 'matronly'. The worst aspect of a cheerful Mrs High and Mighty is that she says 'Bye eeee' on departure. We lost all respect for her when she refused to help KATE regain her daughter from a life of proledom.

MRS POTTER She seems to have had a walking frame since the age of 16 but shows no sign of giving up. Has not been known to speak but her walking frame has been heard to scrape. We imagine that the dreaded and castist Archers Anoraks invite the frame to their events so that they can hobnob with it. Her finest hour was probably the occasion on which, with great silent dignity, she upset some tins in the village shop and sent them cascading to the ground.

MR PULLEN One of the little indulgences the Ambridge cosy establishment allows itself is to make snide remarks about this poor gentleman who has a weak bladder. Naturally he is never allowed to speak and if he did so it would be from behind a lavatory door. There is never any talk about getting Mr Pullen treatment, albeit that his problem has been the topic of sneering for around 20 years, and he has never been permitted any other characteristics whatsoever. He is yet another leaking example of the complete failure of DR DEATH and latterly DR DIM to maintain a proper level of healthcare in the village. In June 2001 his life was greatly enriched when he used his pension to buy a collection of EDDIE GRUNDY's porno-gnomes.

MR SNOWY Before he became a philanderer, NIGEL PARGETTER was a strange androgynous Hooray Henry who used to scrape a living in an ice-cream van of this name. This dates back to the days when *The Archers* was in large part a slapstick routine. But don't knock it – the Mr Snowy ice-cream brought joy to the hearts of millions.

NAOMI By the time you are reading this we hope that Naomi will have proved to be our saviour. If all goes to plan, this 'very fit' student from Felpersham Poly will have been well and truly SORTED by OILSLICK. If there is any justice in the world, Dopey DEBBIE will be back at Home Farm with Mummy and Daddy, licking her wounds and BRIAN will be saying 'I told you so' with a grin on his face that would make the Cheshire Cat look like a pall bearer.

NASTY GINGER CAT To all normal-thinking people, everything about SHULUGH raises the hackles. So it came as no surprise when her characteristically pampered puss Tibby was attacked by what SHULUGH pathetically dubbed 'that nasty ginger cat'. Fearlessly the ginger cat fought, emitting an audible snarl, the likes of which you would only expect to hear on the Masai Mara. Only the intervention of village wimp – the former ice-cream toting NIGEL prevented Ginger from having a go at DAMIEN. Ginger's day will come.

NATIONAL LOTTERY The launch of the Lottery was one of the few SUDDEN NATIONAL EVENTS which didn't go entirely unnoticed in Ambridge. The problem was that it was launched at a time when the PC view was that it was a cynical way of taking money from morons and giving it to artistic fat cats. Hence the only village folk to play it were the Grundys – in fact both FAT CLARRIE and EDDIE played it without telling each other because they were both so ashamed of what they were doing. No one else in Ambridge played it then nor apparently has since, and it is now never mentioned despite having become an integral part of NHS funding and a right-on feature of Cool Britannia. Whether there is a Lottery terminal at the village shop has never been revealed though they do sell scratch cards as we saw when Clarrie blew her winnings on a guitar.

NEIL CARTER It is difficult for Anarchists to like Neil, but we do try. He is an incredibly boring plodder who allowed himself to be bullied by his dreadful wife JAILBIRD into taking the most unsuitable job that he could possibly have taken – that of a sales rep. For ages we were treated to the harrowing scenes of him trying apologetically to sell feed nuts to all the Ambridge farming folk. It was quite clear that Neil was not up to this work and it seemed to be on the cards that he would lose his job and the F-reg. Datsun Sunny that no doubt accompanied it. Yet, amazingly, he kept the job for yonks and we never heard of the trials and tribulations of sales from one year to the next. He seemed to have become the John Harvey-Jones of Ambridge. When Neil eventually ended his employment with BORCHESTER FEED MILLS it was a great surprise that he walked out on them rather than the other way around.

Since he came to the village, Neil has wandered around with a justifiable inferiority complex that has never noticeably improved. Before he married Jailbird he tried his hand, or other parts of his anatomy, with a number of the village ladies, most of whom were way above his social standing and gave him the elbow. He was engaged to a bird called Julie who was a real Brummie townie, but that one never got off the starting blocks. Interestingly Neil is another of the village's many convicted criminals, as he was done for possession of drugs some years ago.

A most pathetic sight for many years was Neil being led on by SHULUGH. It's not surprising that she was later to come a cropper with HARD-WORKING SIMON, because she has always been such a tease. Poor Neil would have given anything to go the distance with her, but she always ended up giving him the brush off. Neil's finest hour was while his Jailbird wife was doing porridge, and he almost had a fling with MO TRAVIS. 'Almost' is about as far as you can ever imagine Neil going when it comes to rumpy pumpy, in fact one has to presume that EMMER and Elephant Man are down to the AID man.

To his credit, Neil finally stood up to Jailbird and confessed his undying love for pigs and returned to a lucrative career as an unemployed labourer. Poor Plodder thought he had finally made it when DEEEVID and ROOOTH announced grand plans to expand the pigs at a time when the rest of Britain was getting out of pork as fast as it could. Working for Britain's worst farming partnership is a risky business at the best of times and it was no surprise when Neil had the distinction of being made redundant before he'd even started the job. Apparently, it had all been a mix up and what they had really intended was to close down the pigs altogether. Being the selfish lot they are, they forgot to tell Neil and he found out on the grapevine. Spurred on by an understandably angry Jailbird, Neil told the Geordie Whinger what she could do with any future job offers, i.e. make sure she asked him and he'd drop everything else and come crawling back. He now keeps body and soul together by doing about eighteen low paid/no paid jobs and has meaningless little enterprises on the go with all the losers in the village.

NELSON GABRIEL Nelson's behaviour in disappearing from the face of the Ambridge earth was bizarre in the extreme. As a former robber and architect of the great Ambridge mail van robbery (a crime for which he was tried and wrongly acquitted) there was a great irony when he began flitting from one Costa del Crime to another. It is understandable that Nelson became weary of the endless procession of middle-class bores who trooped through his wine bar. And it has always been something of a mystery how he ever acquired even the slightest knowledge of antiques, so no surprises when his antique shop was sold off.

The strangest thing about Nelson was that he had a posh voice despite being the progeny of one of the village's carrot-crunching bumpkins. Presumably educated at local rural schools, merely being a criminal does not seem a sufficient explanation for his refined pronunciation.

Nelson's sexuality has always been the subject of great speculation, though we all remember his black silk sheets and the attempted seduction of Jackie Woodstock. He had a daughter who is, ironically, a copper, but in latter years Nelson came over as Borchester's Quentin Crisp.

His eponymous wine bar never seemed to be a great success as it was always a place where middle-class yuppie Ambridge types like SHULUGH, LOATHSOME and NIGEL would go when they needed to talk quietly and earnestly (no doubt spinning out a half bottle of Frascati for four hours). Places where you can always get a table are useful but not much of a recommendation unless you are talking of MFI.

Following Nelson's disappearance in 1998, Elizabeth announced in a dramatic and tearful voice that she had received a phone call from him and we would 'never see him again'. This was somewhat odd given that nowhere on earth is more than a few hours on a long-haul flight.

It was highly suspicious that the next news of Nelson came in March 2001, again via Loathsome. She reported that Nelson was 'dead', though an observant Anarchist pointed out that as they tend to be rather behind the times in Ambridge, she was actually reporting the death of Admiral Horatio Nelson at the battle of Trafalgar. He died peacefully, as we would all wish to go, amid a hail of bullets in a desperate shoot-out in Buenos

Aires. There was one strange addendum in that his daughter suddenly declared that Nelson had wanted to have a great wake in Ambridge attended by all his mates and to be buried in St Stephens. Quite rightly, Nelson had poured scorn on virtually all the boring inhabitants of Ambridge and therefore didn't really have any mates. Apart from a relatively recent friendship with JOAN, he had only consorted with criminals and most of them were shady people who lived away from Ambridge. In the event his funeral was a tacky affair more suited to that of one of the Krays. We assume most of the mourners were wearing dark glasses. As can often happen, a lot of complete tosh was talked about what a wonderful bloke he was but Loathsome's description of him as 'the sweetest man ever' took not merely the biscuit, but the whole packet.

NIGEL PARGETTER A prime example of what can happen when an expensive education is lavished on someone who, in former times, would have walked about the village with a pig's bladder on a stick. Nigel is an upper-class twit who has always wanted to get inside SHULUGH's knickers and probably has done. In fact at one time he used to call her 'Shuli' – a term of affection that had any self-respecting Anarchists running for the safety of the lavatory. Like many in the village he is a convicted criminal, having been charged jointly with SHULUGH of the serious offence of 'taking and driving away'. He married 'Lizzie' as very much a second-best and because she shared his educationally subnormal slapstick sense of humour. In recent years we have felt a little more sympathy with him especially when LOATHSOME was playing away with HORNY HUGH.

For one delicious moment (during the Horny Hugh episode) the nation held its breath when Nigel appeared to be about to go the distance with THE VILLAGE BICYCLE. He presumably fancied her wonga as well as a bit of single wicket, and on her part he was. . .well. . .someone else in trousers. That it came to nought was a national disgrace.

In recent years Nigel has lapsed into complete dull, chinlessness. His attempts to manage LOWER LOXLEY are pathetic. We would like him to do the honourable thing – drink a bottle of gin, ascend THE TREETOP WALK and do a promotional for EXIT.

NURSE To our utter astonishment it was suddenly revealed that there is one at the doctor's surgery. A reward will be given for any information leading to a name or personality.

O

OAK APPLE DAY Another of the complete failures as a theme night to try and revive the ailing fortunes of THE BULL during the dark days of KATHY'S dismal reign. It was attended by the Snells, and that was it. It was a typical example of the total bankruptcy of imagination where the Perkses are concerned. Who was likely to get excited by Oak Apple Day when in those days you could go to a drag night at THE PINK CAT?

OILSLICK GERRARD We first encountered Oilslick when he was a professor at Exeter University where he led Dopey DEBBIE astray – hardly a difficult thing to do. He suddenly turned up a couple of years ago in the middle of the academic year in order to take up a post as Professor of Canadian Literature in Felpersham. As a subject of study it must rival the architecture of Communist Romania for its rich diversity. Dopey immediately fell for his oily charms and Anarchists were delighted when one of his female students made an accusation of sexual harassment against him. Disappointingly it was dropped and Dopey was daft enough to marry him. BRIAN thinks he is a gold-digging prat, and has been refreshingly hostile to him. We hate him because he was not very nice to the late SAMMY THE CAT and an enemy of Sammy's is no friend of ours.

OLIVER FOXBRUSH When he arrived to take over at Grunge Farm, it must have come to him as something of a surprise that despite being Master of Foxhounds for the local hunt, no one seemed to know him. Even those people who are known to hunt such as THE VILLAGE BICYCLE had not met him until he arrived in the village. But being the confident sort, he took this all in his stride and it wasn't long before he was giving the Bicycle the once over. If you can cope with totally silent hounds, you can presumably handle anything. He had the good sense to gut Grunge Farm, removing every last vestige of Grundy tastelessness. It's a relief to have someone with a bit of class coming into the village and his house-warming party must have been a delight, with EDWEIRD wandering round dispensing fox canapés. He claims his divorce was 'as amicable as divorces can be' which is code for 'they don't complain much when they're encased in six foot of concrete.' We'll probably grow to hate him, but his willingness to employ Edweird to do all his maintenance and odd jobs when he should be at school is at least a gesture in the right direction.

ONE-EYED MONSTER, THE Mike Tucker (or Tugger as he calls himself) is one of life's losers and an unreconstructed sexist. As a result of an industrial accident he has had only one eye for some years, but we very rarely hear any reference to this. Not exactly New Labour, he was at one time the trade union rep at Brookfield. He has enough chips on his shoulder to start a MacDonalds restaurant, which is typical of the kind of hare-brained scheme he would come up with.

It is always surprising that anyone is prepared to enter into any entrepreneurial deal with him since nothing he turns his hand to is destined for success – for example, the STRAWBERRY CROP. He is permanently in a state of simmering anger and is very much in the category of people who call their lunch 'dinner'. But of course, as with everyone else, you'll never hear a genuinely bad word pass his lips.

He is a paid-up member of the not totally exclusive bankrupts club and also suffered a breakdown of the type that makes your nearest and dearest remove all the heavy implements from the house. He recovered in that sudden and miraculous way that we have come to expect, but it has left the unpleasant and everlasting mark that causes him to tell anyone with so much as a sniffle that 'Oi've bin there.' He treats brainless BEDDY as Mrs Caveman and expects his food put in front of him on demand. He was ridiculously proud of racist ROY when he managed to graduate with one of those degrees that no one has ever failed. We see Tugger as a short chap who suffers from terminal smallman's disease. One of life's greatest delights is to witness his occasional explosions, such as the time he realized BIG BRENDA had fallen for the charms of SCOTTY.

1 + 1 = 3 It is rarely possible for two people in Ambridge to have a conversation without a third person joining in. This seems to happen particularly when they are discussing something of a confidential nature. Sure as night follows day someone will bound up to them and barge into the conversation with not the slightest degree of sensitivity.

ORGAN FUND Any charity fundraiser will tell you that if you set up an appeal, it is important to structure it properly, to report how much it has raised and to what extent the goal can now be achieved. The Organ Fund at St Stephen's was set up several years ago now, long before the days of TFW who would probably rather see the organ replaced with guitars and a steel band. A number of busybodies got involved in raising funds and at least one event took place. We've never heard another word about what happened or where the money went. But you probably don't have to look much further than who were the churchwardens at the time. One was FAT MAN FORREST.

ORGANIC VEGETABLES Boring though they are, they deserve a mention as they are grown by PAT and TONY. One of the many right-on things to occur in Ambridge is the existence of their organic crops. Considering the rip-off price these things are in our supermarkets as we eagerly pay a premium to buy carrots that are covered in mud it is hard to understand why Tony and Pat go on so often about being hard up.

OVERENTHUSIASM This was the euphemism which was used in court to describe HARD-WORKING SIMON's behaviour which had allegedly resulted in DEBBIE ALDRIDGE receiving some minor bruising. She originally claimed it was actually the result of a RIDING ACCIDENT but as she is a pathological liar it is best not to believe her.

OVER-SIXTIES CLUB Does it still exist? It can't be the most rockin' and rollin' of clubs since its events seem to be highly sporadic. The annual coach trip happens about as regularly as a total eclipse of the sun. Of course one of the things that doubtless hampers its success is the sheer volume of silent people who attend any of its functions. It must be most dispiriting for a guest speaker. Naturally many of its stalwart members have cashed in their chips but there are plenty of people who could have taken their place.

PC DAVIES The 'community beat officer' in Ambridge must have a beat that covers the whole of England as we only see him about once every four years. He doesn't say much, but quiet effective policing is just what they like in the village. It's a case of softly, softly catchy murderer, though he never manages to catch one. When he does speak, he fits the pattern of all policemen in Ambridge since the friendly Colin Drury who left us some 25 years ago – same belligerent voice, no local accent, insensitive manner, last person you'd call if someone broke into your house, last person who'd come if someone broke into your house.

PARISH COUNCIL It is strange that whilst VILLAGE PRODUCTIONS occupy an absurdly disproportionate amount of time we hear virtually nothing of the Parish Council for months, sometimes years on end. Yet the Council must meet several times a year and will have numerous subcommittees. It is also rather odd that an old dipso like GEORGE (ALCOPOP) BARFORD has been allowed to continue as its Chairman for so long. We could really do with a list of all the members because there don't seem to be many people actually on it. The Parish Council is one of Britain's finest repositories for busybodies of which Ambridge has more than its fair share. And whereas Ambridge's only springs into life on special occasions such as when someone wishes to site a nuclear reactor on LAKEY HILL or build a few houses, in the rest of Britain they will have a full-scale meeting if someone forgets to take their dustbin in.

PAT ARCHER If we were to sum up Pat in a few words it would be an economic Uncle Tom (not Forrest we hasten to add). She has always been one of the village lefties and has tended to make life hell for the more conservative and down to earth TONY, whom she has worn down by years of constant nagging. The discovery of the joys of capitalism has largely silenced her political ramblings and she is Ambridge's yoghurt queen, ruling the dairy with a rod of iron. Pat's succession of inevitably low-paid female staff are bullied and generally treated like something the cat brought in – ironic given that her product is something the cat would like to take out.

The role of Pat and Tony is to be always on the cusp of success but never quite achieve it. They are carefully positioned to contrast with BRIAN and MRS HIGH AND MIGHTY who are always one step away from obscene wealth and THE ONE-EYED MONSTER whose fingernails are the only things standing between him and the abyss.

Pat is never far away when there is a death caused by a farming-related vehicle in the offing. She was in the car with POLL DOLL when Kevin's MILK TANKER slammed into them, and of course JAAARN's death by THE FERGIE was another bummer for her. At first Pat coped with the death quite well and was relatively unfazed even by LANCASTRIAN 'TRASHER' TOMMY's assertion that she had effectively nagged Jaaarn to death. Whilst he did not exactly choose the most sensitive time to offer this opinion, it is not without some foundation in truth. All changed for a while when she fell victim to the Great Sausage Betrayal, described elsewhere here in greater detail.

In true spirit of sisterhood, and typically without consulting the rest of the family, Pat invited homeless KATHY and JAMIE TEALEAF-PERKS to move in for an indefinite period, where she was apparently given the bathroom as her sleeping quarters, since no one else was ever able to ablute when they wanted to.

Pat is the epitome of New Labour and faithfully laps up MAFF propaganda. If she were to be told she had to slaughter her animals, Mr Blair would get a thank you letter by return. When he was almost lynched by angry farmers on a visit to Devon in 2000, Pat's only comments were about how much he was apparently going to do for farmers.

If we can be permitted one enormous CASTIST indiscretion, we could point out that she has come a long way since being Jimmy Clitheroe's sister.

PEEEP ARCHER One recurrent theme is the naming of children within the Archer clan. The name is never determined by what is or is not a nice name. Instead it is used as a mechanism to curry favour (for example, the late JAAARN was named John Daniel in order to get a mention in the late DAN's will). So Peeep is actually named after PHIL. And sure enough, helped on by a bit of blackmail it soon paid dividends when Phil announced that ROOOTH and DEEEVID could have Brookfield gratis.

Like all the children of the cosy establishment, Peeep is a precocious little brat. Surprisingly, by the taciturn standards of Ambridge folk, she commenced speaking early. One of her first utterances boded ill for the future: 'There's Stephen. I don't like Stephen.' We knew it wouldn't be long before Stephen took a dive into a slurry pit. And sure enough he's never been heard of since.

Peeep threw a bit of a wobbly when her brother BSE Josh was born. The usual sort of sibling jealousy, but of course it had to be dealt with in a very PC way. Poor old DEEEVID had to take a day off work to parade Josh in front of Peeep's class at school. Much to the chagrin of us all, Josh proceeded to 'fill his nappy' on prime-time suppertime radio. Miraculously, this one visit removed all traces of jealousy.

Peeep was unfortunately disfigured for life at the village fête a few years ago. HORRIBLE HAYLEY applied a toxic face paint to her – just what you expect from someone who spends their life looking after children. As she grows up, Peeep becomes less pleasant by the day. Anarchists were bitterly disappointed when a bull failed to take the opportunity to give her a well-deserved goring. Unfortunately, the amazing KEVIN DUNN put a premature stop to those proceedings. She is essentially selfish and was quite unkind to her poor mother during her illness in 2000, though she was not much better to her father as she kept asking for 'Daddy to read me a story'– a cruel jibe at someone who is illiterate. Her parents got their own back when they set up a fortress against FOOT AND MOUTH and Peeep was evacuated to Glebe Cottage and the clutches of DAMIEN. Within two days she was demanding to be released as Damien was about to achieve his first human sacrifice.

PEGGOI WOOLLEY Owner of the late SAMMY the cat and wife of JECK, Peggoi can be a bit of a pain. Where did she get her rather posh voice? She is another of the characters whose voice bears no relation to her parentage. Mrs Perkins, her mother, was a cockney with a voice to match. Peggoi is worth a copper or two having at one time owned THE BULL, and lives a life of luxury at GREY GABLES.

Peggoi is treated very much as a milk cow by her grandchildren and seems to enjoy dispensing largesse – always with strings attached. The best thing about Peggoi is that she doesn't approve of THAT FISHER WOMAN, since she has no truck with vicarettes. She has stuck to her guns and now worships at All Saints, Borchester, a good Bentley's drive away. Peggoi is also fairly lukewarm about THE VILLAGE BICYCLE ever since she tried to lure BRIAN away from Peggoi's awful daughter.

Peggoi clearly sees herself as Ambridge's conscience and who are we to argue? She is something of a prude and is always more likely to be heard saying, 'I don't think that's very nice' than '***kin 'ell, let's go down the pub and get slaughtered.'

She's a bit of a busybody and tends to go in for a lot of 'third-party sulks' almost always relating to her children or grandchildren. Invariably the way these work is that someone hasn't told her something, she's come to hear of it, and is now known to be upset about hearing it and the fact that she wasn't told.

Although she seems to be in remission for the moment, Peggoi went through a strange phase of being a self-appointed party-enforcer. This meant that she would identify when one of her relatives had a birthday or anniversary cropping up and then, regardless of whether they wished to celebrate the event or not, she would insist that a party be held. In turn, we had to witness the frog-marching of a string of reluctant guests and the victim had to be put into a straight-jacket and sedated before they could be persuaded to attend.

We were a little disappointed that even Peggoi has become so imbued with political correctness that she thought nothing of her unmarried granddaughter turning up preggers again and did not even notice the arrival of a Boer in Ambridge. But she has now become so cool and hip that she suggested GLUCOSE and KATE might as well have just lived together rather than got married. She's one cool cockney.

PERIODS More or less half the population of the world have periods, but in a sedate place like Ambridge we do not need to hear about them. In recent years, the falling standards we have come to expect have reached the village and there are now two or three occasions when periods have raised their heads. BRENDA TUGGER and EMMER CARTER started having them (note that it only happens to the common people), much to BEDDY's surprise and concern, and KATE stopped having them. Anarchists tend to be a bit squeamish about these sort of things, especially when we are about to have our evening meal at 7.00 pm. As it happens, it seems it was only a phase like silly silver-coloured scooters and doesn't appear to have happened to anyone else. Strangely, but much to our relief, we hear much less about MEN'S PROBLEMS.

PHALLUSTAIR BLANDVOICE The current vet is only one of a long string of vets to put it about with the better-heeled womenfolk in the village. Over the years, the dreaded SHULUGH and THE VILLAGE BICYCLE have ensnared more vets between them than MR PULLEN has made trips to the LAVATORY. But Phallustair really takes the biscuit when it comes to charisma bypasses. He actually manages to make the late HANDBAG HEBDEN seem a bit of a player. Unfortunately he is just the kind of cosy character that the Archer clan loves.

Phallustair obviously came on the scene with just one aim – to get goalside of the St Michael label in SHULUGH's sensible knickers, a mission he managed to accomplish despite being two-timed by DR DEATH. Scenes involving Phallustair and Shulugh are always liable to induce severe nausea. They make the archetypal smug couple that in itself creates a need for Anarchists.

It would be nice to know a bit more about the first Mrs Blandvoice, as Anarchists still cling to desperate hopes that he might yet turn out to be a serial killer. Fuel was added to our speculation when he refused to get married in church because he was not prepared to discuss his first marriage with the nosey TFW.

He appears to be oblivious to the sinister nature of his demonic stepson and has irresponsibly given him access to all kinds of animals, allowed him to own a hamster, keep beetles and spend an unhealthy amount of time in the churchyard.

Phallustair is a complete doormat to be walked over by the horrendous Shulugh at all opportunities. As with many other people in the village, he managed to appear without arriving. Perhaps he could DISAPPEAR without leaving – another beloved trick of many loved and hated characters. But if he does not wake up soon and leg it, it will be too late as he is all set to become one of Damien's ritual sacrifices.

PHIL ARCHER Although he is clearly a real stalwart of the village, and now in his seventies, it is difficult for Anarchists to know what to make of the blighter. Phil is very much part of the cosy establishment but he is also pretty boring. It is hard to think of anything he has ever done or said that gets the pulses racing. His judgement over the years has been pretty good. He seems happy enough being married to FOGHORN, and it wasn't his fault that he married someone so combustible before that.

Phil manages to get up the nose of his equally boring son DEEEVID and has been unnecessarily tolerant of the daughter-in-law-from-hell ROOOTH who, ever since arriving as a student, has managed to grab his son and a partnership in the farm. Unlike Foghorn, Phil has the measure of LOATHSOME and KEN TON and recognizes them to some extent for what they are. He has always been lukewarm about NIGEL, whom he has long recognized as the dickhead we all know him to be. But where Phil has a ludicrously soft spot is for the dreaded sanctimonious SHULUGH. As someone who has always been cautious with his money, it was rather surprising that Phil was so ready to bail out his waster of a son Ken Ton when it transpired he owed an unspecified sum to the Aussie revenue.

A few years ago Phil entered some kind of crisis which resulted in him spontaneously becoming a cooking maniac. This was very serious since not only did it get in the way of his running of the farm, but it caused severe friction with Foghorn for whom cooking is her raison d'être. At its height he would insist on cooking Christmas dinner, and was to be found with his head permanently buried in Delia Smith, so to speak. Happily, he seems to have forgotten his new-found hobby completely, and is barely likely to switch a kettle on, let alone cook a meal. But as a cook in recovery, it should never be forgotten that he is always liable to have a relapse and we should be on our guard.

As the patriarch of the Archer dynasty, Phil does not expect to be crossed and there was a wonderful moment early in 1998 when the Foghorn sided with Roooth and Deeevid over the perennially mind-numbingly boring question of whether or not to expand the herd. Poor old Phil was cut to the quick by the fact that even his beloved Foghorn had veered from her automatic pilot. Sensible Phil will doubtless pootle on into senility, at which time he will, like his father before him, be dragged kicking and screaming from the farmyard, finally surrendering to Deeevid and the Geordie gorgon. Although he and Foghorn have finally surrendered Brookfield, it was with a heavy heart as they have had to stand by and watch Deeevid and Rooth make an utter pig's ear of almost every aspect of the farm.

He and Foghorn were both greatly distressed by the battle amongst their children for some of the remaining wonga but he has certainly gone out of his way to divide things up in the least equitable manner imaginable. Deeevid gets the farm, Ken Ton nothing on the basis that the few quid bunged to the taxman a few years ago should keep him quiet, Loathsome nothing because she has stolen her mother-in-law's inheritance and Shulugh gets nothing as she had already stolen her Grandmother's cottage and now has the cheek to want to sell it to her parents.

POLL DOLL Polly Perks was a nice normal woman of a kind sadly lacking in Ambridge nowadays. She was everything that the dreadful KATHY is not in that she was pleasant, friendly and an excellent landlady for THE BULL. She had class (lower) and knew her place. If she had but one fault it was that she was friendly with PAT, a crime for which she was to pay with her life when she was tragically squashed by a MILK TANKER. SID loved Poll Doll and has never properly recovered.

PORTIA A dead Afghan cruelly murdered by PHALLUSTAIR, aided and abetted by HORRIBLE HAYLEY. Beloved pet of MRS ANTROBUS, she was unceremoniously buried before her very eyes.

POSTMAN The postman always rings twice? Don't make us laugh, not in Ambridge he doesn't. There isn't one and hasn't been for years. NELSON almost murdered one when he committed the great Ambridge mail van robbery and Harry Booker delivered post for a while, but he and his wife moved about two miles away and have never been heard of again. God knows how they get their post nowadays. Since they spend all their time shouting and calling in on each other they probably never bother to write anything. There is very little evidence that they ever communicate with the outside world, so perhaps there's no need for one.

PRINCE CHARLES Talking to plants is fine by us, but throwing your gaff open to a load of lunatics who call themselves 'the cast' of *The Archers* is definitely out of order. And that's just what he did in the spring of 2001. Naturally, a furious missive was penned to the Prince pointing out the error of his ways. His response though prompt was bordering on the unsatisfactory since it only thanked us for writing and conveyed his good wishes. It's a good job his ancestors had a bit more bottle, somehow we can't see the Armada having been SORTED by a few good wishes.

PRODUCT PLACEMENT This is not a phenomenon confined to television. Indeed on radio it is in a certain way even more glaring when it does occur. For whilst you can casually leave a box of Kellogg's cornflakes on a table in a television production, you actually have to mention it on the radio. It manifests itself on *The Archers* in a number of different forms. The out and out reference to a brand name is relatively rare, although the manufacturers of WD-40 were no doubt delighted when DEEEVID suggested to someone that 'a spot of WD' might help shift a rusty bolt on a gate. And since his original plug, the stuff has become more popular in Ambridge than SHIRES. Delia Smith got a good airing by Phil in his cookery spasm. *The Teletubbies* were given a merciless promo with DAMIEN and PEEEP both suitably enthralled by this moronic pap. Vodafone were given a nice plug when MRS HIGH AND MIGHTY was heard trying to contact the mobile of MORWENA THE WICKED WITCH. *The Lion King* was hugely enjoyed by KATHY and JAMIE TEALEAF PERKS. Chocolate Hobnobs made a guest appearance and it goes without saying that no one suddenly clutched their stomachs and declaimed them as the food of the devil. Bill Bryson was read with slightly more equivocation by ROOOTH. What is more common is the placement of information advertising such as JAAARN crashing his tractor without a safety cab. The final manifestation is the promotion of certain events over and above the level that would naturally occur within that community – the most notable example being GAY PRIDE and sycophantic endorsement whenever Mr Blair blows his nose. But to give them their due, the BBC is happy to plug the competition on occasions, as evidenced by HORRIBLE HAYLEY consulting Teletext.

PRU FORREST It is many years now since FAT MAN FORREST read *Jane Eyre* and began to see Mr Rochester as a kind of role model. He then packed his wife Pru off to THE LAURELS where she maniacally produced jams and other preserves from the comfort of her padded cell. The official reason for incarcerating her in Stalug Luft Laurel since she was 70 was that she had a couple of strokes. It is far more likely that her moaning murderer of a husband preferred wandering round the village saying 'I miss moi Pru' to the task of looking after her.

It is easy to tell how long someone has been listening to *The Archers*, simply by the fact that if they claim that Pru never spoke, you know they are relative newcomers. For at one time Pru was possessed of a rather ridiculous bleating voice redolent of Larry the Lamb, and would call her husband 'Taarm' rather in the same way that SHARON RICHARDS called the late John 'JAARN'. They had a couple of foster sons – Peter and Johnny – who are just another two of Ambridge's many DISAPPEARED. Given Tom's track record, their continued absence is particularly sinister. Perhaps, for once in their lives, the village cosies should remove the blinkers from their eyes and investigate the oft-dug gardens of the Forrests. Pru was murdered in the most cold-blooded way by FOGHORN who could wait no longer to get her mitts on Pru's recipe book. She turned up to The Laurels with a batch of poisoned scones and since Borsetshire thinks coroner is a kind of margarine, there was no one to cry foul. And were we surprised soon afterwards when PHIL walked into the kitchen at Brookfield triumphantly brandishing the much-coveted recipe book.

PUGSLEY (MRS) This timeless old crone has been housekeeper to generations of Pargetters since the Middle Ages. When you are as established as her, you don't need to lower yourself by speaking, you just bake with dignity and serve.

QUEEN, Her Majesty The. When old Sophie Wessex started slagging off every public figure she could think of, including her ma-in-law, to an imitation sheik, Anarchists could usually have been relied upon to have bayed for her blood. For hitherto we've been royalist to the hilt (except for those who think the monarchy sucks). But we all became republicans on 1 January 2001 when the Queen slung an MBE in the direction of a deluded character who passes himself off as EDDIE GRUNDY. People who don a hat with horns and impersonate others should be given strong tranquillizers, not encouragement and for Her Majesty to become a party to gross castism is deeply disturbing and threatens our whole constitution.

QUEENIE For a misogynist like ZEBEDEE TRING, naming a cat Queenie must have been an act of great self-sacrifice. But then if you've got a female cat you can hardly call it Gary can you? There is a long-established tendency for animals to be neglected in Ambridge and no one knows what happened to Queenie when Zebedee croaked it.

QUIZ Perhaps one of the reasons THE BULL became so unpopular was because of SID's propensity to start some entertainment feature and then discontinue it without comment. In the latter part of 1997 there seemed to be a quiz team that competed regularly and with some success against the silent teams of other pubs in Borsetshire. But this seemed to stop without a word of explanation. When he came up with the whacky and sexist idea of running a women's quiz team during the 1998 World Cup, no one was heard to ask what had happened to the regular quiz nights with the existing team of BERT, ST USHA, etc. Like a volcano it then lay dormant until it erupted once again as a new idea in the spring of 2001. Quiz cheat Fry was this time exiled in the BOONGALOW where he was interned during the FOOT AND MOUTH outbreak but he came up with an unlikely idea that he would participate via the INTERNET, the mechanics of which were never made totally clear.

REG AND BUNTY Having ridiculous names should be no impediment to your grandparental rights and Anarchists have been furious at the callous disregard shown to HANDBAG HEBDEN's parents by the ghastly SHULUGH and PHALLUSTAIR. The adoption of DAMIEN by Phallustair was terribly upsetting for them and they raised their objections in vain. FOGHORN was sent as an emissary to shout at them, which didn't exactly do the trick, but then the Archer mafia simply didn't give a toss whether they had their blessing or not.

RELIGION No one could accuse Ambridge folk of being a bunch of Bible bashers. And when you put your mind to it you suddenly realize that there is something quite sinister about the way religion is treated in this weird place. Appropriately enough most of the residents exist in a kind of Amish community with very little discernible contact with the outside world. There is, of course, St Stephen's but this is clearly a front for all kinds of pagan goings on and it is obvious that THAT FISHER WOMAN is a complete impostor.

Few of the residents ever refer to going to church apart from one or two of the token sanctimonious characters such as the awful SHULUGH and her cosy parents. Yet whenever we hear a service in Ambridge it sounds like a state occasion in Westminster Abbey, with hymns being belted out like nobody's business. On those occasions it is noticeable that FOGHORN is always completely ignoring the service and talking to someone in a huge stage whisper.

Anarchists have pointed out in the past the complete absence of Catholicism in Ambridge – the Reformation was obviously a pretty thorough job in Ambridge. It must have been coincidental therefore that shortly afterwards, a left footer arrived in the obnoxious person of SHEYAWN HAVITAWAY. She thoughtfully brought her own church with her, Our Lady of all Phoney Accents. But sensitive to what the neighbours might think she parked it outside the village. JOE GRUNDY claims to be a Methodist but this would seem to be nothing more than a convenient excuse to avoid St Stephen's. We never hear that he's 'off down the chapel', and indeed whenever he quotes the Bible, which he is prone to do now and then in times of trouble, it is always the fire-and-brimstone passages – hardly the stuff of Methodism.

It's only when you get to the less mainstream religions that the village comes into its own. There is obviously a Hindu temple next door to the village shop, on the other side from the police house presumably. Muslims are not forgotten and EDWEIRD can often be seen shinning up the minaret, swigging from a can of Kronenberg 1664 as he goes. Rastafarians have always found the village a home from home, living proof of which is the wretched FREEBIE.

RIDING ACCIDENT Second only to that SLAP in its deliciousness was the occasion when the simpering Dopey DEBBIE, then Aldridge, came a cropper at the hands of HARD-WORKING SIMON. It is one of those occasions when we have to be honest as witnesses and say we didn't see a thing. You know how it is, when does a football manager ever see the events leading up to his side conceding a penalty? All we know is that there was a lot of shouting on the part of both Debbie and Simon after which Debbie was allegedly a touch black and blue. She immediately attributed her state to having fallen from her long-suffering horse, Tolly, on the riding course. And who are we to doubt her?

Under pressure from THE VILLAGE BICYCLE and SHULUGH, both of whom carried a long-term vendetta against poor Simon, Debbie changed her story and Simon was landed in court. Debbie is clearly unstable and has had numerous unsatisfactory relationships with men. It is almost certain that she was hallucinating (Home Farm's GM magic mushrooms can do funny things) and that Hard-working Simon was just being gallant in carrying the can. The manful way in which he pleaded guilty in order to save Debbie from having to testify in court never received the praise and admiration it deserved. What a shame this misunderstood man is no longer in the village to add his own colour – black with a tinge of blue.

ROBERT SNELL A somewhat sinister figure whose life is entirely consumed by computers and CRICKET. Robert has been known to call his good lady 'Lindybottom', but sadly we rarely get to hear this. He is somewhat lacking in charisma and has been rather unkindly stereotyped as a computer nerd, when of course we all know that no more than 95 per cent of computer buffs can truly be described as such. Robert had a job 'in computers' which no one seemed to know about in any detail, and then it all went pear-shaped (what is wrong with the shape of a pear?) This meant that Lindybottom had to get on her bike and look for menial tasks to help earn the family crust.

Robert is on his second wife, having bored the first one, the absurdly named Bobo into submission. One of the most exciting things he has ever done since his arrival in Ambridge is to almost move to Grimsby – a career move scuppered by Lindybottom's efforts to assist him. Since then he has apparently been 'in work' though the precise nature of this is shrouded in mystery. All of a sudden in March 2001, Robert suddenly saw the light, the heady glow of which was the realization that his wife was an insufferable nutcase. It concerned the uneasy relationship between Linda and her silent stepdaughter Leonie. The poor child, just 25, wanted to buy a house and as all 25-year-old children are apt to do expected her father to buy it for her. It seemed a very reasonably priced property at £5,000 but Lynda Tight-wad thought Robert should be spending it on feng-shueing their goats. Instead, he chose to feng shuei his brain and left the perennially rearranged house. This proved all too temporary as he was back within days, declaring his undying love for Lindybottom and sending us all skuttling to our sick buckets, gadgets that are second only to radios in our households.

ROBIN STOKES A very boring vicar-vet who had two children called 'Salmon Oliver'. He had two characteristics of note. The first was a weird speaking voice that sounded like Noêl Coward singing 'Mad Dogs and Englishmen'. The other was that he suffered from one of the MEN'S PROBLEMS: impotence. He was all set to marry THE VILLAGE BICYCLE but after HANDBAG HEBDEN had tried to mow her down in his kamikaze attack, she suddenly realized that Stokes hadn't got a big enough wad. Robin could hardly be described as 'over the moon' when the Bicycle not only broke off their engagement but rapidly married poor old loaded GUY. He moved away in abject misery, although he probably got the last laugh when he realized how close he had come to being bumped off, for the marriage to Guy only really lasted long enough for him to change his will.

ROGER TRAVERS-MACY He is one of the heroes of *The Archers*. By trying to imitate David Coulthard along the narrow Ambridge lanes, Roger managed to rid us of the least interesting character ever to grace the airwaves – HANDBAG HEBDEN. He wasn't going to be put off by a few horses clogging up the highways, and it certainly wasn't his fault that Handbag was on his MOBILE PHONE at the time.

Roger picked MRS HIGH AND MIGHTY out of the gutter when she was a single mum and married her. But his struggling antiquarian book business couldn't keep the spoilt woman in the style to which she wished to become accustomed. We all thought he had disappeared from the scene until one day he showed up at Home Farm and whisked Jennifer off her feet once again. Poor old BRIAN, a man whose morals are above question and whose old-fashioned standards of decency are a credit to him, was understandably mortified. Travers-Macy by now seemed rolling in it, presumably as he has now gone in to the far more lucrative hard porn business. He gave the awful DEBBIE a flash car – a totally inappropriate gift for a girl who goes round in sackcloth and ashes most of the time. Sadly Roger the dodger seems to have disappeared again. But Anarchists would welcome him back anytime.

ROOOTH ARCHER The whingeing Geordie has assaulted our ears for too many years, ever since she arrived at Brookfield from Harper Adams Agricultural College as a student on work experience. She managed to inveigle her way into Brookfield, marry DEEEVID and is now a partner in the firm. Roooth has produced two sprogs – PEEEP and BSE Josh, the latter sired by BSE ANDY. It is notable that she spends as little time as possible with her children. She is forever palming them off on FOGHORN to look after and it has been suggested that she may well be suffering from Munchausen's syndrome by proxy.

Roooth, like Dopey DEBBIE, is paranoid about being ignored in decision making. This is ironic as she tends to sulk her way into getting exactly what she wants. There is no question that she prefers the company of cattle to children – her enthusiasm for the 'red cows' at Brookfield far outweighs her interest in her children.

Roooth's life was turned upside down in 2000 when a routine medical check-up revealed that she was suffering from terminal fake Geordiness, a disease we would not wish on our worst enemy. In a tribute to Blair's Britain she was whisked into Borchester General faster than the speed of sound where she was attended in vain by elocution consultants. This brought out political correctness in all its most offensive manifestations and we were treated to endless promotionals on 'life after Geordiness'. It's important to realize that just because you have had a major operation, it doesn't need to change your life, particularly your sex life. Thus we have been treated to the unedifying spectacle of Deeevid and Roooth making lewd sexual innuendo in every episode and generally behaving like rutting dogs ever since.

Her relentless wearing down of all opposition has borne much fruit of late. Amazingly, her threat to up sticks to France, which would have sent Anarchists hurrying to the travel agents on her behalf, resulted in a rapid guarantee that she and Deeevid would keep Brookfield. Her endless whingeing about the size of the BOONGALOW finally brought about the eviction of poor old Foghorn and PHIL from their home. There is little to commend her, but perhaps her most revolting characteristic is her tendency to throw a multi-decibel tantrum when she is asked to do some work, particularly anything of a domestic nature. Her reaction when it was suggested that she might look after the holiday cottages to bring much-needed dosh into the perpetually near bankrupt enterprise that is Brookfield was akin to Etna at its worst. Our only hope is that Deeevid will one day discover the true father of BSE Josh and will run off with a Hereford Cow.

ROY TUGGER Roy has long been the working-class member of the rapidly ageing brat pack and for some time was seemingly welded to the bar of THE PINK CAT. As the son of THE ONE-EYED MONSTER, it is inevitable that he will carry traces of spud on his shoulder. Yet for a complete dumb cluck he has had some quite interesting moments. While at his FE college he fell in with two gentlemen named SPANNER and CRAVEN who held strong views on the subject of immigration. In a trice, Roy went from one of the 'silent' to fully fledged Nazi, something for which he seems to have been entirely and unjustifiably forgiven. Whilst no Anarchist could condone their behaviour, there can be few who would not have wanted to post a turd through ST USHA's front door if only in the hope that her then live-in lover DR DEATH might slip on it.

The extremely unlikely coupling of the dreary Tugger boy with KATE ALDRIDGE was never going to be an easy one. Young Tugger does not appear to have any particular interests or ambitions but is increasingly sensible – always a bad sign in anyone.

The murder of his friend JAAARN did raise a number of interesting issues. Tugger had been threatened by Jaaarn just a few weeks prior to his death when Jaaarn told him that if he ever touched 'his HAYLEY' he'd 'kill' him. Though he never got the chance, was it just because Tugger took preventative action? After all, young Roy was already making great strides towards bedding Hayley on the old rebound.

Andrew Motion began to shake in his shoes when Tugger popped up at Jaaarn's funeral with a somewhat finger-down-the-throat poem he claimed to have written himself. Strangely, this poem was reprinted in the *Radio Times* shortly after, when it was said to have been written by someone else. Is the lad actually living in a Walter Mitty world, and is this bit of plagiarism another sign of the built-in inadequacy of the Tugger family?

Mensa have never been troubled with an application form from Roy of the racists but it was quite remarkable when he suddenly claimed paternity of Rastafarian FREEBIE and just showed how lax these things can be when he was declared the father. Since then he has shacked up with HORRIBLE, how Jaaarn would turn in his grave, and is fast becoming the most boring man in Ambridge – an accolade for which there is never a shortage of competitors. Egged on by Horrible, he has behaved appallingly to Kate and denied her the right to give Freebie the proper multicultural upbringing she craves. Just before his wedding it became apparent that he is a cross-dresser but of course Horrible was too daft to realize and swallowed his ludicrous explanation instantly. Any suspicions that he may be a closet intellectual were finally removed when, on the day of his wedding, we witnessed the horror with which he greeted the gift of a book 'Iron John' from OILSLICK. The realization that it contained more than pictures was just too much to bear. But you have to hand it him. He knows how to give a girl a good time. He and Horrible must have been the only couple in British history to have gone on honeymoon to Camden, in a hotel where they will have been able to mix with the pick of London's DSS claimants.

RUSSELLS You can be excused if you don't remember the Russells. They were the smug goody-goody couple described as 'lovely' that TUGGER and HORRIBLE were sent to see as part of their 'wedding preparation'. This is one of the trendy TFW innovations that go a long way to explaining declining church attendances. Even Tugger was unhappy about having to go and see the perfect couple boasting about how wonderful their marriage was. It is difficult to discern how this experience is meant to enlighten a would-be married couple. If you fancy fish and chips, you don't expect to have to meet a satisfied customer before you go to the chip shop. And if the idea is to warn you of the pitfalls of marriage it would be better to send you to a couple who regularly knock ten bells out of each other and whose children terrorize the neighbourhood.

ST USHA GUPTA A token figure who has slotted herself into the life of the village with an almost seamless ease. This is hardly surprising because Ambridge is one of the most liberal-minded communities on earth. No one apart from ROY of the racists has ever made a racist remark, and even the old folk of the village who have never set foot outside the place in their lives are only too happy to welcome St Usha as if she was a sister. The cosy establishment in the village have really gone over the top in their desire to toady to her – particularly noticeable when St Usha was invited on to the Playground Committee when there would have been many more obvious candidates.

It was all something of a mystery when she suddenly became the victim of horrendous racial attacks. Here she was in the middle of a rural village where she was universally loved, and suddenly she was getting turds through the post – that's mail order for you – no wonder then that the village doesn't have a POSTMAN any more.

St Usha may be a top-notch lawyer, but a cook she ain't. As far as we can tell she is completely incapable of even boiling an egg. This is somewhat strange since vegetarians are invariably good cooks, if for no other reason than to save themselves the problems of having to endure the unimaginative attempts of the carnivorous majority to produce vegetarian fare. She will regularly drive to Borchester to obtain take-aways, where the sight of an Asian lady patiently queuing for a veggie madras along with all the lager louts will presumably go unnoticed. St Usha has remarkably few relations. Apart from her brother, we only ever hear of AUNTIE SATIA. When she discovered that

DR DEATH was two-timing her with SHULUGH she provided some wonderfully acrimonious scenes and let her have it with both barrels. Since then she and ROOOTH have become quite pally, neither of them being too enamoured of Shulugh and both sharing an interest in salsa, the noble art of mixing pesto with tomatoes. She has struck up relationships with a variety of men since Death but on the basis that revenge is a dish best served microwaved from deep frozen we rather hope she might get it together with PHALLUSTAIR one day. That would be well worth waiting for.

SAMMY Peggoi Woolley's long-suffering late puss who once drove Peggoi to say the memorable words, 'No more pilchards until I get a decent miaow out of you.' It generally did the normal cat-like things such as getting lost or locked in places, being a bit ill, etc. Had been known to speak somewhat more than TRUDY PORTER. Alas in the dying days of the year 2000, Sammy disappeared for the final time, only to be 'discovered' by Wiwyerm 'curled up near the pheasants'. It didn't take a genius to work out what had happened, even the most resilient of us would curl up a bit if we had to suffer the attentions of Wiwyerm's twelve-bore. To this day, many of us still feel a great loss and sense of bitterness at the demise of poor Sammy.

SAMMY WHIPPLE This man is quite simply a saint. Saddled with a ridiculous Hardyesque name, Sammy worked in the feudal environs of Home Farm where he had successive indignities heaped upon him. If Sammy wasn't being patronized by MRS HIGH AND MIGHTY, or lambasted by BRIAN, he was suffering the humiliation of having daffy DEBBIE bossing him around. Sammy suffered the final insult in 1998 when he was made redundant with the minimum possible redundancy of £6,000. To add insult to injury, DR DEATH, who, remember, was shacked up with Sammy's solicitor, repeatedly made malign smears as to his tendency to swing the lead over his poor health. They don't make shepherds like that any more and the Aldridges didn't deserve him. We had hoped that in his retirement he would decide to take up speech as a hobby. Sadly he opted for the other popular local pastime, total disappearance.

SCOTT A young actor and fancier of both himself and LILLIAN. Like many actors, he does a lot of resting and supplements his income by posing for those glossy brochures that tend to fall out of the Sunday papers before you've even left the shop, leaving you with the dilemma of whether or not to bother picking them up. He has one of those voices that, on radio, gets confused with all the other bland voices and you desperately need people to keep saying 'Scott' so you know who is there. That he is younger than Lillian is hardly surprising since she underwent her total body swap with an octogenarian. As he gets up the noses of her family, we have no hesitation in wishing him all the best. He is certainly one for the ladies and we could hear the gentle tap of his white stick as he chatted up and then deflowered the naive BIG BRENDA Tugger.

SEAN MYERSON Sean is/was (?) our very first declared homosexual. For years, we have wondered about the sexual proclivities of various characters but Sean actually 'came out' without even a by your leave and shouted his sexual preferences from the rooftops. MRS HIGH AND MIGHTY had the hots for him and was clearly disappointed but she didn't give up, and was always keen to have long drawn-out discussions with him on interior decorating. She quite clearly hoped that he would reveal himself to be more of a bi guy.

Like any minority in Ambridge, Sean was almost entirely without sin and it falls to Anarchists like ourselves to uncover the vile character behind the pink exterior. We know him to have been a collaborator in Benefits fraud since he was allowing KATE to work for him when he knew she was claiming dole. Sean was clearly on a mission to see THE BULL closed down so it was hardly surprising that SID was not his number-one fan. Indeed, Sean's first act on taking over THE PINK CAT was to steal an outside bar concession from Sid. Like a number of characters, Sean did not 'arrive', he was just suddenly 'there'. No one knew where he or his partner Peter came from but they were immediately welcomed into the community in that way that will be familiar to all minorities who have moved into rural villages. The departure of Sean following the demise of The Cat has never been commented upon. Does this mean he is still around? Should we be searching the cellars of The Cat to see if he has become the victim of an obscure sexual perversion involving a bottle of Labbatts Ice and a Bacardi Breezer?

SELF-DENIAL We have to award SHULUGH with the Anarchists' Hair Shirt for her observance of Lent. In 2000 she gave up chocolate, unspectacular enough. But in 2001 she announced that this year she was going to collect stamps for charity during Lent. How anyone has the fortitude to deny themselves the used stamps from the letters they receive is beyond comprehension. She must be some woman.

SEX The permissive society has been slow to reach Ambridge. Scenes of rampant sex and debauchery are few and far between, but that does not mean they do not exist. Long-term listeners will know that SHULUGH has been deflowered more times than a Christmas cactus, and well we remember a sordid scene in which she was rogered by journalist Simon Parker in a cornfield. But, in the main, sex is alluded to in the most coy terms – there is occasional talk of 'early nights' amongst the establishment figures. ROOOTH and DEEEVID turned up to a Christmas lunch with hay in their hair and now imply copulative practices on a daily basis, in the same way as the likes of HORRIBLE HAYLEY and formerly SHARON make suggestive sexual references from time to time. There was a disgusting episode in 2000 when all the evidence suggested that MRS H&M had sex with her husband and of course SID and THE LILY blazed a bit of a trail. But Anarchists believe that within the village there lurks beneath the surface every kind of sexual deviancy known to man, woman, and (without a doubt) beast. As we enter the permissive age of the 21st century it has become evident that *The Archers* will soon degenerate into 13 minutes of pure porn. We have it on good authority it is all set to transfer to Channel Five where it will go out at 3.00 am.

SHANE Until early 1998, a prominent member of the non-speaking fraternity. Shane was a member of the ever-growing homosexual mafia that seems to have taken a grip on Borsetshire's catering industry. His only job was as chef at NELSON's wine bar. All one ever heard of him related to tantrums and prima donna-ish behaviour, but then he did have to endure the burden of working for old queen NELSON GABRIEL. He was unceremoniously made redundant when the wine bar was shut down amid a welter of castism surrounding the reasons for Nelson's disappearance. He is now largely forgotten as we reflect sadly that he who lives by the quiche shall die by the quiche, though he did turn up, quiche in hand, at Nelson's wake.

SHARON RICHARDS We have always been somewhat mystified about how GEORGE (ALCOPOP) BARFORD in his role as Parish Councillor managed to get SHARON fixed up with a COUNCIL HOUSE. Housing is not a PARISH

COUNCIL responsibility – this would fall within the jurisdiction of the District Council relevant to that part of Borsetshire. On the other hand, there has only ever been one Councillor in living memory in the village who served on anything other than the Parish Council, and that was the late HANDBAG HEBDEN. Anyway, presumably in return for sexual favours, boring George swung it so that Sharon was able to move from her caravan at Bridge Farm.

Sharon, poor girl, was dealt one of life's sorry hands. She has always had good taste in men, and got together with young CLIVE HORROBIN to produce the delightful and mostly silent KYLIE. She lived with Gerry Buckle, one of Ambridge's vicars in the good old pre-THAT FISHER WOMAN days. Whether he was giving her one was never made clear, but there's no such thing as a free vicarage is there?

The snobby socialist PAT ARCHER always detested Sharon, partly because she used to drop cigarette ash in the yoghurt when she worked for her in the dairy, but more so because she didn't think her good enough for her JAAARN. A talented hairdresser, poor Sharon only needed a break. She loved Jaaarn and, for a while, they lived a life of bliss in the council house. Eventually pressure from the Archer mafia forced her to move to Leeds, breaking Jaaarn's heart in the process. When she returned, she soon saw off the shallow HORRIBLE HAYLEY, who was little more than a Brummie voice and a bunch of sexist attitudes. Sharon's womanly charms were just what Jaaarn needed, and who didn't sympathize with the lovely couple when Horrible Hayley caught them at it? The true un-Christian nature of the Archer community, That Fisher Woman, *et al.*, really came into its own when Jaaarn died and they deliberately didn't make the effort to let Sharon know. She missed the funeral but at least came back to let Hayley have it with both barrels afterwards. Alas we see little of her as there is nothing left to attract her to Ambridge. But it would be rather nice if she came back to give LANCASTRIAN 'TRASHER' TOMMY a quick introduction to the *Kama Sutra*.

SHEYAWN HAVITAWAY Dr Dim's wife is a thoroughly unpleasant specimen. Not the first Irish woman to descend on the village, she has a vicious tongue and was brutally unpleasant to poor LYNDA about her inability to have children. Her dislike of Lynda seems to be attributable only to her desire to be top dog in the village busybody stakes. She has muscled in to the 'Save Loxley Barrat School' campaign, joining all the other childless people who seem to be running it, but she has also become the self-appointed leader of the disgraceful campaign to discredit plans for new houses in the village. Such roles are often assumed by the most recent arrivals. She deserved everything she got when Dim started exploring beneath TFW's cassock. Her work involves Brussels and as she doesn't appear to be a lacemaker she is obviously some form of bureaucrat undermining the livelihoods of many of her fellow villagers. She is very keen to get preggers, which might prove difficult now that her husband has admitted he'd rather have the vicar. No doubt she will be another of the increasing number of locals whose children are fathered as a result of extra-curricular activity. When her child throws its rattle away and demands, in French, a filing cabinet, 400 reams of paper and a ride on the gravy train, we will not be surprised.

SHIFFON GUPTA St Usha's brother is a refreshingly genuine character. He hates white people and sees his sister as a bit of an Auntie Tom. He couldn't understand what she saw in DR DEATH, but then he hadn't seen his trusty sword. Very much 'new man', Shiffon was disgusted by the fact that Dr Death tended to leave all his clothes lying around and expect ST

USHA to clear up and do the housework. He is a rare visitor to Ambridge.

SHIRES The name of the local brewery, and unique in that it only sells the one eponymous beer. No 'special', 'best', or 'winter warmer' – you have a pint of Shires or lump it. Sold in THE BULL, but not at the late CAT. You might have thought that the brewery would have some employees and that once in 47 years someone in Ambridge might have worked there, or an employee moved into the village – not a bit of it.

SHULUGH HEBDEN-BLAND VOICE (MURDERESS) In fact, cosy establishment figure Shulugh Hebden, universally and consistently loathed by Anarchists, is at least a double murderess. To start with it was very convenient that she should be the one, and the only one, to 'find' DORIS dead, given that she was coincidentally the heiress to Glebe Cottage. We all know that she gave her a helping hand, just the odd cushion, Brookside-style. She was probably dormant for several years until she cunningly managed to call husband HANDBAG HEBDEN on his MOBILE PHONE to do a spot of nagging, just as he was trying to negotiate a winding lane full of cars and horses. We strongly suspect that she was involved with THE VILLAGE BICYCLE in the murder of GUY but have never been able to prove it. Shulugh was the acknowledged village bicycle before Caroline came on the scene and it is ironic that they should be such good friends, helping to create the village tandem.

We are often asked why we dislike Shulugh with such vehemence and the reason is that she embodies the sanctimony and goody-two-shoes smugness of the Ambridge establishment. She is a dreadful do-gooder and has a veneer of a complete absence of malice. She has frequently been nominated by

Anarchists as the person we would most like to see immersed in a vat of boiling oil. In addition to her successful career as a murderess, for which she remains unconvicted, she does have a conviction for 'taking and driving away' which does not make her the ideal choice for a church-warden.

Her attitude to HARD-WORKING SIMON was highly hypocritical. Remember that the Shulugh who took exception to Simon's dalliance with HARRIET WILLIAMS was the same Shulugh who has led men such as NEIL CARTER a merry dance and then stole DR DEATH from under the nose of her then good friend ST USHA. Indeed she has had more blokes than GEORGE (ALCOPOP) BARFORD has had hangovers. Shulugh no longer needs to work, having made a packet out of the insurance wonga from her late husband Handbag, though she dabbles half-heartedly at the stables, built up over the years by her boring aunt. As Estate manager, working for Rodway and Watson, she milked the business and ran the office like a social centre. Any time anyone wanted free photocopies they only had to turn up. Shulugh was frequently compromised by the fact that members of her family were tenants of the Estate. Justice was done in the end as her career ended with her instant dismissal for gross misconduct in testifying in favour of the layabout Grundys against her own employer at the tribunal. The notion of declaring an interest never seems at any stage to have occurred to her. Shulugh has become increasingly self-indulgent and self-centred in recent times. The extent to which she gradually sought to seduce DR DEATH and her appalling treatment of PHALLUSTAIR was quite shocking. Many of us were moved to chunder by her attitude to the great Brookfield succession row as she simpered 'I'd be happy if Mum and Dad left me an old plant pot.' Yet when it came to selling Glebe Cottage, her main concern was to squeeze the highest possible price from her parents to whom she was proposing to sell the place. She even sought to drive the price up by encouraging the boring Barfords to show an interest. In her own way, Shulugh pokes her nose into everyone's affairs and sees herself as some kind of Henry Kissinger as the village and family peacemaker. So it is particularly refreshing when LOATHSOME tells her to bog off, as she tends to do from time to time. Her indulgence of Damien and his weird supernatural ways is making it almost certain that he will spend most of his adult life pushing draughts around in a secure institution and confiding in his fellow inmates that he can fly. The future for Shulugh is probably one of cosy and stomach-churning bliss until Damien begins to sink his fangs into his cousins. Mind you, we would always be very interested in seeing the exhumation of Doris.

SID PERKS Yet another criminal, for a long while Sid was not even legally entitled to hold the licence of a pub. Over the years he has, on the face of it, eschewed his criminal ways and become the mainstay of THE BULL. For a while he suffered huge competition from the local gay bar, THE PINK CAT, where naturally most of the village folk preferred to drink. Possibly this was a reaction to the hare-brained theme nights he put on to try to attract the punters. For The Bull to be a success KATHY had to go. You simply can't have a pub where the landlady harbours a pathological hatred of customers, cooking and serving behind the bar. Fortunately, he saw the light and traded Kathy in for THE LILY, a true professional of the bar. Takings shot up in an instant as The Cat fell victim to the cleavage vote and they all came back to The Bull. He has had to pay a price because he has sold most of his share to THE VILLAGE BICYCLE so has effectively returned to where he started, as a manager rather than an owner. Sid is very very boring and very very stupid but his strangulated chicken noise when he gets angry would be irreplaceable.

SIGNATURE TUNE Interfering busybodies at the BBC who feel compelled to change everything have occasionally tampered with our signature tune. The daily version is a reworking of a previous version, but the most outrageous interference was to substitute the normal orchestration for the ridiculous accordion-dominated row that now greets us on a Sunday. The accordion is not a musical instrument but a hand-operated kazoo, and Anarchists have never accepted the Sunday signature tune. It is a memorial to meddling. The revered signature tune has been used to great dramatic effect in the past although nowadays they don't seem bothered to use it so. For example, a dramatic ending would usually be given a part of the tune starting Da Da Da Da Diddle idlle Da, Da Da Da Da Diddle idlle Da, Da Da Da Da Diddle idlle Da, etc. before then going into the usual tum te tum te tum te tum. Sad isn't it?

SINGLE WICKET TROPHY Despite the fact that most people were only too glad to forget the awful HANDBAG HEBDEN when he rather cruelly drove into a horse and killed himself, SHULUGH insisted on donating a trophy to his memory. This is an irritating habit widely practised in amateur sport and culture and results in a proliferation of pieces of meaningless silverware, turning AGMs into interminably boring events. They also result in acrimonious infighting, associating the dear departed with an annual commemorative fist fight.

There are in fact two trophies bearing this name because when the late JAAARN won it he had the good sense to file it in a drawer out of sight. He forgot where he had put it and was forced to have a replica made. Happily they have different inscriptions. One says 'to a very dear friend', the other says 'to a true and trusted friend' though the trust did not seem to extend to him not running you over when he was on the phone – if you were a horse.

Nowadays, in PC Ambridge, the women are allowed to compete for the trophy and it almost goes without saying that they are far better at cricket than the menfolk.

SIR SIDNEY AND MERCEDES GOODMAN This couple are definitely 'new money'. He was knighted in Harold Wilson's resignation honours list for services to scrap metal and Old Labour. She's a permanently tanned old slapper with about as much taste as Posh Spice. Like attracts like, so when they come to Ambridge they hob nob with the new money but get little attention from the real class such as THE VILLAGE BICYCLE.

SLAP The most glorious moment in two decades was when HARD-WORKING SIMON allegedly slapped SHULUGH. It was widely agreed that she deserved it for years of sanctimony and cosiness. Indeed even the generally left-of-centre journalist LIBBY PURVES famously wrote that, 'Someone had to slap SHULUGH'. Anarchists however take the view that Simon, one of nature's gentlemen, merely took the blame for SHULUGH hitting him. We all heard a slap but none of us saw it (a bit like the RIDING ACCIDENT). Readers of the Anarchist newsletter actually voted by a large majority that what in fact had happened was that MOUNTAINEERING TEDDY had fallen from the mantelpiece, upsetting a bowl of cold custard which had fallen face down on a stone floor. You'll just have to make your own mind up. Whatever the cause of this small noise, SHULUGH didn't half make a fuss about it, went into purdah for about two weeks, until she blabbed to THE VILLAGE BICYCLE who of course did her best to escalate the situation. In typical churchwardenly fashion, SHULUGH sought to blackmail Simon by saying she'd publicize the slap if he tried to sack the idle JAILBIRD CARTER from the Estate office. Now there's professionalism for you.

SMOKING AND DRUGS These play a disappointingly small role in Ambridge PC life. KATE was heard to exclaim 'I'm dying for a fag' once. She has also been one of the few people to introduce the wonders of dope to the village, although it was brought in by her then housemate JOLYON GIBSON. So successful was she in this that her parents spent a very cheerful evening with her and enjoyed a particularly elevating soup. Of course if BRIAN lived up to his reputation as a disciplinarian he should have been tough on crime and marched her to the police in true Jack Straw fashion.

The other person to have brought dope into the village was NEIL CARTER, via a girlfriend many years ago. The only mentions we ever really hear of smoking are highly judgmental comments from parents when children have been caught smoking behind the bike sheds or, since not many people in Ambridge have bikes apart from WIWYERM GRUNDY and LYNDA SNELL, over at LAKEY HILL. There have just got to be some magic mushrooms on LAKEY HILL or over in MARNEYS. The lovely SHARON RICHARDS enjoyed the odd ciggie or 50, and there has been mention of GEORGE (ALCOPOP) BARFORD and his pipe. But Ambridge still awaits its first heroin junkie with eager anticipation.

SOLLY AND HEATHER PRITCHARD These have to be the most peculiar people ever to have darkened our nightly doorsteps. Purporting to be the parents of ROOOTH they are obviously Caribbean and generally turn up en route for the Notting Hill Carnival. We know that Solly is not a Geordie because he was heard to utter the words 'You shall have a fishee in a little dishee', such a racist stereotype of our Tyneside brothers and sisters as to render him liable to a ducking in the Am. They are very dull people and can consider themselves lucky to have warranted an entry at all.

SORTED Ambridge folk are very 'can do' people, which is the only plausible explanation for the enthusiasm with which they all talk of getting things 'sorted'. It is a verb much over-used in the village and not merely confined to the lips of the village lowlife but issues just as comfortably from those of tiger-hunting DOG WOMAN, Dame JOAN PARGETTER, PEGGOI or the upper-crust VILLAGE BICYCLE. Everyone is just as likely to use it regardless of creed, colour, age or presumed vocabulary size. If you concentrate very hard during a conversation between any permutation of Ambridge folk you could be forgiven for thinking you were listening to a soundtrack from *Brookside*. Even SHEYAWN, the doctor's-wife, was using the word after being in Ambridge for five minutes. There is nobody who fails to 'sort' things, and the word comes up a dozen times per episode.

SPANNER This was one of the gentleman colleagues of ROY TUGGER who decided to persecute ST USHA on the basis that she was completely unreal and lived with the appalling DR DEATH. Because he went a bit too far in putting a turd through her letter box and giving her a free sample of his ammonia fragrance. He was thrown into jail along with his good mate CRAVEN. So far as we are aware they are both still on Death Row. Whereas CLIVE, who was imprisoned for a spot of armed robbery, was quickly out and about again, these two have never surfaced to date.

STRANGE LEWIS Once NELSON had disappeared, JOAN PARGETTER was desperate for someone to talk to since her son and daughter-in-law would barely give her the time of day. As luck would have it, she suddenly found Lewis, presumably when she was turning out some old cupboards. In true Borsetshire style, he came from nowhere but turns out to be an architect and male nanny. We could understand it if he was a youngster since Architecture and Parenthood is just the kind of degree course you would do at Borchester Poly. But Lewis sounds to be beyond his first youth. The removal of charisma is the kind of operation that might usually be tricky to obtain on the NHS, but Borchester having the finest hospital in Britain carries out this treatment as if it was routine. And with Lewis, it was an unqualified success. He has no personality at all but wheels FREDDYNLILY in their pushchair most of the time and seems permanently to be designing structures at LOWER LOXLEY despite the fact that all their renovations and building works must be complete.

STRAWBERRY CROP Increasingly dull in its annual reappearance was the joint venture between THE ONE-EYED MONSTER and NEIL to grow strawberries and run it as a pick-your-own. Since both Neil and The One-eyed Monster operate with an inverted Midas touch, there is always a different plague to hit it. In 1997 it was destroyed by rain, and what wasn't destroyed was eaten by KATE's alternative friends. During the Nazi period of Ambridge, SPANNER and CRAVEN mistook it for Donnington Race Track. The other problem is that there never seems to be anyone available to man the shop so most of the strawberries just walk. Following another unsuccessful season in 2000, they had the bright idea of abandoning the enterprise altogether.

SUDDEN NATIONAL EVENTS Ambridge folk are always caught out by events in the world outside their village. They either ignore them completely or one person in the village makes a brief allusion to it and that is the end of the matter. When Princess Diana was killed, there was a hasty mention, a weird monologue from FOGHORN in St Stephen's (where she didn't actually mention it), and that was it – no books of condolence or special events. On the day of the funeral, life in the village carried on as if it had never happened.

Few national disasters are mentioned in Ambridge, and there is never any question of anyone in the village having been involved. The explanation for all of this is probably that, as far as we can tell, most of the villagers never set foot outside the place, and would therefore be unaware of what was going on. Apart from one or two unlikely souls who seem to have Radio Borchester piped into their brains, no one listens to the radio or watches television. Newspapers were a rarity until recently other than the *Borchester Echo* which is probably produced somewhere in the village using a John Bull printing outfit.

SWEARING However angry they get, and they do get very angry, people in Ambridge hardly ever swear. Those who would be most likely to swear – DEEEVID, TUGGERS, EDWEIRD, SID and NEIL – never resort to bad language. Strangely it is the women who are most likely to conjure up the odd expletive when pushed to the brink. THE VILLAGE BICYCLE has taken solace in foul language on at least two notable occasions, each a respectable few years apart. On the occasion that JECK WOOLLEY shot the LYNX she said, 'Why did you bloody do that?' She also described her stepson, the much-maligned HARD-WORKING SIMON, as a 'shit'. DEBBIE called the self-same Simon a 'bastard' during his bout of OVERENTHUSIASM. She also said 'bugger' when the phone wouldn't work at the time of the post office visit by CLIVE. An aural pinpointing has it that THE ONE-EYED MONSTER called someone a 'bastard' on 27 March 1983. EDDIE has managed a respectable 'bloody' from time to time. New ground was broken on 21 March 1999 when LANCASTRIAN 'TRASHER' TOMMY uttered the word 'piss'. We had a welcome 'shag' from Eddie when he told the public bar of THE BULL what SID was up to with DOREEN, but there's precious little else to report. Perhaps 2002 could be declared 'The Year of the F Word'.

TAIL-BITING One of the many nasty animal-related problems suffered by farmers but only mentioned once in a blue moon. *The Archers* was originally designed in part as a farming information programme, so one cannot help but feel sorry for any farmer who tuned in to the first episode in the hope that he might find a cure for tail-biting in pigs. But all he needed was a bit of patience for, sure enough, some 46 years later he will have heard his answer. Anyone could have told him: house the pigs on a bed of straw.

TAMAGOTCHI Ambridge never fails to surprise us with the aspects of modern life that it ignores and those it takes to its bosom. ROBERT SNELL, a serious computer person, was one of the first people in the country to obtain one of these children's toys. LYNDA, ever ready for a child substitute, was only too delighted to look after it when Robert was away on a business trip a few years ago. Since it is a pocket-sized object it is rather surprising that Robert felt it necessary to leave it in her care rather than take it with him. In retrospect it was a particularly bad decision on his part, as she killed it.

THAT FISHER WOMAN TFW has become one of the Anarchists' most detested characters. She embodies virtually everything we hate – political correctness, superficial 'niceness', a characterless voice, and the fact that she was immediately welcomed by the establishment within the village. She has been such a malign influence on the village that she warrants a lengthy discussion in a separate chapter.

THOSE PEOPLE It was a sad day indeed when 'Those People' left Keeper's Cottage in autumn 2000, not least because it created a space for the layabout Grundys. Their departure had at least been eased by their never having arrived, but one could not help but feel sorry that they had never been integrated into village life to the extent of having been given the occasional mention. Never mind, for when the great history of Ambridge is finally written, Those People will have their place, however humble. And Anarchists vow never to forget them.

TITCOMBE The gardener at LOWER LOXLEY, and probably the character with the silliest name in Borsetshire though no one ever laughs at it. He's not helped by having no Christian name, but then Morse seemed to manage OK. Titcombe was treated like dirt by JOAN but is now patronized by the dreaded NIGEL and LOATHSOME. You might have thought the days when young upstarts could call a loyal employee by his surname are long since gone, but then perhaps it's his Christian name.

TOKEN OLD FARMING RETAINERS Seasoned listeners will know that there is always an old yokel who works at Brookfield, is given special dispensation to speak and must always have the same voice. Anarchists cannot necessarily remember the first ones but take for example Ned Larkin who popped his clogs back in 1967. There was no mention of him dying, he was simply replaced seamlessly by his son Jethro who had exactly the same voice, and eventually we heard occasional allusions such as 'remember poor old Ned'. At least, thanks to DEEEVID, we knew when Jethro shuffled off this mortal coil. He was replaced eventually by BERT FRY who, though only in middle age when he arrived, had the same old decrepit voice that is standard issue for his role. There are numerous silent farming retainers who are suddenly invented and in many cases never alluded to again. They make excellent workers – they never go in the pub or the shop, never gossip, just simply toil.

TOMMY CROKER QUARTET, THE JECK WOOLLEY's favourite function band for events at GREY GABLES. They are a cross between Motorhead and The Dead Kennedys – a fine bunch of musicians. We never actually hear them and this makes them the ideal band for those occasions when you don't want to shout to make yourself heard. They tend to play most of their gigs in Wetherspoons pubs.

TONY ARCHER You can always recognize Tony by the substantial chip on his shoulder. Although it falls somewhat short of the giant spud that adorns the epaulettes of THE ONE-EYED MONSTER, Tony has always had a problem about not being his rich sisters. Being married to Ms PAT ARCHER, who inflicts the double whammy of being both a feminist and Welsh, is a cross he has had to bear for some time, and Anarchists tend to find his 'call a spade a spade' mentality quite refreshing for the most part. He's a hard-working chap, although it is written in his tea leaves that a good 50 per cent of anything he touches will turn into the proverbial brown stuff. In his heyday Tony was quite a stud and it is very disappointing that he has been so reluctant to put it about since he got married to Pat. It's such a pity he didn't marry the fragrant Mary Weston to whom he was once engaged, life might have been so much kinder to him. His decision to go organic was rather PC but quite ahead of its time.

Since the death of JAAARN, Tony has become rather dull. He has a growing and alarming tendency to be nice to people and to get less agitated about things. He seems to have acquired the philosophy that once your son has been squashed by a tractor it doesn't really matter if someone wants to put a pipeline through your farm. Whilst in some respects this is an understandable position it could lead to a worrying increase in tractor sales to property developers.

Recently he has celebrated his 50th birthday, a joint event with EDDIE at which it was revealed for the first time that he had friends from outside the village. It's such a shame they couldn't have made him a false passport and uniform to enable him to attempt a bold escape from Ambridge to visit them.

TRACY HORROBIN It is very sad that we never hear a peep out of young Tracy. By all accounts she is everything that her awful social-climbing JAILBIRD of a sister is not – fun, a live wire, attractive, in fact a really nice girl. Naturally Jailbird rarely mentions her, but she is a real credit to her hard-working mum Ivy and Anarchists would like her to be given her rightful place in village life. One option is for NEIL and her to strike up a relationship. It is very noticeable that Tracy never pops round to Jailbird's, presumably because she wouldn't be welcome – too much of a prole. Tracy is the sort of girl who believes that there is generally something better to do than work, a fine philosophy to which more people should subscribe. Nevertheless, she has held down some pretty high-flying jobs in her time. For a while she was under-manager at the Dairy where she had the daunting challenge of having to manage FAT CLARRIE. Anyone who has tried to motivate a tub of lard will know that it is not always the most straightforward proposition. Tracy moved on to work at Lower Loxley where her true love Silent Owen is cook. But the poor girl received such appalling treatment from the Pargetters that she was soon resting again. We say, give her a chance. A Horrobin is worth 20 Archers any day.

TRAFFIC NOISE Traffic in Ambridge works on the tree falling in the forest principle. Every now and again, someone (usually LYNDA) becomes concerned about traffic in the village. When this happens we hear a constant sound of heavy lorries and cars being driven too fast as a background to every outdoor scene. Indeed we could be forgiven for assuming that Ambridge is in fact an M5 service station. Yet as soon as the campaigner tires of the subject we are back to the peace and tranquillity that we all love. No one seems to realize that the best riposte when one of the village busybodies starts up a petition about heavy lorries or whatever is simply to suggest they forget about it and it will go away.

TREE BRANCH The murder weapon used by DEEEVID ARCHER to kill the TOKEN OLD FARMING RETAINER Jethro. It is only because members of the Archer family seem to enjoy an immunity from prosecution usually reserved for foreign diplomats that he has never been brought to book.

TREETOP WALK In a desperate attempt to turn LOWER LOXLEY into some kind of visitor attraction, the combined brainpower of village idiot and former ice-cream salesman, Loopy NIGEL together with that of failed consultant LOATHSOME LIZZIE came up with this wacky idea. Nailing a few planks together and sticking them up a tree doesn't exactly sound very enticing but the Ambridge locals are easily pleased. Anarchists are quite supportive of this particular aspect of the enterprise since it can only be a matter of time before the whole thing collapses. The important thing is to make sure the right people are on it at the time. In a dry run for the disaster, Doreen Rogers attempted to murder JAMIE PEACOCK-TEALEAF-PERKS by pushing him off. The trouble is that Doreen's brains are in her appendages and she forgot that it's best not to push someone when they are on the bottom rung of the ladder nor when they have a good covering of feathers. If we could entice DAMIEN up there together with the ghastly PEEEP, all we then need is a force ten gale.

TREGORRANS, THE There's no real class in Ambridge nowadays. It's mainly new money. John and Carol TREGORRAN and their privately educated daughter Anne were dead posh, kind to the riffraff, benevolent and superior. They sort of fizzled out without any explanation. They belonged to the era of Lawson-Hopes, Brigadier Winstanley and Ralph Bellamy. They had a maid called Nancy – there are no known maids or housekeepers in Ambridge now (with the possible exception of Mrs Brown who, if THE VILLAGE BICYCLE hasn't murdered her, used to look after the late GUY PEMBERTON and was presumably inherited along with the Dower House).

Carol had her own market garden and vineyard. The village aristocracy would regularly get pie-eyed on Manor Court wine. When the Tregorrans were spirited away, Manor Court and the vineyard must have gone with them because they have never been mentioned since. In 2000 the Tregorrans made a top secret and silent return to Ambridge and were smuggled into FOGHORN's 70th birthday party with blankets over their heads to avoid the prying lenses of the paparazzi. Amid tight security, they spoke to no one, visited none of their old haunts and disappeared into the night.

TRUDY PORTER For many years, Trudy's only claim to fame was the elevation of her chest: flat. She is one of those characters who has been around so long that she must be well into her 40s by now. Yet whenever she is mentioned, it is as if she is no more than a flighty teenager. Trudy has worked at GREY GABLES for over 25 years and has always been referred to in a somewhat sneering and dismissive way. Just because she doesn't want to talk. But who would want to talk if the only people to talk to were JECK, LYNDA, THE VILLAGE BICYCLE, JEAN-PAUL or HIGGS?

When a junior management position was created at Grey Gables to replace the awful KATHY PERKS, who was departing to have her sprog, Trudy finally came into her own. As with any job selection in *The Archers*, the applicants are invariably people we've heard of and so the choice was between the educated and enthusiastic Lynda Snell and the silent Trudy. Poor old Lynda never had a chance because she gets up The Bicycle's nose, so Trudy got the job and has rarely been heard of since. Indeed, if we did not know better we might believe that 'someone' has forgotten that Trudy got the job, since Lynda always seems to be standing in when The Bicycle is away. In the summer of 2001 Trudy faced allegations of hypocrisy when she allegedly reported that WILLIAM and SCOTT were 'hardly speaking'.

TWINNING Ambridge has been twinned with Meyruelle since September 1994. Meyruelle is the setting for 'an everyday story of garlic-eating, beret-wearing lamb burners'. As with many Ambridge activities there is never any continuity with their twinning. You can go years without any excursions taking place or even a fleeting reference to it. Then it will suddenly dominate life for three months – it is almost volcanic in its behaviour. When the village gets 'twinning fever', FAT CLARRIE starts trying to turn her pot noodles into exotic French dishes and SID remembers that he is actually running boules tournaments on an ongoing basis. There have, of course, been visits each way, though it would appear that the majority of those residents from Meyruelle who come over to Ambridge are Trappist monks.

UNCLE RAY A distinctly dodgy children's entertainer, hired for the birthday party of JAMIE TEALEAF-PERKS. No one was very forthcoming as to the nature of his entertainment and given the unerring negligence of Borsetshire social services, it doesn't bear thinking about. But we would suggest a bouncy castle might be a safer bet next time.

UNDERWOODS Borchester's department store, it is always full of people from Ambridge and no one else. People like MRS HIGH AND MIGHTY seem to live there, and it appears that there is nothing which cannot be found in the place. Underwoods is always spoken of in respectful tones and one gets the impression it is the Harrods of Borsetshire. This is rather strange since it is obviously one of the dwindling number of independent stores and such places tend to be redolent of Grace Brothers rather than Harrods. The village poor only visit Underwoods on special occasions and then they are invariably patronized by Mrs H & M who expresses great surprise that they can afford to be there. No one ever visits a supermarket, and why should they when they can go to Underwoods Food Hall and stuff themselves with PAT's overpriced yoghurt? In fact there are only three retail outlets ever referred to in *The Archers* – Underwoods, 'the cash and carry' and the village shop.

VEGETARIANISM There have been plenty of vegetarians in Ambridge over the years. Virtually every young woman in the village: LOATHSOME, KATE, and LUCY have at least dallied with it long enough for us to be given endless lectures on the cruelties of meat production. ST USHA is one but that's all to do with her religious beliefs.

VENETIA AND NICK The nicest residents Ambridge never had. This delightful normal couple were all set to buy April Cottage. Indeed, due to Borsetshire's rather unique conveyancing laws they had the decorators and carpet fitters in before they had even exchanged contracts. Unfortunately they found themselves next to the layabout Grundys and FAT CLARRIE was determined not to have neighbours who pronounced their consonants and did an honest day's work. She had set her heart on April Cottage going to the dreary KATHY and her thieving son and drove poor Nick and Venetia away with a scandalous exhibition of noise and vulgarity. This served to lower the value of April Cottage and if JECK had not become so senile he should have sent the Grundys back to Meadow Rise.

VILLAGE BICYCLE, THE Caroline Bone arrived in the village as a cook at THE BULL. The establishment tend to regard her with affection, but the truth is that she is a calculating self-centred manipulator who has been laid more times than an Axminster carpet. She thought nothing of deserting poor old SID to work in competition to him at GREY GABLES, and how ironic that she would eventually inflict the final humiliation on her erstwhile employer by becoming the major shareholder in The Bull.

Caroline's finest hour was when she seduced BRIAN ALDRIDGE, much to the distress of MRS HIGH AND MIGHTY. But as a rule you will find that she has had a sexual relationship with any remotely professional person who ever shows his face (or any other part of him) in Ambridge. In most cases she leaves behind a broken heart but she has certainly done well financially. When her Uncle, Lord Netherbourne, pops his clogs, she will probably cop a whole load more dosh.

Caroline's conquests also include vicar-vet ROBIN STOKES, Dr Matthew Thorogood, and former Estate owner CAMERON FRASER. In fact Cameron was stolen from her by the equally scheming LOATHSOME, but Caroline was undaunted. As soon as Fraser did a John Stonehouse, she had her claws into the new owner, the loveable old buffer GUY PEMBERTON.

Here we saw Caroline at her most cunning. She hatched an evil plan – to marry poor old Guy and then drive him to an early grave. Caroline was well aware that the ghastly SHULUGH had the hots for HARD-WORKING SIMON and was fearful that if that relationship should continue she could be kissing goodbye to serious wonga. She duly married Guy and then proceeded to make his life a misery by endlessly telling him unsubstantiated tales about Simon's relationship with HARRIET WILLIAMS. Eventually Guy could take it no more, his heart gave out, and The Bicycle inherited the Dower House and half THE BULL. Not bad for a few months' work.

Poor Guy was hardly cold in his grave when The Bicycle's mind turned to whom she could seduce next. Unfortunately she had exhausted every middle-class or above male in the village. She advertised in the lonely hearts section of *Borchester Life* (one of those publications which had never been mentioned before or since). Inevitably, of all the millions of people she could have met, she managed to talk to someone and actually arrange to meet him without realizing until she got there that it was someone she knew: the LOONY LARRY LOVELL. After that experience she played hard to get with GRAHAM RYDER who obviously was simply not up to her bank balance. After a brief pause, she made a bee line for the next professional to move into the village OLIVER FOXBRUSH, another man oozing wonga from every pore. Not above a bit of rough now and then, The Bicycle has clearly been playing Lady Chatterley and getting a regular service from WIWYERM GRUNDY who lives rather too conveniently and inexplicably under her roof.

VILLAGE POND So far as we are aware, the pond is completely full of vomit left over from the GCSE celebration party organized by LANCASTRIAN 'TRASHER' TOMMY in August 1996.

VILLAGE PRODUCTIONS Urgh, urgh, urgh, argh. . . Every year we have a tedious pantomime or Christmas show, and nowadays we often have a summer one as well. The storyline is always the bloody same. LYNDA always wants to direct it, others always try to wrest control from her, but they always fail. No one, except BERT FRY and the Grundys, actually wants to be in it. No one wants to attend rehearsals and we always have endless scenes with people pretending to act – quite ironic really, particularly when someone like BORING CHRISTINE gets involved. The people whom the director most wants in the production never want to be in it. And the people who do end up in it are permutations of the same narrow bunch of village cosies.

The most awful thing about village productions is that we have to listen to weeks of rehearsals culminating in the performance itself which usually occupies the whole of an evening slot. What we hate about these productions is not so much the fact that they are repetitive, cosy and dull, but that there are millions of other things that must go on in the village at the same time that we simply never hear about. We accept that it might be odd suddenly to dispense with these shows, but the fact that we don't hear every tedious description of the proceedings does not mean they are not happening. For much of the year it is like listening to *Midsummer Night's Dream* FM.

WALTER GABRIEL Even non-*Archers* devotees know the name of Walter Gabriel. But it is a wonder that, when Ambridge has been populated with people like that, we have ever survived to the 21st century. Walter was a ridiculous, incredible character who wheezed and giggled in a manic way and whose sole contribution to village life was to say 'Me old pal, me old beauty' and 'doh' *ad nauseum*. Walter had a monotonous tendency to inflict his woodcarvings on small children.

WAYNE FOLEY It was a great day for broadcasting when Radio Borsetshire suddenly appeared on the airwaves. It is obviously a kind of Radio Caroline outfit, broadcasting illegally from a canoe in the Am, because no listings can be found for it in *Radio Times* or similar organs. Apart from BIG BRENDA who makes the tea, there is just one other employee and that is the dreary hack Wayne Foley. Running on few staff is quite normal for a radio station and it is often difficult to get a reporter to cover in person any event less than a massacre by a mad axeman. But Foley will actually doorstep people about minor issues such as Borchester Land's tiny housing development. Presumably the station plays military music pending his return.

WEATHER This is a very important subject in a farming community. The success or failure of crops can depend on it, yet it is mentioned surprisingly rarely in Ambridge. One possible reason for this could be that when they do start to discuss their weather it is sometimes completely different from that experienced by the rest of us. Once, the harvest was interrupted by torrential storms at a time when the whole of Britain was caught in the middle of a drought. Snow is unheard of which leads us to suspect Ambridge is somewhere in the Mediterranean. Farm vehicles in Ambridge can be falling foul of black ice and people bemoaning the cold weather while the rest of England enjoys the mildest winter in living memory. Many farmers in 2000/2001 experienced saturation making it impossible to cultivate their fields. Happily no such problems in Ambridge where the Am was at its usual trickle.

'WHAT ARE YOU DOING HERE?' This and other slightly less aggressive derivations such as 'What brings you here?' or 'What can I do for you?' are stock phrases which are trotted out with unbelievable regularity. In a small village where people are constantly going to encounter each other, this rather 'in-yer-face' confrontation seems quite unnecessary, yet amazingly no one ever seems to mind being asked. Never do we hear a 'mind your own business'. The enquiry is always greeted with a courteous explanation to justify one's presence on earth.

WIWYERM GRUNDY As a child, Wiwyerm was the kind of waster that is commensurate with having feckless neanderthal parents. He got up to all the normal delinquent activities and caused the Grange Farm fire which resulted in thousands of pounds worth of damage and a very hot dog. He would play truant from school and his parents would shrug their shoulders and shout a bit. He showed an unhealthy interest in animals and an unhealthy disinterest in girls. One good bit of business his family did carry out for him was to persuade the VILLAGE BICYCLE to be his Godmother. As The Bicycle doesn't believe in small change, Wiwyerm has been the beneficiary of a stream of lavish presents including bikes, cows and latterly accommodation. Being a gigolo doesn't seem to have bothered him unduly. Having come of age he is now the proud owner of a clapped out old car adorned courtesy of his mother, Ambridge's queen of taste, with a couple of large furry dice.

X The letter X is the bane of any self-respecting A–Z compiler's life. Even the London A–Z baulks at an X. Sadly, Ambridge is no different. You might expect that during the course of 50 years someone would have launched a successful career as a xylophonist, but of course the residents of Ambridge are largely philistines and the percentage of musicians has always been negligible. Nevertheless, if we may be permitted the most naff and vulgar distortion of the English language imaginable, we will here discuss the. . .

XTRA EPISODE 1998 saw one of the greatest cons in the history of mankind. We were told that we were to get an extra episode on Sunday nights. The fact is that this is constructed entirely out of the minutes casually lopped off each weekday episode. The result is we are being expected to listen more often but are not getting anything extra.

YOGHURT PAT ARCHER's yoghurt is one of Ambridge's only known exports. It is only a matter of time before a pot is found to contain one of TONY's toenail clippings, or perhaps some of UNDERWOODS' customers die of salmonella. We all know that any success for this unfortunate family is only ever destined to be short-lived.

ZEBEDEE TRING No A–Z can be without its Z either, but in the absence of a zebra crossing or zebra park in the village, we will have to make do with Zebedee Tring. He was a really miserable old goat, with a ridiculous old person's voice. He used to go in THE BULL but had no character at all, save for the fact that he spoke with unadulterated bitterness, probably because he had such a silly voice.

Zebedee used to be abusive to women for no apparent reason, calling them 'woman'. This was all before the PC *Archers* we all love so dearly today. It would be wonderful, were he alive today, to see how he would cope with the likes of THAT FISHER WOMAN. Zebedee died back in the early 1970s. The only other point of interest was that he used to drink scrumpy in The Bull, and one can't help wondering whether The Bull still serves scrumpy as no one ever asks for it. The Grundys occasionally drink it but only their home-made stuff.

Archers Listeners – 57 Varieties

There are several varied and valued categories of listener to *The Archers*: some hold their heads up high and declare their loyalty while others will deny even knowing where Radio 4 sits on the dial and will not turn a hair as the cock crows thrice.

I've been listening since the end of Dick Barton – these listeners are by definition old. They clearly identify themselves as serious long-term players, although the way they refer to a kind of seamless continuity from the days of Dick Barton 'Special Agent' does sometimes make you wonder if they would have become just as attached to the shipping forecast if it had been put in the same time slot.

The wife listens to it so I can't help hearing it sometimes – these are the same people who collect autographs from celebrities explaining, 'It's not for me, it's for the boy.' They know every detail of the plot and will give themselves away within fifteen seconds of the beginning of the conversation by demonstrating the fact.

I have it on in the car sometimes – these are apologists. Like the previous type, they don't really want to admit that they are completely hooked because they feel there is something not quite decent about it. They are the type of people who, if you were to tell them that you did not possess a television, would hastily tell you that they only have a 'small black-and-white one', as if this demonstrated anything apart from general weirdness. Not only do they listen to *The Archers* in the car, but you can regularly see them in a supermarket car park having arrived at 7.08 p.m. sheepishly emerging from their vehicle at 7.15.

I only hear it occasionally but it doesn't seem to matter how many episodes you miss, you can always catch up – this is a comment frequently made about soaps and invariably accompanied by ladles of smugness. So far as *The Archers* is concerned it is palpably untrue. There are too many things that only occur once in a millennium in Ambridge and if you miss that crucial episode you will end up with a totally distorted view of the place.

I'm a great Archers *fan (but not really)* – These are people who go out of their way to tell you how much they share your love of *The Archers* but then give themselves away as people who occasionally forget to switch it off after the news. They give themselves away by telephoning you at 7.10 pm, suggesting meeting at 7.00 pm and looking completely blank when you refer to some cataclysmic Ambridge event that has just occurred.

If you listen to *The Archers* you are a good egg and all other personality flaws (homicidal tendencies, etc.) can be forgiven, but Archers Anarchists are invariably people who have come out as fully-fledged unapologetic listeners. We put in sixty-five hours a year, plus a few hours of repeats. We don't answer the phone during episodes and we don't accept social engagements before 7.15 pm, but then we don't get invited to many so that helps a bit.

A Breath of Fresh Air
Is Helen the Hazel of the New Millennium?

We analyse the immense contribution of Helen Archer in resuscitating Bridge Farm

Anyone who challenges the cosy scone culture of Ambridge is to be embraced. The relatively recent arrival of a vocal Helen together with a brand new Sloaney voice and modern farming expertise gives rise to cautious optimism.

Helen Archer is one of the many characters who have managed to acquire an accent which is totally at odds with their origin and upbringing. Her childhood was spent in more or less total silence, yet even in her early teens she gave the occasional sign that she might turn out to be 'one of us'. Anyone who can break into Peggoi's cottage and turn it into a theatre of adolescent debauchery is worthy of our admiration.

After the death of Jaaarn, Helen suddenly came out as a Sloane Ranger with a splendid 'OK-ya' voice. For the more long-in-the-tooth listeners who hanker after the lovely Hazel Woolley, Helen looks like she may well fill the void. One of the most striking similarities was the tendency for each to turn up, cause havoc and then depart from the scene. However, it seems that 'Helin' (as some people, including her mother, irritatingly call her) is becoming a rather more permanent fixture though she is apt to lapse into silence for many months.

As someone who has never done a hand's turn in her life save for filling the odd yoghurt pot, Helen is admirably qualified to lecture her parents on marketing and brand image. She immediately saw that Brum Nanny Sausages were never going to be a real earner. And she consistently espoused the view that the organic pork industry would not be best served by someone whose day should be entirely taken up with the career of looking after other people's children.

To give Helen her due, something we are always pleased to do, she is one of those rare people in the village (the other is Brian) who actually want to see something run efficiently. Those who remember the Estate office prior to the arrival of Hard-working Simon Pemberton (bless his cotton-enriched socks) will know that it was run like a holiday camp largely for the convenience of its staff. Shulugh and Jailbird Carter would spend all day making personal calls on the office phone, entertaining passers-by to coffee and a chat, and working the office photocopier round the clock to produce leaflets for all the busybody community groups in Borsetshire.

Similarly the dairy at Bridge Farm had become a repository for the idle. Clarrie would turn up when it suited her, forgetting all the health and safety measures, and Tracy Horrobin would just not bother showing up at all. Helen recognized this and really tried to inject a bit of urgency and businesslike behaviour into the proceedings. Many profitable opportunities for the dairy had been squandered under the lax regime of Pat. For years Fat Clarrie has doubtless been gorging herself with churn-loads of cream on a 'one for me, one for the pot' basis.

It was Helen who saw what thousands of Anarchists knew Bridge Farm had been crying out for – a Hazard Analysis Critical Control Point Study. It was so blindingly obvious to most of us but no one but Helen had bothered to implement one. When she suggested this to Clarrie, it has to be said that Clarrie's response was embarrassing. She made the classic mistake of anyone who has a single-figure IQ of trying to be clever. When Helen patiently started to outline her systems and structure for her HACCP (as we aficionados call it), Clarrie jeered 'Systems and strategy, eh? Let me guess, you learned about this at Reece Heath, didn't you?'

Clarrie is presumably the kind of person who walks into a doctor's surgery and when prescribed an antibiotic says 'Oh, I suppose you learned that at medical school, didn't you?' What we do have to remember about Clarrie is that it is for people like her packets of salted peanuts are produced bearing the legend 'This product contains nuts.'

Helen is a real people's person, with an easygoing but efficient manner – the sort of person who would give you her last Rolo, and then send you a bill. Her efforts to introduce a training regime at the dairy were admirable. The extent to which Pat had allowed things to slide became apparent when Helen discovered an employee knocking around whom no one else ever seemed to have noticed.

Unfortunately Colin Kennedy was apparently more influenced by Clarrie and therefore was sullen and resentful of Helen's efforts. As a former teacher he should have embraced the opportunity to learn and grabbed the chance with both hands. Alas, he was obviously the sort of teacher who thought that yoghurt pots were primarily intended as the raw materials of tedious infant sculptures rather than as receptacles for yoghurt. It is a mystery how he came to be on the payroll of Bridge Farm without anyone realizing, almost redolent of the ghost-workers in the pre-reconstructed newspaper industry.

But Helen's real achievement was to enable the blossoming of Tracy Horrobin. She took to the new training like a duck to a Malteser (an interesting phenomenon if you are prepared to surrender a Malteser in the cause of science – children should be supervised).

The bitter feud between Fat Clarrie and Tracy served only to highlight all that is bad in Ambridge. Clarrie, having fought Helen tooth and nail, and poured scorn on all her training initiatives, expected that when Helen decided to create the much needed management function of assistant supervisor she would be first in line for the job. This despite the fact that she couldn't be bothered even to produce a simple flow diagram for Helen. Tracy on the other hand had recognized the old maxim 'If in doubt ask', and had enlisted the help of the MENSA-rated Jailbird to help her colour in a very attractive flow chart. Thus Tracy had demonstrated herself a willing and enthusiastic worker and eminently deserving of promotion – the first time a Horrobin had been promoted since the Am last froze over.

Fat Clarrie was outraged that Tracy had used her gumption and had been prepared to better herself. She duly tried to stitch her up, but luckily Helen had learned about people like Clarrie at Reece Heath in her Fat Employees with Attitude Problems classes. Clarrie was annoyed that Tracy, having become 'management', had the temerity to ask her to make a cup of tea. But if you can't get your staff to make you a cuppa, what's the point of promotion?

Tracy fully justified Helen's faith in her by displaying an imaginative form of 'hands-off' management. Under Helen she was able to demonstrate her creativity, and almost immediately added a new flavour to the yoghurt range. Ash-flavoured yoghurt would have been a bestseller among all right-thinking non-PC people if only Tracy's genius had been properly recognized.

Helen really made an effort to persuade Clarrie to inculcate some basic standards of hygiene into the dairy routine. But it was a painfully uphill struggle. When it comes down to it,

Clarrie is the kind of person whose ambition stretches no further than to be one of the people pulling moronic faces behind John McCririck on Channel 4 Racing. Helen's only management fault was that she did not immediately ask Clarrie to clear her desk. That task would have entailed nothing more than the removal of several forgotten items of decaying foodstuffs, a couple of Mills and Boons and one of those highly amusing postcards saying 'You don't have to be mad to work here but it helps.'

Lancastrian 'Trasher' Tommy seems to have a bit of a problem with his sister's management style but this can be attributed to the more laid-back 'manyana' way in which they work up North. He needs to learn that, for Southerners, efficiency comes somewhere between cleanliness and godliness. He also has to recognize the limitations of his own abilities, which are playing cricket, projecting diced carrot and running Roooth a close second as international whingeing champion.

A firm believer in the family unit, Sloane Helen was justly outraged that Horrible Hayley continued to hang around like a bad smell long after Jaaarn's death. So Helen's pointed references to Hayley as an outsider were quite befitting. After all, Hayley had had something of a hand in Jaaarn's demise, having as good as told him he could stick his engagement ring through the nose of one of his pigs. There are those who thought Helen was a trifle unpleasant, with her endless carping to Hayley about her not being part of the family, but sometimes the truth hurts and you have to be cruel to be cruel.

As the great sausage saga unfolded (you will find it well chronicled elsewhere in this book), Helen's perspicacity really came to the fore where Hayley was concerned. 'Am I the only one around here who can see what her game is? She's a gold-digger, after a share in the farm.' The plain answer to her rhetorical question is that she was by no means the only person who could see through Hayley, you can add several hundred baying Anarchists. But it was comforting that Helen at least was not taken in.

Helen is by no means hard-hearted and many people must have warmed to her as she gently dealt with her mother's bout of sausage-induced depression, shouting at her in tones that put Foghorn in the shade and enthusiastically tipping Prozac down her throat.

One of the recurrent problems in *The Archers* is that some characters metamorphose into cosy goody-goodies. It was very alarming when Helen suddenly seemed to be under the misapprehension that she had made a bit of a horlicks of managing the dairy. She suddenly came over all tearful and Pat had to be taken out of her strait-jacket for an hour or so to 'sort it'. Then, having justifiably lambasted Lancastrian 'Trasher' Tommy for his selfishness in dragging the noble name of Bridge Farm through the slurry, she suddenly admitted that she admired what he was doing. Helen should always remember that remorse is for softies.

Helen received little initial acclaim for her willingness to sacrifice her degree by helping out with the Bridge Farm shambles. There are not many students who could find time to run a dairy while in the middle of a degree course. And in the face of all her adversity she still managed to walk off with the Reece Heath Prize for Business Student of the Year. So stick that one in yer yoghurt pot, Clarrie!

On her 21st birthday in 2000 Helen was at last acknowledged for the graft she had put in and, somewhat to the chagrin of the idle Lancastrian 'Trasher' Tommy, she was given the key of their new organic shop. Sadly, once again her business experience slightly let her down when it came to recruiting staff. She started off OK by recruiting some anonymous oik called Peter, a typical product of a modern university education, i.e. when asked to give change from a five pound note for two yoghurts priced 50p he goes into a coma. She then made the fundamental mistake of employing the simperingly tedious Kathy Perks. Her record of bringing The Bull to the verge of bankruptcy by complaining to and about the customers presumably made her the obvious shop assistant. Within minutes of her arrival she was trying to tell Helen how to run the place and it must have come as a great relief when the Pargetters were daft enough to add her to the weird Lower Loxley staff. Since then Northern Kirsty seems to do the front of house stuff while Helen makes the strategic decisions such as which way round the yoghurt pots should face.

Like all strong leaders, Helen has had to cope with back-biting and unpleasantness from her jealous inferiors and it was no surprise when Horrible Hayley failed to invite her to her Hen Night, an event so nauseating that it had the same effect on most of us as a meal of two-year-old sun-baked haddock. Helen managed to shrug this off but she is the only person around who still mourns the death of Jaaarn and knows that the last thing he would have wanted was to see his true love become a Tugger.

One of our disappointments is that Helen has yet to devour the village menfolk. The only hint in this direction was mention of Trevor, the designer of acceptably modern yoghurt and sausage labels. It was quite obvious that Trevor's designs were well and truly set on Helen's King's Road knickers rather than yoghurt labels. But Trevor needs to learn that Sloane Rangers don't knock around with people called Trevor. In fact, does anyone?

If Helen is truly to emulate Hazel, and we desperately hope she will, then she needs to turn her attention to blokes who are to all intents and purposes in a happy relationship already. The problem is that most people in that category are already in her family, where divorce is unknown. But is that really a problem? It was once famously recommended that you should try anything once except folk-dancing and incest, so perhaps we could look forward to Helen seducing Tommy at a barn dance.

Don't Forget to Flush
Things That Never (or Rarely) Happen in Ambridge

While there can be no question that *The Archers* is anything other than real, it is nevertheless surprising that so many everyday things simply don't happen in Ambridge. Archers Anarchists can justly claim to have exerted some influence in these matters, for we find that certain things mysteriously occur for the first time when we point out their absence. It was with quiet satisfaction that we noted one of the first ever references to a television programme when Eddie admitted his previously well-hidden addiction to *Coronation Street*. That he should have chosen to watch a non-BBC soap was particularly laudable. Unfortunately, he seems to have forgotten his enthusiasm for 'Corrie' as he has never mentioned it again. Rare indeed are any references to children watching more than the occasional dose of televisual pap. This must be very satisfying to all the educationalists who tell us that very nearly all children watch TV for twenty-four hours a day.

Going into the Closet
Even the title of this chapter has been somewhat overtaken by events. When the BBC addresses some of these important omissions from Ambridge life, the result tends to be rather like the fabled No. 9 bus – you wait forty-five years for someone to

go to the lavatory and then suddenly everyone's permanently in the kasi. Until recently it was at least a habit confined to typically vulgar men, so imagine our shock and revulsion when Lynda Snell, blazing the trail for the women, suddenly announced she was off to 'powder her nose'. Deeevid was later described as being 'in the Gents' at the Cat and Fiddle, which could have set some tongues wagging in that particular watering hole. But after a brief period when everyone was suddenly emulating Mr Pullen, we're back to prolonged constipation.

Aerial Absence

Modern broadcasting devices such as satellite television have largely passed by Ambridge. More unusual is the complete absence of dreadful commercial music stations that so many people have as perpetual background to their work. You would expect the proletarian villagers, such as Jailbird, Clarrie, Eddie, Neil, Mike Tugger, etc., to be inseparable from 'Wazzock FM' (broadcast twenty-four hours a day from Felpersham). Not that anyone usually listens to any form of radio; even Radio 4 is ignored by Mrs Antrobus, Foghorn, Phil, Peggoi and other likely listeners. Which leads us on to the perennial puzzle of why no one in Ambridge listens to *The Archers*. It is possible to envisage a wonderful scene where Foghorn is shouting away, clattering about in the kitchen at around 7.05 and is forced to complain that she can't hear herself shout above the noise of the radio featuring her shouting away. You get the picture? It would be tremendously helpful to the cause of anti-castism if, every so often, someone would say, 'I must get home to listen to *The Archers*.'

We have to acknowledge the existence in recent years of Radio Borsetshire but it's a pretty unusual set up, being Britain's only county-wide talk radio station. The standard of interviewing is quite Paxmanesque.

No News is No News

Until recently there was no apparent means of obtaining newspapers in the village, with the obvious exception of the *Borchester Echo*. This presented no immediate problems as no one ever seemed to want to read one. But in 1999, Robert Snell broke all the rules in the book by going into the village shop to buy his Sunday papers.

This was an amazing feat, because there has never previously been any mention of the shop being open on a Sunday. Surely we would have heard *ad nauseam* if Beddy Tugger or Jailbird were being expected to work Sundays and Jeck would have been making his constipated firm managerial noises all over the place. Not content with just buying a paper in a one-off aberration, Robert proceeded to buy a newspaper for the following few Sundays and it seemed to have become something of a fixation with him. He simply couldn't stop talking about how much he was looking forward to reading them. So severe was his addiction and so infectious that even the illiterate Fat Clarrie started buying a tabloid, presumably for the pictures. Local media moguls were obviously impressed with the new zest for news in Ambridge because out of nowhere suddenly appeared the *Felpersham Advertiser*. The news blackout was soon imposed and Sunday papers are once again reserved as an occasional treat. For obvious reasons, no one ever does a paper round.

It is probably due to the lack of news that people in Ambridge are so eager to read the obituaries in the *Echo*.. When Nelson was killed, the locals were queuing up to buy the *Echo* just to read some ill-informed hagiography written by Mrs High and Mighty..

Famous Faces

There is no one famous or even of minor celebrity status in Ambridge, and never has been. Most villages can offer the odd celeb, often because they are the only people who can afford the house prices – whether it is a popstar, footballer, actor or businessman. Perhaps Ambridge is just a very ugly village populated by very ugly people and Mrs Antrobus.

Woeful Welfare
The Social Services are completely absent from Ambridge, particularly surprising given the number of wayward children and the apparently grinding poverty that afflicts so many of the characters. It was only in early 1999 that we learned of 'all the staff' at the doctor's surgery – presumably a silent army of nurses on permanent standby to remove the nits from the hair of the Grundys and Christopher 'Elephant Man' Carter. The ease with which Damien was adopted by Phallustair despite fierce opposition from his doting Hebden grandparents was a wicked scandal.

The Fourth Emergency Service
In the good old days there was Wharton's Garage and Fat Man Forrest's adopted son Peter Stevens who was a car mechanic. Nowadays there is no one within miles if you break down or need an MOT or service. Which perhaps doesn't matter because there seems to be no requirements for these in Ambridge any more. Strange, because Peter seemed to be kept pretty busy.

Throw Away the Key
Another thing that seems to be absent from Borsetshire in general is the release of prisoners. At the time of writing it is several years since Spanner and Craven were jailed for mistaking Usha Gupta's letterbox for a sewage treatment works. Since we now live in the touchy-feely world where murderers are let out of prison after a year or so with an apple, a

balloon and a going-home present, it seems extraordinary that these people have languished for so long at Her Majesty's pleasure. In fact, Her Majesty must be becoming rather bored with their company. Similarly we might have expected to see Clive Horrobin back in the bosom of his family before now.

Wheelie Strange
There are some very mundane absentees and one such example concerns refuse collection. No one ever puts their bin out. Indeed the thorny and sensitive issue of whether or not they have wheelie-bins has never so much as surfaced. Yet wheelie-bins have rent in twain many a community. Surely, from time to time we should be able to witness a snarl-up in the farmyard at Brookfield or Home Farm as the dustcart attempts to manoeuvre itself, accompanied by the silent barking of excited farm dogs. It should perhaps be acknowledged that Foghorn did allegedly inform the newly arrived Sheyawn Havitaway of the day that the bin men came, but since we never hear them perhaps she was just relating an historical event.

Till Death Us Do Part?
Divorce is not quite an unknown phenomenon in Ambridge but contestants for the Dunmow Flitch could fill several coaches. The divorce rate is way below the national average and in the few cases where anyone is divorced it tends to have happened before the arrival of the character in the village. Robert Snell divorced the ludicrously named Bobo long before he married Lynda and moved to the village. Kathy Perks's first husband, Steve, breezed into the village momentarily but it was all done and dusted without him staying. Boring George Barford was already divorced when he arrived, as were Phallustair Blandvoice (or so he says, we see it differently) and Robin Stokes.

The strangest feature is that the trend in Ambridge is completely different from that in the rest of the country in that there is actually a decline in the divorce rate. In the past we at least had Mrs High and Mighty Aldridge divorcing Roger the Dodger, a man who never received due acclaim for murdering Handbag Hebden. Greg Salt, a kind of prototype Mike Tugger divorced Nora, who eventually shacked up with Boring George. And, of course, dear old Jeck Woolley divorced Valerie. The recent divorce of Sid and Kathy is just a sop thrown in to discredit our theory and anyway Kathy is a serial divorcer. It should be noted that Sid took the whole business very seriously and when he confirmed that the decree absolute had gone through he remarked in a dignified way that it was not 'a cause for celebration', a sentiment that was only slightly dissipated when he immediately walked into The Bull and announced 'drinks all round, on the house'.

'The Appeared'

Perhaps the most intriguing and sinister absence is that of anyone's past, with the exception obviously of the indigenous population. A fair number of new characters have arrived in the village over a period of time but virtually no one brings much of a past with them. When you pause to consider some of our bastions of Ambridge life, we know very little about whence they came. Brian Aldridge turned up around 1975 loaded with wonga to the extent that he could buy a farm but never has any relation of his come to visit him nor has he ever visited them.

Similarly Sid – you might have thought that some of his old criminal mates would call by to chat about the good old days. Pat had her Uncle Haydn, who preceded her to Ambridge, but could not a few other relations find time to prise themselves away from their sheep to see her occasionally? The Snells are not the most exciting people in the world, but wouldn't there be the occasional Sunningdalese visitor or wouldn't Lynda want to go back to tell all her old neighbours what a mark she has made in her new area? Neil Carter had relatives back home when he first arrived in the village but he seems to have forgotten them. Phallustair, of course, has no visitors but we explain this elsewhere. Since there has to be an irritating exception to every rule, Horrible Hayley brought her silent grandparents to the village to be photographed guzzling wine and eating strawberries. In fact we were probably witness to the first silent drunken grandma on British radio.

Even those who do have relatives only seem to have them on a temporary basis, perhaps when they first arrive, and then they cease to exist. We had the occasional visit from Terry Boring-Barford, who had inherited every bit of his father's boringness with some to spare, but that was long ago and daughter Karen has never appeared. Dr Death had no relations, but he'd probably disposed of them. Even St Usha can only muster two relations. No one comes to see the awful Haveitaways or TFW, but then who would want to?

Anarchists have long discussed the vexed subject of 'the disappeared' but perhaps we have neglected to point out that there must be many people in Ambridge who are 'the disappeared' to their own relations. Somewhere in some far forgotten corner of England there is an old withered Aldridge. Tied to an unpruned tree is a yellow ribbon, blowing pathetically and forlornly in the breeze.

Housebuyers' Heaven

Not all the things missing from Ambridge are to be regretted, and the arrival of Smarmball Doctor Dim and his Missus indicated one of the benefits of living in this particular village. Many frustrated house-buyers and sellers were green with envy at the speed with which the Haveitaways were able to view 'The

Cottage formerly known as Honeysuckle', sell their own property, carry out the surveys and move in, all in just four weeks. Most of us find that it takes about that time to get an estate agent or solicitor to return our calls but in Ambridge it is Nirvana.

And it didn't stop there. Naturally the cottage did not have adequate space to accommodate the doctor's enormous bedside manner and so an early extension was essential. Since the demise of SDP councillor Handbag Hebden, whose political party seemed to go the same way as him, there has been no consistent form of local government in Borsetshire apart from the Parish Council. Thus it would appear that it is a complete haven from any kind of planning regulation since Token Brumvoice Jason was constructing one of his famous extension-cum-demolitions before you could say planning consent.

Break Away?

The song 'We're All Going on a Summer Holiday' is more or less taboo in Ambridge. Certainly holidays are not unknown, but they are very few and far between. In the rest of the country most people with an average or higher income can be expected to have one or two holidays during the year. But it would seem that you can only expect a holiday once every few years if you live in Ambridge and it is unusual for more than one person or family to be away at the same time. People don't even go away for short breaks. Even the well-to-do such as Jeck and Peggoi, Brian and Jennifer and Bicycle Pemberton don't seem to manage a holiday every year.

Ironically, or perhaps inevitably, when someone does have a holiday it is likely to be a big one and will be the talk of the village, e.g. Foghorn and Phil on the occasional trip to see wastrel son Ken Ton, or Usha and TFW on their dreadful walking holiday. The other feature of holidays when they do happen is that they are invariably taken with the utmost reluctance. Someone will always fight tooth and nail against the idea, either on grounds of cost or because 'there's far too much to do on the farm'.

Clarrie manages the occasional trip to Meyruelle, although people in Ambridge forget about their twinning arrangements for years at a time. It is rather painful hearing her struggle with her French and we can't help feeling she would be more comfortable with an annual week in Torremolinos, where she could get a decent piece of battered cod and chips with a nice lard dressing.

Sport in Question

It takes a great deal to get anyone in Ambridge interested in sporting events apart from those that occur within the village. There can be no other corner of the British Isles where boules is discussed more frequently than football with a reference ratio of about 60:1. The usual pub bar conversation of a Saturday night when the afternoon's footie results are dissected piece by piece just never takes place. During the World Cup there were one or two references to the competition but never to the results. No one ever backs the winner in the Grand National and until the Boat Race is relocated to the Am it doesn't look like we're going to hear anything about that either.

There was, however, a single and rather peculiar reference to the Cricket World Cup in summer 1999. It was mentioned that failed ex-feed rep Neil Carter had been given a ticket to the semi-final in Edgbaston by one of his old customers. It is an extremely unlikely form of corporate hospitality where someone decides to bestow such favours upon junior former employees of their suppliers rather than their own customers, but such is Borchester life.

Wimbledon got a couple of mentions in 1999. Unfortunately

Foghorn stayed in to watch it on television on a day when it was completely rained off, but she didn't seem to notice – probably sat there quite happily without even switching the TV on. People from Ambridge never go to Ascot or Henley, which is just as well as the Anarchist HQ is in Henley and we would be most upset to bump into any of them.

Louts There is no consistency in loutish behaviour and vandalism in Ambridge. It tends to switch itself on and off which is strange because there is never an obvious reason for it to stop. Edweird and his mates were causing minor trouble on a regular basis crawling over the church roof and damaging cars at The Bull, but now Edweird has become Richard Branson without any prompting. It's not as if anyone is being tough on the causes of loutishness, it simply evaporates. Total tolerance: a recipe for the rest of the country perhaps.

Cultural Deserts Ambridge is bereft of any true culture. There are no proper artists, just the occasional dabbler and Poppy the Cow. There are no classical musicians apart from third rate organist Phil or the harmonium playing Dog Woman. There are no authors apart from Mrs High and Mighty who is really in the 'I used to write a bit' category. And the few poets such as Horrible Hayley or the lad Tugger are simply risible.

Grunge Farm
The Rehabilitation of the Grundys

It is a well-documented phenomenon that age tends to mellow people and, with a few honourable exceptions, former revolutionaries tend to become establishment pussycats. Sadly, this has happened to the Grundys in a big way. For those listeners who can recall the days of Dastardly Dan, there will be strong memories of the constant vilification of the Grundys by the Archer establishment. No one ever had a good word to say to a Grundy and voices would immediately intone with rank hostility the moment Joe or Eddie joined a conversation. In those days the question, 'What are you doing here?' would literally be spat, though perhaps with less frequency than we have to bear today. Grundys were lazy slackers, poachers and ne'er-do-wells. The only exception was the silent Susan Grundy, who was a typical Ambridge cooking guru – a kind of Foghorn on Mogodon.

Anarchists would have loved the Grundys of yesteryear. Any enemy of an Archer is always a friend of ours. But tragically and for no accountable reason, people over the years have started being nice to them. There is no justification – Joe is still a foul-mouthed old goat, Eddie is still a poacher, thief, con artist and fraud and they all still whinge on ceaselessly as if the world owes them a living. Their children complement each other quite well but seem to move in opposite directions. You have Wiwyerm who, while at school, was more interested in rearing pheasants than getting a good crop of GCSEs. He has gone from the kind of layabout that would do his dad proud to ridiculous goody-two-shoes, though he plays a good Mellors to The Bicycle's Constance. Meanwhile Edward went through his childhood as a bit of a pansy – painting eggs and singing cherubically when he should have been going round looking for smaller children to bully. Mercifully Edweird now seems to be coming bad and shows encouraging signs of developing into the best youngster in the village since Clive Horrobin. Clarrie's voice is just too ridiculous for us to waste any sympathy in her direction.

A major turning point in attitudes to the Grundys occurred when Hard-working Simon Pemberton sensibly decided that Grunge Farm would be better suited to a major flax plantation than a scrap metal and turkey yard. He rightly gave them notice to quit and Wiwyerm helpfully set light to the place by dropping a lighted fag end, resulting in a particularly hot dog. All of a sudden people in the village came rallying to their defence. The likes of Deeevid were to be heard calling Eddie 'mate' and the awful Shulugh was going out of her way to help them with their insurance claims. This of course was another criminal conspiracy because an insurance company would not expect to be paying out on damage caused by arson on the part of one of the beneficiaries from the claim. The one person who didn't lift a finger to help was Jailbird Carter, who knows a bunch of wasters when she sees them.

Jailbird had for once in her life acted like a loyal employee, remaining absolutely shtum when Fat Clarrie kept asking her why the insurance hadn't come through. Clarrie tried the old blackmail trick of, 'Oi thort we was meant to be best friends', and unfortunately Jailbird turned turtle and rather belatedly let her in on the flax plans.

There is no proper explanation as to why the Grundys are and always have been totally penniless. They were tenant farmers, employed no staff and had a complete monopoly on turkey production, breeding a unique kind of silent, gobble-free turkey. At any given time Fat Clarrie has approximately five full-time jobs albeit of a staggeringly menial nature. It is hard to imagine that Grunge Farm produced anything at all since no one seemed to work it. Eddie would do any other kind of work, however lowly, rather than farm his own land. He has always felt entitled to line up with all the other hired hands seeking 'tractor work'.

Statistically, if you devote your life to inventing illegal or semi-legal scams, some of them are going to work, yet everything touched by a Grundy goes belly-up.

Wiwyerm has become a nasty case of poacher turned fascist as he marches round the covers in the country park threatening to shoot people's dogs and insolently telling his father to 'Keep orf moi paaatch.' If he was a real old-style Grundy he'd shoot the dogs without asking questions first and would turn up at Keeper's Cottage with a few brace of pheasant for his dad to sell. Perhaps we are speaking too soon, for he has time on his side. Even Gregarious Greg Turner, who initially had the good sense to pour scorn on the idea of employing offspring from one of Borsetshire's leading criminal fraternities, is now reduced to fawning adoration of Wiwyerm's every step. Wiwyerm has done several ridiculous things that are anathema to the Grundys of yesteryear, notably selling Posh Spice to pay off his parents' debts, and paying his keep. Where will it end? Will he be taking holy orders when he should be nicking from the collection plate?

When the Grundys finally went bankrupt, it was under somewhat surprising circumstances. Borchester Feed Mills foreclosed on them for £8,000. It was a mark of the fecklessness of the Grundys that they had incurred such a large amount on food bills when they never really appeared to have many animals. Presumably Fat Clarrie was eating her way through it. Typically, they went to celebrate their bankruptcy in a yuppie wine bar, Bannisters in Borchester, where Fat Clarrie was entranced to find 'newspapers on sticks'.

Fortuitously a large tower block called Meadow Rise had suddenly turned up in Borchester, providing some excellent and appropriate accommodation for them all, though Wiwyerm was soon seduced to The Dower House. Eddie got a job that must have stretched his intellect to near breaking point as a deliverer of take-away curries. Anyone familiar with Indian restaurants will know that it is perfectly usual for them to be staffed by unemployed English farm labourers. The good thing is that he took the opportunity to pour a vindaloo over Oilslick Gerrard.

Although they had sent most of their belongings to storage, presumably at the local refuse tip, Eddie did have the presence of mind to retain a lump hammer, which came in very useful when Joe decided that there were three more ferrets in the flat than was necessary.

Despite having a perfectly good roof over their head, bankrupt Eddie suddenly seemed to find that he had enough money to buy a caravan. Since all homes in Ambridge are mobile it was rather bad luck that it was spotted on Borchester Land and there was a revolting scene when poor Brian suddenly interrupted Fat Clarrie when she was starkers in the shower. It would have been enough to turn him vegetarian.

The caravan moved on to land owned by kindly Neil Plodder-Carter though the only plot he would allow them to use seemed to be three inches away from Tugger territory.

Ever since they lost Grunge Farm, Fat Clarrie has continued with all her jobs while Eddie has done sporadic labouring jobs, yet they seem to have amassed sufficient dosh to rent Keeper's

Cottage which must be able to command a fairly high rent in an area where accommodation is so short.

Recent indications show that the Grundy's are enjoying undeserved success on two rather ludicrous fronts. Eddie seems to be doing a booming trade in sexually explicit concrete garden ornaments, though perhaps the tax man will begin to take an interest in this enterprise.

But what absaolutely defies all credibility is that senile Joe Grundy has beaten his fast encroaching dementia to appear twice weekly on his Radio Borcetshire chat show. 'Joe's Dribbles' now seems to have an avid listenership consisting of bonkers Bert Fry and Mrs Potter. Since Radio Borcetshire is a BBC station, the taxpayers should demand a reduction in their license fee until this pap is removed.

The Grundys who vacillate constantly between dishonesty and stupidity, have become an embarrassment. Nowadays they are regarded as lovable rogues and the moment anyone becomes lovable they lose our support. It is quite unacceptable that their rehabilitation should have been so easy. Eddie is a lazy git and they deserve so much less in life.

Braveheart
Jamie Perks

For some unaccountable reason Archers Anarchists have occasionally been accused of negativity. 'Is there no one for whom you have a good word?' whimpers the occasional faintheart as they hastily try to conceal their Archers Anoraks membership cards. We have just two words to stop them in their tracks – they are 'Jamie' and 'Perks', consecutively, contiguously and with profound respect.

There is no doubt that Jamie will become a great man. We are all familiar with those people in life for whom, in their formative years, the bread lands butter side down on so many occasions that there seems no alternative but to stop buttering bread completely. Yet miraculously they reappear poking their defiant heads above the brown stuff. Such a sprog is Jamie Perks.

We have to admit culpability in neglecting Jamie. We completely overlooked him in our original A–Z, didn't even give the little blighter a couple of lines. Yet just consider what he has had to contend with.

Firstly he was born a Perks. No one is really called Perks – at least there are only three in the Reading phone book, hopefully three rather small, passive Perkses. His mother rejected him before he was even born. She was going around the village refusing to discuss her pregnancy and for a while the mere mention of 'baby' within earshot of Kathy drew the same response as saying 'sausages' to Pat. She vaguely warmed to the idea of being a mother as time went on, largely because she realized that it would give her at least a temporary excuse to keep away from serving in The Bull and all those dreadful customers. You can never underestimate what Kathy will do to avoid cooking and the catering business – she even lent her saucepans to the depressingly one-dimensional Sheyawn.

His next problem was being given a perfectly good traditional name like James and having it automatically converted to 'Jamie'. The thing that parents don't realize when they name their children is how ridiculous those names will sound when the child grows up. Even Kate twigged this one when she eventually decided against calling her child 'Baby', though she rather lost it when it came to the next one.

Jamie has never been permitted to see his half-sister, Lucy, because she is one of 'The Disappeared'. For several years he was apparently kept in some kind of cage, possibly with Eccles the peacock, since his sunny silent tones were never heard in The Bull and only recently does anyone talk to him. We are virtually certain that he has been brought up to all intents and purposes as a peacock. But the good thing about Jamie is that he doesn't let little things like this get him down. And all of a sudden he showed the mettle of a true champion at the noble art of egg-rolling.

What marked Jamie out as a true braveheart was not so much the mere fact of winning in this rather absurd sport but that he was prepared to take on all the forces of evil ranged against him in the person of the awful Damien. While that dreaded possessed child had his black heart set on victory, Jamie fearlessly showed that the forces of good are still alive in Ambridge.

But realistically, though we admire him, Jamie is perhaps

foolhardy. You don't cross the Archer mafia and live to tell the tale, and no one can honestly fancy his chances in later life against the darker forces of Damien. You will not have to wait too long before hearing, 'It was a complete accident – Jamie and Daniel were just playing together when Jamie fell into the Am. Daniel tried to rescue him but apparently the game they were playing involved Jamie having a large quantity of house bricks in his pocket and a lump of concrete tied to his leg.' Many of us held our breath when he almost came a cropper on the Treetop Walk and there was little doubt that he was having to muster the forces of good in the face of Damien's curse.

In the meantime he fights back against all the odds. Often left in the care of the Angel of Death, Horrible Hayley, he rarely squeaks out but accepts life's lot. He has a voice of sorts that emerges on saints' days and other festivals but it is 95 per cent peacock, 5 per cent human.

In 2001 there was an occurrence that threw into doubt the assumption of his Peacockness. By now he had moved with his awful mother to April Cottage where they were living next door to neighbours from hell, the Grundys. Fat Clarrie suddenly declared that her wedding ring had disappeared and though we all assumed she had eaten it, to our surprise it was revealed that Jamie had stolen it. There was no proper explanation and it was all hushed up, but it suddenly clicked that Jamie is more magpie than Peacock. For once in his life, Eddie actually raised a sensible point when he questioned if they wanted a kleptomaniac living next door, though if he had not allowed his corpulent spouse to harass the admirable putative owners of April Cottage, Nick and Venetia, the question would never have arisen. But overall, Anarchists were delighted. To have another thief in Ambridge is just what the doctor ordered.

From the Cutting-room Floor I
The Arrival of the First Mrs Blandvoice

Archers Anarchist militants have broken into the BBC strong-room and obtained some dialogue which is currently being withheld from adoring listeners. It concerns the vital matter of the first Mrs Blandvoice. Listeners will well remember how Phallustair suddenly refused to have a church wedding with the awful Shulugh when he realized that he was going to have to discuss his first marriage in a no-holds-barred session with That Fisher Woman. Wrongly, many people assumed he just could not 'bear to bare' his soul to a woman who is so clearly a theological impostor. But the truth was far more interesting. The following transcript liberated from the cutting-room floor makes fascinating reading.

The scene is the village shop on a summer afternoon. Beddy Tugger and Jailbird Carter are quietly pilfering stamps, falsifying Child Benefit claims and engaging in desultory conversation.

Beddy: At least Mike's getting some tractor work. Oh, sorry Susan, I didn't mean. . .

Jailbird: Oh, that's all right, Betty, Neil's quite enjoying clearing dogs' mess from the village green. He doesn't need tractor work.

Shop bell rings and a woman in her thirties enters, complete with horribly disfigured face.

Beddy: What brings you here?

Jailbird: Yeah, what the f*** do you think you're doing – a member of the public coming into a shop?

Quasimodette: Well, actually, it's awfully nice of you to ask but I didn't come in to buy anything. I'm looking for the home of someone called Phallustair Blandvoice-acid-thrower.

Jailbird: Do you mean Shulugh's husband?

Quasimodette: No, he can't be anyone's husband, he's still married to me.

Jailbird: But we've got a Phallustair Blandvoice here in Ambridge. He's the vet.

Quasimodette: Oh, no, he's not pretending to be a vet again, is he?

Beddy: *(gulping)* Pretending?

Quasimodette: I'm afraid Phallustair is a very sick man. He spent ten years in prison after eating two of our children.

Jailbird: *(with enthusiasm)* Oh, that's nice, I've been in prison, too. We can have a good old natter about it.

Quasimodette: While he was in prison he started reading one or two books about veterinary science and when he was let out he immediately set himself up as a vet. He's got no qualifications at all.

Jailbird: (*proudly*) I haven't got any qualifications.

Beddy: (*with a voice resonant of a monkfish choking on a Brillo pad*) So, did he come back to you after leaving prison?

Quasimodette: Oh, he came back to me all right, just long enough to redesign my face in an acid attack. I went to the police, but they let him off with a caution as long as he went to live somewhere off their beat. I haven't seen him again, though he still sends cards to the children.

Beddy: But I thought you said he ate the children?

Quasimodette: No, I'm talking about the other five. Sorry, we haven't really introduced ourselves, have we. I'm Quasimodette Blandvoice.

Jailbird: Very pleased to meet you. You remind me of my Christopher.

Exit Quasimodette.

Jailbird: What was I saying? Oh, yes, tractor work.

The Great Sausage Betrayal
From Pork to Prozac

*'Those blessed sausages, they've
caused so much strife in this family.'*
Pat Archer, 8 March 1999

Spring 1999 was largely devoted to one of the most riveting plots ever to be served up on the airwaves. The degree of acrimony arising from this situation was sufficient to send poor Pat from Bridge Farm to Funny Farm. It all stemmed from the somewhat deranged plan of Horrible Hayley and Lancastrian 'Trasher' Tommy to produce organic sausages. Everyone accepts that there are a number of risks associated with allowing a team headed up by a serial poisoner to go into food production, yet strangely this never actually came into the equation.

There was an early hiccup in the whole enterprise when Hayley, with all the relevant experience that comes from looking after toddlers, excitedly told Tommy how they would be able to produce 'different kinds' of sausages. A completely nonplussed Tommy asked, 'What do you mean?' and Hayley had to break it to him that sausages were not actually grown from seeds – they could, in fact, be subject to variations in ingredients, thus resulting in different flavours. Once over this little hurdle it looked as if they'd be laughing all the way to the abattoir, but sadly it was not to be.

Initially Tony and Pat were as enthusiastic as two terminally miserable people can be, but it was the intervention of the excellent Helen that turned the tide. Helen managed to persuade her parents that if the sausages were to be marketed without a newly revamped Bridge Farm label then a great plague and pestilence would fall upon the farm. We can only assume that with the death of Jaaarn still fresh in their minds they just didn't want to take the risk. For although we have nothing but respect for Helen's marketing expertise, it is not immediately apparent that the labelling of sausages is that important. It is not unusual for sausages to be sold loose, in which case they wouldn't have a label at all.

Much to the chagrin of Britain's most unlikely coupling of entrepreneurs, Pat and Tony pulled the plug on the whole venture at Helen's insistence and refused to fund it.

Ambridge may lack many of the facilities and services available in most medium-sized villages but one thing it does have is a resident venture capitalist. Indeed, there is hardly a person below the age of thirty in the Archer family who is not up to their eyeballs in debt to Peggoi Woolley. Hayley and Tommy went hot-foot to Peggoi to see if she would stump up the readies. Peggoi, always partial to the occasional sausage, was only too pleased to get involved initially. But not having the blessing of Pat and Tony turned out to be like having a bad reference from a credit-checking company, and when Peggoi learned that these sausages were to be produced without a state-of-the-art label she immediately changed her tune.

Desperate, Hayley and Tommy considered other ways of raising the capital. They overlooked the obvious solution, which was to steal from poor old blind Mrs Antrobus, but this was presumably because Hayley regarded Mrs A as a long-term investment. Ironically the modest funding eventually came from the most unpredictable of sources, the very people who had withdrawn it in first place. When it came to Tommy's birthday (and what a jolly affair that was!) Pat, despite having talked of nothing else for the previous month, had not been able to think of anything to get him for a present and therefore wrote out a cheque, thus inadvertently solving the Brum Nanny Sausages cash-flow problem.

The subterfuge had only just begun. Cash duly secured, the next problem was that, for some reason best known to himself, the butcher who would construct the sausages required the leeks ready chopped. Preparing leeks at Bridge Farm would have been akin to setting up a charcuterie in a synagogue and, by a cruel twist of fate, Hayley did not seem to have a sink in her flat at Nightingale Farm. This meant that an accomplice was needed in this vicious plot. Step forward Jailbird Carter. Well used to harbouring criminals, the temporary loan of a sink was chicken feed to her and she even helped in the dirty deed.

The next obstacle in the whole ghastly business was that when Hayley and Tommy were about to set off, armed to the teeth with pigs and leeks, Pat suddenly decided that a trip to the abattoir was her ideal day out. They only managed to deter her by gently convincing her that she was completely bonkers.

The denouement came with the triumphal arrival of Lancastrian 'Trasher' Tommy back at Bridge Farm accompanied by fifty pounds of organic pork and leek sausages. Having gone to inordinate lengths to produce these comestibles in the utmost secrecy, it was rather bewildering that he was so quick to flaunt them before the unstable Pat, particularly bearing in mind her deep-seated sausage phobia.

On cue, Pat completely trolleyed it on sight of the offending sausages. 'Get out of my sight', she said to her errant son. It's difficult and inappropriate for us to make a value judgement and the jury could go either way in determining the sanity of an eighteen-year-old who chooses fifty pounds of sausages as his coming-of-age present.

But that was by no means the end of the matter as Helen, by now famous for her numerous unannounced appearances when everyone thought she was meant to be at college, suddenly showed up. Her antennae had picked up the word 'sausages' and she launched a complete rocket attack on the whole project. Hayley was suddenly cornered like a rat and her veneer of syrup fell away as she lashed out at Helen, accusing her of all things under the sun. Pat was forced to retreat to her boudoir with a touch of the vapours.

It further transpired that the leeks were, of course, stolen from Pat and Tony, a crime for which hanging would be akin to a total reprieve. Needless to say, Brum Nanny sausages were eagerly snapped up by the odd but appreciative Borsetshire public. Never mind the problems of rural transport, people were travelling from miles around, turning up at Bridge Farm at all hours of the day to get half a pound of the contentious bangers.

But Pat and Tony were adamant. No matter how many millions of sausages were sold, if they didn't have one of Trevor's as yet unproduced labels, they were illegal. Pat was actually confined to her bed for at least two weeks, suffering from the constant pressure to permit the illicit production to continue. It can't have helped matters that, during this time, Foghorn would appear on the hour every hour to attempt to pour soup down her throat, while the insensitive Tommy wanted to revive her with a constant regime of bangers and mash. It became like a slapstick 'Don't mention the war' routine. Nobody seemed capable of talking to Pat for more than about twenty seconds without mentioning sausages and this would immediately cause a relapse. For weeks, Pat could be reduced to tears by the mere mention of the 'S' word.

Perhaps the most amazing incident in the whole debacle

occurred at 7.15 pm on Sunday, 21 March 1999. Lancastrian 'Trasher' Tommy, suffering from a kind of reverse syndrome to his mother's whereby he could think of nothing but sausages, suddenly declared that the attitude to Hayley over the whole business 'is really pissing me off.'

The nation stood stock still. Sunday roasts being taken from their respective ovens went crashing to the floor. Those roasts in a more advanced stage of the cycle lodged in their eaters' throats. Birds stopped singing. After forty-eight 'piss'-free years and despite the numerous provocations during that time – armed robberies, murders, outbreaks of foot and mouth disease, TB etc., etc., it took a few pounds of pork and leek sausages to trigger off the first ever 'piss' in Ambridge. Whether or not anyone in the village noticed is open to conjecture. The signature tune hastily cut in the moment the word was uttered, and by Monday we can only assume that all villagers in the know had been sworn to secrecy.

Things went from bad to worse at Bridge Farm. Pat was by now a mere step away from Château Insane as she seemed unable to recover from the whole sausage ordeal. For someone with such a generally short fuse, Tony had played a blinder and taken on the role of mediator with relish for the task. Thanks to Helen's tip-off, he had stepped in to ensure that Horrible Hayley would not become a partner in the burgeoning sausage empire. Hayley had sufficiently poisoned the mind of Lancastrian 'Trasher' Tommy to ensure that he was going to go round like he'd lost a fiver and found a euro for some time to come. It was noticeable that for several weeks around this time, he was permanently off his food. It is a wonder he was not treated for anorexia.

One day towards the end of March, the deranged Pat suddenly turned on poor Tony and accused him of being hard on Tommy and a 'bad manager'. Not content to stop there, she went on to say that this was exactly how he had treated Jaaarn. Tony was stung to the quick and suddenly adopted a strangulated voice like that of Charlie Drake singing 'My Boomerang Won't Come Back', asking, 'You're not blaming me for John's death, are you?' But, oh yes, she was, and there was no stopping her. All of a sudden we thought we were in heart-attack territory as Pat, like a wailing banshee, came over all unnecessary.

Poor Tony was so shaken by the whole business that he couldn't remember the number 999 to call an ambulance. Totally overcome by the all-pervading demonic influence in the village he kept dialling 666. And there we were left at 7.15 pm on a Friday night with a good old-fashioned cliffhanger, wondering whether by Sunday night Horrible Hayley would be busy writing poetry and TFW would be getting ready for more pagan festivities.

But, alas, this was the cruel 1990s and by Sunday, Pat was back to being quietly doolally in her bedroom with the curtains closed. Apparently it was nothing more than a bit of sausage-induced hyperventilation. Tony seemed to have forgotten that he was currently standing accused of murder and merrily suggested to Pat that she may feel better if they took a trip to look at Brian Aldridge's top-security genetic research establishment. There's nothing like a double-headed sheep or a field of talking barley to make you feel better when you've been hyperventilating.

Eventually, someone decided that as Pat had spent the previous six weeks in bed and was rapidly becoming like a walk-on part in *One Flew Over the Cuckoo's Nest* it might be worth getting the doctor in. The BMA has an agreement that all doctors in Ambridge will be great ambassadors for the profession, so we can only assume that they must have had a brief falling out with the BBC during the time Dr Death was there. Dr Dim is back in the groove as an all-round nauseatingly good guy who dispenses bucketloads of sympathy whether or not it is requested or deserved.

Despite the fact that Dr Death had apparently neglected to mention in Pat's medical notes the small matter of her losing her son, Dr Dim was soon on the case. Within minutes he had set Pat well on the road to being our first Ambridge junkie.

After her huge fracas with the Bridge Farm gang, Horrible Hayley was completely gob-smacked by the revelation that Pat might be suffering from 'depression'. Her reaction was, 'I can't believe it.' What the million or so listeners couldn't believe was that she should be so surprised that Pat should be depressed by having an East End-style gangland war fought out in her farmyard – over pork and leek sausages.

Thankfully, marketing guru Sloaney Helen got her way and the sausages were duly given their labels, emblazoned with the name that had advertising agencies dropping their collective jaws with admiration, 'Bridge Farm Organic Sausages'. Unfortunately, the very appearance of these labels led Tommy to go off the deep end in a manner not seen since his gracious appreciation of his eighteenth-birthday celebrations.

As the weeks wore on, the whole subject of sausages was reduced to the status of an unstable semi-dormant volcano. At Helen's birthday party it was actually Pat who mentioned the war with a, 'How are the sausages coming on, Tommy?' The nation held its breath, but there was no need to worry because this was False Jollity Awareness Day at Bridge Farm and fuses were to stay intact. In fact the only enduring memory from Helen's festivities was the revelation that Pat is tone deaf and cannot sing in tune. Her rendition of 'Happy Birthday' will linger in our ears for far too long.

Anyone who thought that Pat was cured was in for a bitter disappointment. When they get hold of a new idea, they hang on to it for grim death. And, after all, the idea of someone going around Ambridge like a permanent wet weekend was so novel, you could hardly blame them for milking it a bit. Much to the chagrin of the pharmaceutical industry, the happy pills that Pat was eventually forced to take did not have an instantaneous effect. But then, if the rest of us had sons with the temerity to set up a small-scale sausage-making enterprise, we would all doubtless find that it needed more than a few milligrams of Pfizer's finest to set us back on the straight and narrow.

When the drugs had failed there was urgent consultation over what steps to take next. It was felt that Pat needed to talk to someone who might understand what she was going through, a task probably best suited to someone from a family of butchers. TFW made the occasional very fleeting appearance and it is on the extremely rare occasions when TFW visits the sick that you really do realize she is no more a vicar than Joe or Eddie Grundy.

She was of no help whatsoever for the most part, merely repeating, as if it were some kind of mantra, 'I'm a good listener', a phrase which would induce any self-respecting recipient to administer a knuckle sandwich. Surprisingly little was seen of Horrible Hayley and it appeared that her ostracism had been pretty thorough. She and Pat had a couple of 'glad we're still friends' sessions and then didn't speak to each other for months. Suddenly the psychiatric establishment's secret weapon was unleashed – just the person you want to see when you're on the edge – jolly old Mike Tugger. The counselling role fitted him like an ill-fitting glove and he made a few awkward visits to Pat, telling her, 'Oi've bin there. Oi know what you're goin' through.' Sensibly, Pat realized that the only way to avoid further visits was to get better. So off she went for a four-day visit to a nunnery in Wales, returning in a frame of mind to take on the sausage-producing world single-handed.

The first thing she did when she got back was to retract her comments about Tony being a murderer. This came as a huge disappointment to many, but we have to be stoical about these things. The greatest turnaround came when she offered to help Tommy with his sausages at the Farmers' Market. It then became obvious that the place she had visited in Wales that had brought about her recovery was not a religious establishment at all. In fact it was the equivalent of one of these courses for arachnophobes where they end up holding a spider. By the end of her four days of brainwashing, Pat was able to hold a sausage. It's just wonderful what can be done nowadays. As Pat's Welsh relations would no doubt tell us, 'Never say di.'

Treachery!
Mutiny in the Ambridge Cricket Team

Apart from boules and whingeing the most popular sport in Ambridge is cricket. Good old-fashioned cricket played on lazy summer afternoons and washed down by gallons of warm Shires. Like many village teams, Ambridge CC has had its ups and downs over the years. The frequent banishment of players to the realms of 'The Disappeared' does little to bolster the club's fortunes, but it has generally kept its head above water and occasionally enjoyed modest success.

At the helm have been a succession of captains motivated by a mixture of pride, bile and the inability to say no when asked to take on the job. The demise of one-time Captain Handbag Hebden caused the inception of the dreaded Single Wicket Competition, a contest that has brought recurrent grief and bitterness over the years. But the darkest day in the club's history dawned at the end of the 1998 season.

The club captaincy had drifted into the hands of Sean Myerson. It was one of those classic situations where nobody would take on the role and then when a relative outsider agrees to do it, some of the more long-in-the-tooth club members mutter darkly about 'upstarts and interlopers'. The main objector was former club captain and homosceptic Sid Perks. His dislike of Sean was on two somewhat different grounds. His stated objection was that he 'batted the wrong way', a dreadfully un-PC notion in a village such as Ambridge, where coaches to Gay Pride rallies are regularly oversubscribed.

But Sid's main problem with Sean deserved considerably more sympathy than it was generally accorded. In essence, Sean moved the focal point of village cricket from the Bull to the Pink Cat. Warm beer is one thing but warm lager is quite another, and Sid was justifiably miffed when he lost a load of trade to another pub that was not even in the village. Anarchists have long suspected that the Cat was, in fact, a caravan, as it seemed to have moved around a lot over the years, particularly in terms of its proximity to the village.

The 1998 season was not a good one for the Ambridge Cricket Club. They had frequent difficulties in mustering a team, which meant that the likes of Eddie Grundy were called up – always portentous of looming defeat. Results were appalling and the genial veneer of Sean gave way to snarling defensiveness.

The high points of the local cricket calendar are the games with Darrington which, over the years, have taken on the same intensity as an 'old firm' Rangers and Celtic match. Fat Man Forrest and Dan would turn up in days gone by, with Walter Gabriel in tow, all tooled up with broken bottles and Stanley knives. If you didn't end up with a good glassing, it was a pretty dull affair. Dirty tricks galore have been pulled over the years to try to get one over on the other side. Still fresh in the memory is a half-baked plan by Loopy Nigel and Dr Death to lure the best Darrington players away to non-existent county trials on the day of their match with Ambridge. But in 1998 it was all hopeless.

Sean's solution to the problem was to suggest a merger between Ambridge and Darrington, a suggestion so crass and insensitive as to defy belief. It was the kind of idea that could only come from an outsider with no sense of history. He convened secret talks and tried to enlist the support of the few decent Ambridge cricketers: Deeevid, Racist Roy Tugger, Lancastrian 'Trasher' Tommy and Dr Death.

The latter was a lost cause, as he was too busy making mincemeat of the Hippocratic oath. A general meeting was called to discuss the proposal and Shulugh was very much to the fore, invoking the name of Handbag and saying how he would have turned in his grave at the very idea. He would probably have turned somewhat more, reaching a creditable spin, at the idea of his wife making whoopee with the local doctor.

Ultimately loyalty won the day and there were just two Judases, in the form of young Tugger and Sean himself. Ambridge is an unforgiving village and Sean was punished for his treachery by having his voice box removed for several months. To add insult to injury Sean callously won the Single Wicket Trophy when he was meant to let Lancastrian 'Trasher' Tommy have it as a consolation for having his brother squashed by a tractor.

Deeevid and Lancastrian 'Trasher' Tommy deserve the highest praise for their loyalty. Having lost the captaincy of Sean, there was the usual unseemly wrangling and desperate search for a successor. Unsurprisingly the job went to Phallustair Blandvoice, one of the few speakers in the village who had not already held the uncoveted post.

There had been some question of bringing back Sid. With Sean now off the scene he seemed rather keen to return. He saw himself in the vein of some ousted Third World dictator returning to pick up the pieces. Instead he was given a spurious title of club manager on the strict understanding that it was to be completely meaningless. Initially he was happy enough with this but, of course, the main benefit to Sid was the fact that the focal point for village cricket was once more returned to the

Bull. Presumably the Pink Cat had yet again got itchy feet and moved on up the road.

By the following season, the likes of Beddy Tugger had completely failed to realize the seriousness and truly treacherous nature of what had happened. She was heard cheerfully to say, 'You heard that Darrington beat Edgeley' as if half the village would suddenly don the Darrington colours in honour of her pig's bladder-toting son and the treacherous Mr Myerson.

It's not easy to make the Single Wicket Competition interesting. Once you've lost the trophy and all the characters have won it, what is there left to say? In 1999 there was the question of whether the traitors should be allowed to compete. The rules of the competition say that if you live in Ambridge you are allowed to enter the competition even if you have absconded to the enemy team. But you do have to live in Ambridge. This racist rule was introduced to discriminate against people from Penny Hassett, a nearby village in which all the residents are Somalis.

Roy Tugger, fearing a lynching, decided that discretion was the better part of cowardice and declined to take part. Sean Myerson also declined, but not until he'd wound up Sid to the point where he was pawing the ground. We were treated to some further discussion about Sean's proclivities and Sid's views when Right-on Kate suggested that one in ten of the male population is gay and therefore there must already be a gay member of the cricket team. Sid almost choked on his muesli at this concept.

It's certainly the case that Lancastrian 'Trasher' Tommy has a rather camp voice, but we don't actually know a full eleven members of the team so it's not too easy to 'out' someone. On the other hand, Darrington might have two gay members which could mean that Ambridge need not have any. Funny business, statistics.

The 1999 SWC was dull as ditchwater. The reserve trophy

made a brief appearance while we went through the rather weary ritual of the current holder once more having such a huge house that they are able to lose a large tacky piece of mock-silverware. What we always have to remember is that Shulugh is unaware that there are two trophies, though why she should be concerned about this is open to question.

A new cricketer was born in the form of Elephant Man Christopher Carter. We all knew he was bowling when we heard the shrieks from the normally silent village children and the sound of mothers' aprons being desperately hidden behind. It was noticeably un-PC of someone to describe Christopher's bowling as 'unorthodox'. Most of us thought he had put his trunk to excellent use in bowling out Eddie Grundy.

Sheyawn Haveitaway, obviously in training for the coveted position as the village's most sickly irritating nice person, bowled out Tony. The ultimate in bathos was attained when Lancastrian 'Trasher' Tommy picked up the award, although it was generally agreed among Anarchists that everyone else had thrown the game rather than have to put up with a repeat of the previous year's sulkathon. They didn't fancy having to go on permanent suicide watch at Bridge Farm – never the jolliest of places at the best of times.

One of the reasons that the team is so awful is that doctors and vets always play far too important a role, only to disappear at key moments to do unimportant things like tending sick people and animals. It was just such an occasion when Phallustair had been called away, presumably to murder a dog, that Sid stepped in to captain the team. His great tactical decision was to use nomark Neil Carter as a bowler on the basis that the opposition would be so surprised by the use of a non-bowler that their wickets would clatter. Sure enough, that is exactly what happened. And some people say *The Archers* aren't real. Bah.

Sid has found it exceptionally difficult to keep his ten-foot hooter out of playing matters, though we have to sympathise to some extent because super-wimp Phallustair is so obviously out of his depth. Indeed since Sid has taken on self-appointed duties as an intelligence gatherer, the team has shone.

The Cricket Club Dinner is usually a date worth putting in your diary. A few years ago, it was gatecrashed by the genial Mr Barraclough, devoted son of the late Mrs Barraclough, who accosted Dr Death in front of all his mates and accused him of murder. In 1999 Shulugh booked a Colonel Bridgwater as the guest speaker and he proceeded to spew forth a stream of offensive and risquÈ jokes. In a PC place like Ambridge, that must have been rather a hoot.

The long-term future of the cricket club should be fairly rosy, with the exploding birth rate in the village and it was no surprise when in 2000 Roy Tugger came crawling back to ACC with his tail between his stumpy legs.

2001 has been a strange year for the club so far. By the end of June there had been no mention of the game. Even the beloved single wicket had apparently fallen victim to an epidemic of amnesia. Perhaps they were planning to move the season to the Autumn. Now that would be different, Ambridge cricket invoking fond memories of woolly mufflers and cocoa.

Role of Rogering
The Sexual History of Shulugh Hebden-Blandvoice

Known amongst Anarchists as Britain's most sexually active churchwarden, Shulugh Hebden-Blandvoice has never been reluctant to put it about. Newer listeners may only be aware of her penchant for the medical and veterinary professions, but the awful Shulugh has more notches on her bedpost than there are hassocks in St Stephen's. As far as we can determine the chronological order is as follows. Please bear in mind, however, that when you are dealing with numbers as huge as this, it is impossible to guarantee accuracy and we have had to rely on the human frailties of fading memories, together with one or two castist publications and hagiographies. We would also like to pay tribute to Anarchist Murray Craig, who wrote a learned treatise himself on this same subject and first alerted us to the full extent of St Shulugh's promiscuity. Indeed Mr Craig strongly asserted that 'Carolide', as Jeck Woolley adenoidally calls her, has wrongly been accorded the title of 'Village Bicycle'.

RICK Shulugh began as she meant to go on. This was her first recorded bloke, a married music freak in his thirties from Borchester Tech (now known as University and famous for its useful honours degrees in Contemporary Lager Drinking and Lego Modelling). Although it is always said that this relationship began when she was fourteen, Anarchists strongly believe that she was really only eleven and it was typical of the BBC's tendency, even then, to sanctify Shulugh and gloss over her many indiscretions. Needless to say that Foghorn, although her voice was about two octaves higher in those days, was like a John Dory on heat while this relationship was going on.

WELSH BILL He was actually quite a nice guy, who had the advantage of having more than the shared brain cell employed by most of the characters in Ambridge. His cardinal error was that when he went for tea at Brookfield he failed to consume the statutory eight plates of Foghorn's scones and, more seriously, dared to discuss farming with Phil. It is sometimes the case that people do not realize that the Archer Mafia rule Ambridge and can do no wrong. Bill gave Phil the benefit of his opinions and even in those days the superficially saintly Shulugh would never do anything to jeopardise her inheritance.

ALL THE YOUNG CONSERVATIVES Remembering that this dates back to the days when Young Conservatives ruled the world, we are talking about serious numbers of blokes here. It would be invidious to single out any individual, although we know that loopy **NIGEL PARGETTER** was well in there, together with **TIM BEECHAM**. Tim was a member of the Borchester Branch of the Assassins, whose idea of a good night out was to drink yak's blood and brandy cocktails and throw up over the Lawson Hope memorial seat.

Another was **CHARLES HODGSON**. It was never quite clear why she didn't last longer with this bloke, because he was a well-loaded toff and very much a man of the horse. Perhaps his only crime was that he wasn't hung like one.

NEIL CARTER He was always sniffing around, and Shulugh may or may not have gone the distance with him as her bit of rough. She certainly led him on often enough.

HANDBAG HEBDEN She started knocking around with him a long time before their marriage and, in a style that she was to continue later on, she managed to indulge in some concurrence of bedfellows. For some years there would always be, as a standard character, a scribbler from the Borchester Echo. This tradition has ceased without explanation. **ROBIN CATCHPOLE** was one such person and breezed in and out of Shulugh's bed for a month or so. But he was only the warm-up act for a successor journalist, **SIMON PARKER**, who gave her a good old-fashioned seeing-to in a cornfield, upsetting a whole load of listeners who were so revolted that they couldn't face their suppers for several days.

Ludicrously, we were meant to believe that the cornfield incident was Shulugh's 'first time'. Perhaps the words 'that day' would put it into a more realistic context. Interestingly it was when Parker was offered a job outside Ambridge that Shulugh refused to leave the village and the relationship ended – the same stunt she was to pull after seducing Dr Death many years later.

Some Spanish waiter called **PEDRO** and a complete **AUSTRALIAN SHEARING GANG** can be added to this immodest list, along with all the other male members of the Club 18-30 holiday groups or whatever travel companies she went with on her overseas holidays.

NICK WEARING The next in the queue, he was a bit of a lad, another rich farmer's son who worked his way around the available Ambridge womenfolk before pausing with Shulugh for a while. She went round the world with him except that he went round a bit more of the world than she did because he left her in Bangkok. Bearing in mind that Elizabeth was dumped by the great Cameron Fraser in a similarly remote and inhospitable location (the M1 services), it is coincidental but entirely understandable how these two sisters lend themselves to being abandoned.

BEN WARNER Another bit of rough for Shulugh was the burglar-cum-tramp Ben Warner with, whom she appeared to indulge in the occasional threesome, supplemented by Jackie Woodstock. This was also concurrent with her extremely lengthy engagement/courtship with Handbag Hebden. Throughout her marriage to Hebden she continually reverted to Loopy Nigel, whose charms are clearly well concealed over the radio. If it had not been that he was an SDP councillor with a mobile phone one could have felt quite sorry for Mark.

Hard-working Simon Pemberton Pausing briefly to catch her breath when Hebden went to that great district council meeting in the sky, Shulugh's next port of call was Hard-working Simon Pemberton. All went smoothly enough and her bedsprings were duly put through their paces until she decided to play the pot to Simon's kettle. Just because he was giving some much-needed comfort to his former love, Mrs Harriet Williams, Shulugh went all huffy. Conveniently forgetting the string of blokes she had quadruple-timed, she became all churchwardenish and hit him.

PHALLUSTAIR BLANDVOICE She then went solo for the longest time in her history, until Phallustair Blandvoice arrived on the scene. Listeners will recall that the Village Bicycle immediately had her sights set on Phallustair, but it was all a bit complicated because he was more interested in Shulugh, whilst Graham Ryder was drooling over the Bicycle. To further complicate matters, Shulugh had gone into one of her temporary iron-knickered 'Oh, I've suddenly remembered I'm a churchwarden' modes and was not taking the Phallustair bait.

The fact that the Bicycle wanted Phallustair was sufficient to ensure that Shulugh would deny her best friend the opportunity, so there followed an extremely tedious period of Shulugh playing hard to get. But eventually she swore undying love for the drippy bloke and, within days of this, was seducing **DR DEATH** in an infamous and stomach-churning 'I want you now' scene.

With apologies to any more of the Ambridge males we might have omitted, we reckon that (seasonally adjusting the figures for the shearing gang, Young Conservatives and random holiday partners) Shulugh has managed to get through an average of two or three men per year since she has been fourteen.

Careful study of the types of men she has ensnared over the years will indicate a gradual change from the initial alternation between farm hands and wealthy farmers' sons to the present day when she insists on professional qualifications and a healthy bank balance.

Of course the burning question is who's next? There are a number of obvious possibilities. Dr Dim is certainly in the market for a bit of extra marital and another favourite has to be Oliver Foxbrush, given Shulugh's tendency to go after the Bicycle's conquests. But if it was up to us we'd be particularly enchanted if she could strike up a relationship with the excellent Matt Crawford. Is there a God?

Something of the Night
The Sinister World of Damien Hebden

Shulugh's son, Damien, was the result of numerous experiments in genetic engineering. Anarchists never lavish much pity on Shulugh, but her endless attempts with Handbag Hebden to conceive naturally before giving birth to a Dalek did at least demonstrate a degree of tenacity. He is living, if a little extraterrestrial, proof of the dangers of GM trials.

In a desperate attempt to exorcize the obvious demonic characteristics of the little brat, Shulugh went through the motions of giving him a christening. It has to be said that none of the church services at St Stephen's is what we would regard as 'normal', and the guests at the christening all turned up with cloves of garlic and iron stakes, so essential in his presence. The idea of calling him Daniel should be recognized for what it was, a rather over-used PR stunt in Ambridge whereby you give a child a name in honour of the most financially loaded relation. It is meant to be a good investment for the future.

Thus the late Jaaarn was christened John Daniel in the hope that some of ancient Dan's wonga might percolate through to the impoverished crowd at Bridge Farm. Needless to say, when Dan was fatally savaged by a sheep, Jaaarn inherited diddly squat – not that it would have made any difference as it turned out. Damien was christened Daniel because the avaricious

Shulugh, already having copped Glebe Cottage when she murdered Doris, was determined to butter up her parents in order to stay in the frame for a bit of Brookfield in due course. It was a similar motivation that led to Peeep being named after Phil.

Damien has never really had a decent chance in life. His mother is a confirmed nymphomaniac; indeed, not only is she confirmed but she's a church warden as well. Damien must have become confused by the endless procession of men trooping through the house. As Joe Grundy so brilliantly encapsulated the situation, 'First the doctor, then the vet – it's a good job there isn't a dentist in Ambridge.'

Early signs of Damien's demonic nature appeared when he alternated baby gurgling with lucid, properly structured sentences, apparently being able to switch between them at will. He gradually abandoned the gurgling, but maniacally insisted on answering all questions with full sentences. 'Do you like going to feed the ducks, Daniel?' would be answered not by a simple 'Yes' or a decent grunt, but by, 'Yes, I do'.

Mountaineering Teddy, a gift from the much-missed Hard-working Simon Pemberton, seemed to play a formative role in Damien's development. Since Shulugh has long since ceased to refer to it, we can only assume that she incinerated it in a pagan ritual before Damien's very eyes, no doubt adding to his torment.

Another factor which will have done much to distort Damien's outlook on life is Phallustair's propensity to lie to him. Phallustair is one of those people who delights in confusing children by building up a huge world of non-existent people, such as Father Christmas, the Tooth Fairy *et al*. Filling the little brat's head with stories of animals that speak and magic is enough to send even a normal child completely over the edge. Perhaps the final straw came when Phallustair claimed that a certificate in a frame on a wall was about to sound a trumpet fanfare – a notion so ludicrous that it should have sounded alarm bells throughout the village.

In a weird reversal of normality Damien has increasingly sought the comfort of his mother's bed as he has got older. We have the grotesque prospect in years to come of nineteen-year-old Damien banishing Phallustair from the bedroom on the grounds that the bed is too small for three. In fact, maybe we should be referring to him from now on as Oedipus.

Damien is noticeably restless and ill at ease when he has to accompany his sanctimonious mother on one of her numerous trips to church. The presence of so many crosses clearly does his head in. When he had to attend the Palm Sunday service in 1999 and TFW was handing out palm crosses to all comers, he was beside himself and tried desperately to concentrate on the more secular side of the proceedings. His principal interest was the thorny question of whether the donkey would or would not 'do a pooh'. (See 'That Fisher Woman: The Case Against'.) This was not a one-off because after the same service in 2001, Shulugh commented that immediately after the service he stuffed the palm cross in her handbag.

As time goes on, listeners must be prepared for intermittent manifestations of the forces of darkness. Incidents will occur which at first sight may appear unfortunate accidents, but as they mount up it will become apparent that the hand of the Devil is well and truly at work.

An example of this has already arisen – the knee-capping of Foghorn, an early and amazing triumph for Damien. In the light of the plummeting standards of *Archers* language, it was what one might uncouthly describe as 'a piece of piss'. All he had to do was to deposit a toy car on the stairs at Brookfield. Foghorn was in full flight, rushing downstairs with bedding for her B&B guests, and Bob's yer uncle. Nice one. Foghorn was naturally completely blind to the fact that Damien was to blame and instead said it was all the fault of the guests for whom she was fetching the bedding. We live in a strange world in which B&B guests should sleep without bedding and toy cars are regarded as a legitimate form of stair-carpeting.

Damien revelled in his grandmother's discomfort and was later described as having got 'carried away playing with Jill's crutches'. Numerous comments from other characters give testimony to his true nature, including: 'Inside every little angel there's a devil trying to get out' and 'He's a little monster.' So you don't just have to take our word for it.

We have heard how Damien will insist that the dreadful Shulugh plays his favourite tape of 'children's songs' on car journeys. But what she and Phallustair are too dense to realize is that if you play the tape backwards you can hear concealed messages – 'I'm going to trip my Granny', 'The Devil is king', 'Jamie Perks is next' being just some of them.

Whereas most well-adjusted six-year-olds have nice normal toys like sub-machine-guns, air rifles and Swiss Army knives to play with, Damien has an inflatable crocodile. This is doubtless to get him used to the genre so that he can have the real thing to terrorize the neighbourhood with by the time he is five. That would not be altogether bad news, as a crocodile in the Am would do wonders to spice up the tedious raft races.

Foghorn may be smugly limping around congratulating herself on surviving the assassination attempt, but there are two other members of Damien's family who have a fatwah out on them. BSE Josh and his stepfather Deeevid conspired to dispose of Damien's 'Muzzi'. After Josh had ceremoniously dragged it through the farmyard, Deeevid calmly incinerated it with the same cool detachment with which he killed the badger and murdered Jethro. But few would want to be in those people's shoes with Damien just waiting for his moment.

Damien's cousin Peeep is a similarly sinister little girl who appears to be consumed by hatred for all around her. She had lain dormant for a couple of years since commenting on one of her school colleagues, saying, 'There's Stephen, I don't like Stephen', but was moved to squeak once more when urged by her mother, Roooth, to play with Damien. 'I don't want to. I'm fed up with Daniel', she quoth, presumably because she had tired of playing the much loved children's game of Vampires and Victims. But it is yet another indication that Damien is a malevolent force. Out of the mouths of babes. . .

Deeevid, by no means the sharpest knife in the drawer, has noticed recent signs of Damien's weirdness and was recently moved to describe him as 'a strange little soul'. This is a fine example of litotes when you consider we are talking about a child who takes a delight in 'teaching hedgehogs how to poo', a subject that would seem a trifle unnecessary in the national curriculum of those particular beasts. Increasingly to be found playing in the graveyard it is patently obvious that Beelzebub's representative in Ambridge is in desperate need of a damn good exorcism.

These You Have Loathed

In order to become members of the Archers Anarchist Experience it is necessary not only to bite off the head of a chicken but also to bare your soul to reveal your Archers-related preferences. This gives us invaluable data that we are now able to share exclusively with the wider public. We are constantly assailed by commercial organizations (usually manufacturers of anoraks and supermarket meals-for-one) seeking access to our mailing lists. It is important to state that under no circumstances would we consider acceding to such requests.

Naturally the most loved or hated characters are something of a movable feast according to their antics at the time. We carry out an extensive survey at least once a year. The following list is the top ten most hated characters as nominated by respondents to a survey of some 45 million anarchists during a two-week period in April 2001. Independently analysed and authenticated as a scientific sample by a top pollster, it makes stunning reading.

One or two misguided critics of our movement will look at this list and see its near total domination by Ambridge's womenfolk as evidence of misogyny on our part. It may therefore be helpful to point out that 60 per cent of our members are

1	Horrible Hayley
2	Roooth
3	Shulugh
4	Loathesome Lizzie
5	Kathy
6	Peggoi
7	TFW
8	Jailbird Carter
9	Foghorn
10	Deeevid

themselves women and this list reflects the views of our mass membership.

It is important to stress that non-appearance in the top ten should by no means be taken as a sign of affection. There were no less than 36 people nominated in this category, though it has to be said that the top four were way ahead of the others.

There are a number of changes since the last poll, but the most impressive new entrant must be Horrible Hayley who has never previously made the top ten, yet has come in straight at number one. This has to be attributable to her having played a complete blinder in terms of obnoxiousness for many consecutive months during which time she has stolen Freebie from her true doting mother, extorted huge sums of money from the poor Dog Woman and had the most sickly, syrupy marriage imaginable.

Roooth has consistently been challenging for first place, but even after a spectacular year of non-stop whingeing she has not quite made the top spot. This is also the first time that the awful simpering Shulugh, the Manchester United of Ambridge, has slipped from that coveted position. But there seems little doubt that after another year of utter hypocrisy she will reclaim her usual place.

These You Have Loved
(And Ignored)

Extensive statistical research has found it much more difficult to identify a strong list of characters in terms of popularity. Indeed, many respondents said that they found it virtually impossible to nominate anyone they really liked.

1	Brian
2	Matt Crawford
3	Lillian
4	Edweird
5	Marjorie
6	Joe
7	Lynda
8	Dopey Debbie
9	Fallen
10	Eddie

Brian has consistently been popular with Anarchists due to his having some traces of a sense of humour and a healthy disregard for the cosy people in life. Particularly gratifying is the elevation of Matt Crawford, the conscience of Borsetshire, whose sensitive approach to village affairs has won the hearts of many of us.

Lillian's arrival, straight in at a creditable third place, would seem to owe much to her sudden man-eating tendencies, not to mention her sudden metamorphosis into someone with the general demeanour of a Pie and Mash Shop proprietress.

As usual there are still one or two people who don't rate even a single nomination for either category. These include Beddy Tugger, Doreen Rogers, Lancastrian 'Trasher' Tommy, Kirsty, Auntie Satia, Solly and Heather Pritchard, Jeck Woolley, Oilslick or Wiwyerm. And there's only one thing worse than being talked about. . .

'Do You Mind If I Stand?'
The Perils of Sitting Down in Ambridge

Anyone who is the wrong side of eighty would do well to stay on their pins in Ambridge. Anarchist investigations have revealed a disturbing number of incidences of 'death by sitting'. In the rest of the world people die of *something*, but in Ambridge they die 'peacefully in their chair'. Doris Archer, Fat Man Forrest and his wife, Pru, Martha Woodford, Mabel Larkin and, we presume, her husband, Ned, all seemed to meet their end in a sedentary position. The first thing elderly people in Ambridge should do is to get rid of their armchairs and sofas. It could make a real difference to their life expectancy.

Of course, the truth is that innocent furniture is being made a scapegoat for murder. For example, spot the connection in these two facts: Shulugh found Doris dead in her armchair; Shulugh inherited Glebe Cottage.

The deaths of Fat Man and Pru were even more sinister. It would be usual to hold some kind of inquest when a husband and wife popped their clogs within days of each other in the same old folks' home, but in Ambridge this coincidence went quite unnoticed. Instead it was seized upon as a good opportunity for another pagan funeral with Horrible Hayley, the Angel of Death, more or less officiating. The motive for murder was revealed soon after this double death when Phil triumphantly presented Foghorn with Pru's recipe books, with the words, 'You knew she was going to leave them to you, didn't you?' There can be no doubt that Phil and Foghorn had ample motive, as serial cooks, to remove Fat Man and Pru from the scene. But it was most unfair that a couple of blameless armchairs should once again carry the can.

Poor Martha Woodford actually died from the neglect of her so-called friends and neighbours. No one had mentioned her for months until suddenly she was found quietly dead at home, doubtless in a chair. Perhaps it would be helpful if MFI, Ikea and the rest could invent a symbol to designate the safety of its furniture in terms of general mortality rather than mere fire resistance – a tasteful skull and crossbones would do the trick.

Mrs Perkins, Peggoi's mother, was described in the *Book of The Archers* as being found by Mrs High and Mighty Aldridge 'sitting peacefully in her chair'. This was just another example of an Archer conveniently being at the scene of death. And we shouldn't be misled by all this 'peacefully' stuff. When you are dead in your chair you are hardly likely to be doing the Lambada, are you?

Bill Insley was similarly found at home in his chair although, as with Doris, there was another pair of worrying facts to bear in mind. Bill was 'found' by Neil. Neil was a beneficiary of his will. Perhaps this is why Neil, though in many ways a complete divot, seems sufficiently tuned in to the inherent dangers of a sedentary life in Ambridge, because he was recently heard to say, 'I've spent more time in a tractor cab than I have in my own armchair.' And if he knows what's good for him, he'll keep it that way.

Castism
How to Avoid It

It was the need to challenge castism that brought Archers Anarchists into being. Listeners will doubtless agree that the radio is a far superior form of medium to the goggle-box, whose presence aggressively dominates the living rooms of the majority of our population. It enables us to sharpen our listening faculties and powers of imagination, an activity that television denies us.

Castism is a cruel betrayal of all the efforts we have made to respond to and embrace the wonders of radio. It cocks a snook at the loyalty we have shown as *Archers* listeners. We willingly indulged the late Dan Archer, Patriarch of Ambridge, in his need for four radically different voices throughout his lifetime. No one was discourteous enough to suggest that this was anything other than an endearing idiosyncrasy. But, in return, the BBC, demonstrating crass insensitivity, permitted the publication of four equally different photographs of 'Dan'. Not even the greatest master of disguise could seek to pass off four people of different build, height, skin texture etc. as the same person. So what on earth were we meant to think? The fact is that we didn't need to see photos of Dan because we had already decided what he looked like.

Over the years, things have gone from bad to worse as castism has increased. The tendency for characters from *The*

Archers to make 'public appearances' at shows, fêtes and other functions is quite deplorable. What is particularly upsetting is that it can be difficult to avoid encountering these imitators. The argument 'You don't have to look at them' is of no relevance if you are ambling around some country show only to find yourself suddenly face to face with a hat with horns. Similarly, if you are standing in a queue for a cup of tea and the person in front of you starts chatting away at 190 decibels, you may unwittingly have invaded the airspace of Foghorn.

Unfortunately, castism is not confined to offensive photographs and characters exposing themselves in public. A more subtle form is the tendency of people to talk about 'actors'.

The formation of the 'official' fan club of *The Archers*, a BBC-controlled mafia known to its many enemies as Archers Anoraks, has done much to encourage the growth of castism and the perpetration of castist remarks. The Anoraks produce huge quantities of tacky merchandise, much of it inevitably bearing attempted photographic representation of things which should by rights be confined to the mind.

It is difficult to understand what kind of warped mentality can lead someone to listen to *The Archers* and then cough up £1,500 to go on a cruise with a bunch of luvvies claiming to be 'characters'. Any genuine listener will know that very few people in Ambridge ever go on holiday, and the idea of any of them going off on a cruise together is risible. Yet these castist cruises are regular events. Has anyone ever heard someone in Ambridge say, 'I'm off for a couple of weeks on a freebie cruise with a load of Anoraks'?

A particularly unpleasant manifestation of castism from the dreaded Anoraks is called 'The Ambridge Experience'. It consists of a weekend in some fat cat country house hosted by Foghorn. The idea of paying vast sums to be deafened for two days seems quite perverse.

Archers Anoraks are regularly advertised at the taxpayers' expense on Radio 4. Archers Anarchists can lay claim to some slight influence in that the BBC now invariably describes the Anoraks as 'the only official fan club'. This is a strange phenomenon afflicting many institutions that attract fan clubs, namely the tendency to label themselves 'official'. It is difficult to conceive of any benefit that can be derived from being 'official', save for the fact that you will probably be charged more and restricted in your freedom to criticize or comment upon the institution concerned.

Ideally, Borsetshire characters should remain in that walled county. But sadly this is difficult to enforce, so we have to give you a few handy tips on avoiding castist situations. No one can be completely safe from castism, but if you follow the simple precautions outlined in our ten point plan below, you will greatly reduce your chances of becoming a victim.

1. Avoid agricultural shows (gratuitous appearances by numerous 'characters'). This has the added benefit of allowing you to miss out on people with green wellies, four-wheel drives and straw hanging out of their mouths loudly blaming whichever government happens to be in power for the fact that they have to get up early and milk cows.

2. Never buy country and western records/CDs. Eddie Grundy has a nasty habit of releasing them from time to time and putting his face on the sleeves.

3. Beware of any archive material from the late 'Eddie Grundy Fan Club'. Worthy though it was, Eddie was prone to appear in person at its functions, and alleged pictorial representation would follow in their newsletters.

4. Do not go to see any enticingly worded events at art centres, e.g. 'An evening with *The Archers*'. Remember that the only genuine evening with *The Archers* occurs nightly, except Saturdays, at 7.02 pm

5. Avoid paying four-figure sums of money to go on big boats. If you really want to see a load of water, just leave the bath running.

6. Never buy the *Radio Times*. They take a delight in publishing random castist photographs without warning. They also publish an offensive item called a 'cast list'.

7. Never buy a broadsheet newspaper when there has been a 'big' story in *The Archers*. With true contempt for their readers' capacity for simple comprehension, they take the view that it is impossible to write a story about a radio programme without illustrating it with a photograph.

8. If you ever buy or receive any Archers-related book, other than those bearing the Archers Anarchist seal of approval, be aware that it is virtually unknown for any of these to be free of castism – both photographic and verbal. If you feel it is absolutely necessary to have the book, ensure that someone removes the photographs beforehand. Even then, you are liable to find heavily castist content within the text.

9. If you suddenly hear a monotonous Geordie whingeing sound, run for your life – Roooth's loose.

10. If someone says to you something along the lines of 'Did you know the actor who plays **** has died?', try a subtle form of put-down such as, 'And what actor plays you, sad git?'

Educated Ambridge
The OfSTED Report

In these days of constant talk about class sizes and league tables it is something of a national scandal that nothing has been done to address the appalling level of education in the village of Ambridge and presumably its surrounding area. Sadly the priorities there seem to be 'Fornication, fornication and fornication'. We can only assume that OfSTED inspectors refused to go into Borchester because they don't want to admit the complete failure of the teaching profession to produce a properly educated pupil from the town or its environs over the last twenty to thirty years.

Not that people haven't occasionally gone on to further education. One or two high-flyers have tried in vain to complete the odd vocational course in Applied Stamp Licking or Comic Reading. So, once again, it falls to Anarchists to expose the educational performance of Ambridge's children.

We thought the best way of producing a report was to look at the educational histories of a number of characters through the years from a range of families in order to demonstrate that we are not talking merely of a flash in the imbecilic pan. What we will seek to show is that, regardless of family background or the cost of their education, Ambridge children are as thick as two short planks.

ADAM MACY is the exception that proves the rule. He allegedly graduated from Newcastle University but, as he has never been seen or heard since, we take this with a pinch of Brian's genetically modified crops. If he genuinely did get through university it is nothing short of a miracle, because his schooling was a complete joke. Partly because he'd had rather an excess of dads, thanks to his mother's sexual peccadilloes, he was refusing to work at school and Brian poured large wads of his hard-earned cash into third-rate fee-paying schools. His total disappearance is extremely sinister and we believe his 'appearance' in South Africa was a cruel hoax.

DEEEVID ARCHER was the classic Archer dumb cluck. He went to a boarding school despite his mother's socialist principles, and what a waste of wonga that turned out to be. He failed his maths A level repeatedly, which goes a long way to explaining the parlous state of the finances at Brookfield in recent years. University was about as likely as Roooth cooking a decent meal, so instead he followed in the footsteps of a number of the educationally if not financially challenged and went to agricultural college.

DEBBIE OILSLICK actually went to Exeter University, but before anyone gets over excited at this exceptional example of scholarliness, it has to be pointed out that she only lasted a year. She succumbed to an acute attack of what might nowadays be referred to as Woodheaditis. It all came about because she was studying the extremely useful subject of French Canadian Literature, a course which was later to stand her in such good stead in the lambing shed.

It is also written in the tea leaves that if there is an unsuitable bloke within a radius of 100 miles, Debbie will become magnetically drawn to him. Such was the case with her lecturer in the aforementioned subject, Simon Oilslick, who has, of course, reappeared with a vengeance. To be fair to her, with a pedigree of one failed year at university behind her, Debbie is still a contender for Brain of Borsetshire.

LOATHESOME LIZZIE, whose brains have always proved elusive, failed her Eleven Plus, which, in the state sector, would have condemned her to an early teenage life among the great unwashed. Happily, Red Foghorn rode to the rescue with another minor private boarding school. She was expelled from that school, an honour not even bestowed on the Grundys.

Without any qualifications she went to the penitentiary for all the Ambridge thickoes formerly known as Borchester Tech, now laughingly renamed 'University'. But Elizabeth even manage to fail at the tech, a feat never previously achieved, even by Ambridge youngsters. The stresses and strains of studying Contemporary Sandcastle Studies had proved too much. She never really ventured back into the world of academia and has not since acquired any skills in anything other than mother-in-law baiting.

The mystery of why anyone would want her to present courses in marketing a couple of years ago was soon solved when it was revealed that these courses involved a mattress and a bloke called Horny Hugh. Perhaps we are being slightly unfair to Elizabeth, as she has at least become a practitioner of the world's oldest profession.

THE LATE JAAARN ARCHER Jaaarn was a canny self-made sort of chap from an entrepreneurial perspective, but as far as academic achievement was concerned there is no evidence that he was any better than the rest of the village. He was another of the victims of at least a partial private education and was sent to a place called Brymore – a name that is more redolent of a young offenders' institution than a seat of learning. There was never any serious question of a university education, although being squashed by a tractor rather limited his future educational options.

KATE ALDRIDGE eschewed every educational opportunity and failed to achieve even the most rudimentary qualifications. She started off at the posh Cheltenham Ladies' College, where she just ran amok, and was transferred to the local sink school, Borchester Green, that houses all the low-life such as the Grundys, Horrobins, Tuggers and Carters.

So appalling were Kate's results that the educational psychos even got involved and we had an amusing period when the Aldridges were dragged into 'family therapy'. Brian diagnosed that this was a load of sociological nonsense and gave it a wide berth. After a great deal of pointless hoo-ha Kate went to Borchester Tech, the repository for recidivist non-achievers. All she succeeded in doing there was to make friends with some of Borchester's finest, such as Messrs Spanner and Craven – purveyors of fine excrement.

KEN TON ARCHER There is a very misleading line in the *BOA* which describes Ken Ton as a 'star pupil' at Borchester Grammar. The words which should have been added were 'relatively speaking'. It is quite obvious that, within a catchment area of the most obtuse children ever to walk on Bishop Cyril's earth, it is not difficult to star. It presumably entails being able to write your name, maybe tie your shoelaces and find your way home with the aid of a school bus. That he failed to go on to university but instead went into the 'merchant' navy says it all.

LANCASTRIAN 'TRASHER' TOMMY The first we knew about Tommy's education was when he came of voice, albeit a Lancastrian one, and threw both a huge party and up in the village hall to celebrate the completion of his GCSEs. And there his education ended. He embarked upon some NVQ course in farming. For those who are not up to date on modern pre-/post-millennium qualifications it should be explained that an NVQ isn't one. So Tommy has basically signed up for an NVQ in moping around the farm with an attitude problem, which he looks like achieving with room to spare. To this day the subject of any further attempts at education has never been mentioned.

LUCY PERKS Girls in Ambridge perform slightly better academically than boys – a rare example in *The Archers* of life imitating life – and Lucy appeared against all the odds of a broken and fractious home to get through Nottingham University and emerge with a degree. True it was in Environmental Science and so presumably concentrated on how to build a treehouse or tunnel near a proposed motorway site. But, in the eyes of the Lord, a degree is a degree and in the village of Ambridge it is as rare a sight as a barking dog on one of their farms. Note again that as with Adam she has completely disappeared since 'graduating'.

SHULUGH HEBDEN-BLAND VOICE is another educational disaster. According to the aforementioned *BOA*, Shulugh was actually regarded as 'backward' at her primary school. This could explain a lot – whether they were talking about her intellect or favourite posture. She went to Borchester Grammar, but as per usual there is no evidence of her getting any qualifications of note because she went on to that scholastic graveyard 'Borchester Tech' to do a secretarial course.

She took a number of examinations at Rodway and Watson, which seemed to involve numerous failures and retakes, and her very gradual promotion doubtless owed more to sexual favours granted to Mr Rodway than to any endeavours on her part.

When she was ceremoniously booted out of the firm for gross misconduct there was never any mention of her having any estate management qualifications that she could tout round to other companies. More recently she has once more donned a dunce's cap, this time in the form of a horse rider's hard hat, as she has struggled with horse-riding exams. It really has been painful to behold.

ROY TUGGER Poor Roy has manfully tried to crawl out from the abyss that is life as a Tugger. The *BOA* actually tells a downright lie, describing him as 'bright'. Let there be no mistake here, Roy is about as bright as a 20-watt bulb. We have to remember that this is a bloke who was prepared to go to court to prove that he was the father of a Caribbean baby. His education has been a paradigm of Ambridge learning, culminating in about one and a half GCSEs and a painful course of study at what he cringingly describes as 'Uni', from where he emerged, to his parents' eternal pride, with a BA Hons in Gum Chewing. A glutton for further education, he is now a trainee assistant junior sub-barman at Grey Gables.

SHARON RICHARDS It is one of the great unfairnesses of Ambridge life that Sharon was effectively banished from the village following the death of her beloved Jaaarn. Anyone would think that it was she, not Horrible Hayley, who had callously turned down his proposal of marriage, thus inducing him to put the Fergie on autopilot. But we digress. Sharon was not allowed to emerge from school with any qualifications lest she show up the comparative ignorance of the Archer mafia. So the peak of educational excellence so far as Sharon was concerned was a YTS placement with a hairdresser.

Herein lies yet another Archers mystery, for Sharon dropped out of this taxing form of quasi-employment as soon as she was swept off her feet and on to her back by the debonair Clive Horrobin. Anyone with experience of the hairdressing profession will know that the junior employees do not get anywhere near a pair of scissors. Their role is confined to making tea, washing customers' hair and asking them if they are going on holiday (or, during the period 1 August to 24 December, what they are doing for Christmas), in readiness for the stylist who will repeat the question moments later.

A YTS placement with a hairdresser would, of course, be somewhat below the rank just described. This role would include going out to buy the tea, sweeping up hair and rifling through corporation rubbish tips in the hope of unearthing the odd five-year-old copy of *She* magazine for the delectation of waiting customers.

The mystery is that Sharon was always deemed to be an excellent hairdresser and a whole variety of the Ambridge women would regularly beg her to cut their hair. She must therefore have been possessed of a wonderful innate talent requiring no training at all. We live in hope that she will return to the village one day as the owner of a string of successful salons. But the fact remains she was no academic.

WIWYERM GRUNDY No one would expect Wiwyerm to be the local chairman of MENSA and his educational performance was generally predictable. Grange Farm was the kind of place where, in a more normal village, the Social Services would have had their own parking space, such would have been the frequency of their visits.

Wiwyerm was a professional truant for some years. The most remarkable thing was that while he seemed to miss about four days' schooling in every five, he never came up with any explanation other than 'study days' or 'teacher training days'. Yet half the people to whom he trotted out these falsehoods gave him the benefit of the doubt.

Wiwyerm seemed set to escape school unencumbered by any GCSEs, but an unholy alliance of the completely uneducated George Barford and Jeck Woolley conspired to entice him to do a masters degree in Keepering. How academic study can equip you for a life wandering around woodland in Wellington boots and a wax jacket, carrying a gun, is open to question. But, all in all, this gentleman very much matches the scholastic standards of the village.

DAMIEN's education was always going to be a challenge, if only because his horns would prevent the wearing of a conventional cap. The much crapped upon Bunty and Reg, parents of the late Handbag Hebden, showed an early interest in the matter. Seemingly unaware of his demonic nature, they wanted him to go to a local church school. The likely consequence of sending him to St Beelzebub's and All Vampires was unimaginable, but Phallustair came out as violently anti private school.

Though it has never prevented Foghorn from sending her children to boarding schools and grammar schools, she is also totally opposed to such things. Old footage of *The Archers* from when her voice was a veritable high-pitched scream and more like a police siren than a foghorn has her remonstrating with Phil over plans to send their children to Borchester Grammar.

For the sake of other children, Damien should, of course, be educated by a governess. But Phallustair for once seemed to exert influence over Shulugh, because she decided to send the brat to the local sink school at Loxley, thus setting the seal on a guaranteed career for her son as a demonic dunderhead. Life at school will never be easy for him as he's hardly likely to be very popular in the scrum during games lessons and will probably feel a little self-conscious in the showers, though it would be wise not to laugh at him.

EDWEIRD Despite attending a cathedral school as choral scholar has now reverted to Grundy type and is very much following after his brother. Even though educational standards have reached a point in the rest of Britain where 99 per cent of people get a grade A for all their GCSEs, Edweird looks set to be one of the 1 per cent.

FALLEN The news that she was 'really getting down to it' rather surprised us at from an educational perspective as we all expect her to declare herself up the duff any moment now. We still await her GCSE results but it would be hard to predict anything above the Ambridge average.

EMMER CARTER Borchester Green Comp really put the bog into standard and Emmer graduated in 2000 with a stunning crop of GCSEs: one B and three Cs (3Ds, an E and an F in maths). Unsure what to do she sought careers advice from Shulugh, someone who really has some experience of being brick thick. She recommended that she take a job washing-up at Lower Loxley and the former bedwetter now seems set up for life.

The attitude of people in the village to education is generally very negative. Tony Archer was quoted as saying, 'Exams never did me any good', while the likes of Boring George Barford and Eddie Grundy more or less colluded in allowing Wiwyerm to bunk off school. Poor Clarrieluv has done her best to maintain educational standards in the household, but it is rather pathetic listening to her giving help with revision: 'What's the past tense of Avwaar?'

Ultimately and ironically, this whole discussion is itself academic. If you are going to pursue a career in tractor work, poaching, whingeing or murder – a list that accounts for most of the Ambridge population – education just doesn't matter.

The Winter Cuckoo
Things That Only Happen in Ambridge

One of the many joyous facets of Archers Anarchists is the network of unfortunate people who notice every little wrinkle in our glorious programme. They are vigilant to the last in spotting those peculiarities in Ambridge life that set the villagers apart from the rest of us. The equivalent idiosyncrasies in television can apparently be found in *Coronation Street*, where someone orders a pint of beer, begins drinking it and is then clearly seen to have more in the glass three seconds later than he had moments before. But on radio pointed ears of the highest specifications are needed to do a proper monitoring job.

Cheep Cheep

While many of us just regard birds as things that tweet in a rather pointless and random way, Anarchist Chris Webster has dedicated his life to the recognition of Ambridge birdsong. He suggests that anachronistic tweeting is endemic in the village, but his most dramatic observation to date was the presence of cuckoos in September. Ambridge has always had problems with this particular bird. There have been years when it has been deemed compulsory to impose a 90-decibel cuckoo throughout the conventional duration of the traditional British cuckoo season. It has been all they can do to silence the thing for the indoor scenes and keep it from going in the village shop.

'I'm Off'

But out-of-kilter birdsong is a mere chirrup from the range of things that only happen in Ambridge. There is an abnormally high incidence of 'seeing oneself out'. OK, we all see ourselves out from time to time when visiting the infirm or elderly, though we tend not to make such a song and dance about it; but in Ambridge, seeing yourself out seems to be obligatory. The act of seeing yourself out occurs independently of mood, but anyone who is in a bit of a strop will precede their explained exit with an 'If you'll excuse me – ', followed by a pause.

There are certain allied phrases that are only used by people in Ambridge. No one outside of the village would conclude a conversation in which they have become annoyed with the words, 'Well, I'll bid you good day, then.'

Cassandra Calling

Another idiosyncrasy in Ambridge is that accidents are always presaged by most of the villagers, but the victim to whom the mishap will befall is invariably too stupid to see it coming. For example, the slack on the steering of the Fergie was well flagged up before poor Jaaarn took it for a spin. Whenever someone says, 'You need to mend that **** before someone falls in it/eats it/chokes themselves to death, etc.', you know that the urgent repair will not be carried out and the predicted calamity will duly materialize.

In a similar vein, people in Ambridge take a long time to ask the most obvious questions. Deeevid quite obviously knew who had been trashing the GM crop, but Roooth took a day or so to tackle him about it.

Anno Domini

Old age certainly happens in Ambridge – in a big way. People carry on toiling, and are clearly expected to do so, in a way that probably wouldn't even occur in the Third World. The fact that Joe Grundy was pushing eighty in no way spared him from the rough and inarticulate edge of Clarrie's tongue for failing to do a major share of the housework and cooking, as well as a full day on the farm. Eddie treated him as if he was a skiving teenager when he demurred at the idea of getting up and doing the milking of a cold winter's morning. Even recently Eddie has no respect for his age, expecting him to assemble a heavy flat pack bed for Kathy Perks.

Presumably connected with their outstanding longevity is the ability of all the old folk to retain their faculties. No one who speaks ever suffers from anything more than the occasional temporary bout of dementia and that seems to take on the seriousness of a minor summer cold. They might demonstrate rather loopy behaviour for a week or so (one remembers fondly the temporary madness of Martha Woodford, who was talking to ghosts, turning up in her nightie at dead of night to spring-clean the village phone box, etc.) but normal business is soon resumed. In the case of Martha, her full faculties returned to the extent that, a year or so later, she was taking a lead at a public meeting pontificating about abstruse areas of planning law.

The knack of reacquiring one's mental ability after previously appearing well on the road to senility, (sometimes referred to as Saundersism), was certainly enjoyed by the late Fat Man Forrest and has also been blessed upon Jeck Woolley. As we have so many old folk in Ambridge, it is something to look out for.

Surprised to be Young

But it's not only the elderly who behave in a unique manner, the youngsters have a tendency to forget that they are young and then suddenly behave in what they presumably imagine to be a stereotypical way. Take Wiwyerm Grundy, who only appeared to discover the existence of some 'mates' when his GCSEs were finished. Most people of his age, with no expectation of passing any exams, would have been out on the town during their exams, yet Wiwyerm's great mate Stuart hardly got a mention until this point. Then, true to *Archers* form, it was complete overkill with 'Stuart this, Stuart that' every other sentence. Alarmingly, all references to Stuart suddenly ceased at a time that coincided with Wiwyerm being given his first gun.

PC World

Samples of political correctness discovered in Ambridge have been found to be several times higher than recommended levels for public safety. This leads to uniquely unusual reactions in matters such as health. Mrs Antrobus's reaction of joy on discovering that she would 'only' have to wait at least eight months for her cataract operation was so startling that we half expected her to burst into a rousing chorus of 'Things Can Only Get Better'. Similarly the love that some farming people in Ambridge have for Tony Blair is bordering on the obsessive. Indeed it is surprising that the Prime Minister has so often persisted in visiting rural areas like Cumbria and Devon where he has been harangued and jeered when he could have been showered with rose petals and borne aloft in triumph by the grateful folk of Ambridge. When instances of foot and mouth had decreased to a piffling 15 a day, Mr Blair declared it 'sorted' and Deeevid and Roooth threw open their gates in celebration.

Silence is Golden

Only in Ambridge is there a whole set of people who steadfastly refuse to speak when spoken to. Even Mrs Potter, a sprightly walking-frame scraping 250, managed to stay silent when she knocked over a load of tins in the village shop. This despite being shouted at in a patronising way by Beddy Tugger, a woman who generally has to wait a considerable time before finding anyone sufficiently far down the social order to warrant being patronized by her.

Things which one would expect to emit a noise only do so when mentioned. The barking of dogs is as rare as hen's teeth. Sheep in Ambridge only bleat at shearing time, in the same way that traffic only makes a noise when it is under discussion. Lynda Snell only suffers from hay fever when she is talking about it, but otherwise her nasal passages are crystal clear, even when the pollen count is at its highest.

Mundane Fads

People do things spontaneously but simultaneously without any apparent co-ordination. For example, all of a sudden everyone seemed to be eating pasta. It was not as if it was National Pasta Day or Fettucini Fortnight. People, after nearly half a century of virtual pasta-free living, simply decided they could no longer live without the stuff and it was two fingers to the honest British spud. Peggoi even described pasta with vegetables as 'a treat'.

Obedient Children

The brats of Ambridge are noticeably quieter than most children and invariably do what they are told. 'Don't do that Freddy' is the strongest level of remonstration you will hear and it never needs to be said a second time. Frequently you will hear that 'the children are all in bed' and it is virtually unheard of for one of them to start screeching or reappear. Although you might occasionally hear the odd gurgle or suppressed whine sparking the comment 'I'd better get x home' it is never more than the most muted and unobtrusive sound.

A Speedy Recovery

People in Ambridge generally recover from any illness with great speed and no lingering symptoms. The One-eyed Monster, Foghorn, Alcopop Barford and Pat all recovered from depression without ever looking back. Jeck recovered from heart problems, Brian recovered from epilepsy, Damien recovered from arthritis, Loathsome recovered from heart failure and Roooth recovered from Geordiness. All thanks to the NHS.

Urghh

The principal unique feature of Ambridge, for which we should never cease to give thanks, is that only in that village can there be such a high density of people upon whom you would wish to unleash a firing squad.

From the Cutting-room Floor II
The First Mrs Blandvoice Calls at Glebe Cottage

It is a perfect summer's day and Ambridge's winter birds are in full cry. The First Mrs Blandvoice (Quasimodette) has knocked at the door of Glebe Cottage, door bells being at something of a premium in Ambridge. The door opens and it is Damien, looking fully possessed.

Quasimodette: (*in a voice sounding as if she has a peg on her nose and a bag over her head – like a Virgin Trains on-board sound system*) Hello, is Mummy or Daddy at home?

Damien: My daddy is a test tube and my mummy is out looking for someone to bonk.

Quasimodette: Well, is your Uncle Phallustair at home?

Damien: Yes, he is.

Quasimodette: Will you go and get him for me, then, please?

Damien: Yes, I will.

An unsuspecting Phallustair comes to the door.

Quasimodette: Hello, Phally.

Phallustair: Oh, pooh. . .

Rushes past Mrs Blandvoice, throws a saddle over Tibby the cat and disappears into the distance.

Quasimodette: Would you like to come and live with me?

Damien: Yes, I would.

Quasimodette: Well, come on, then, let's go.

Exit Damien and Quasimodette, hand in hooked claw.

Post-mortem

Painstaking research has revealed that listeners have been duped about the true reasons for the death of characters on several occasions over the years. Here are just a dozen instances where we are proud to be able to put the record straight.

1. Death of Handbag Hebden
What actually happened was that Mark was following one of those lorries with a message on the back reading, 'Well driven? Call 0800 123452'. He was so impressed by the impeccable driving exhibited by the driver of the vehicle that he immediately called the number on his mobile to log his congratulations. He was totally distracted and the rest is history.

2. Death of Grace Archer
Grace was in fact sniffing lighter fuel at the stables. Of course an Archer could never be thought to have done such a thing so a cover-up was launched.

3. Death of Ralph Bellamy
No one seemed to notice the coincidence that Lillian had managed to chalk up two consecutively dead husbands in a very short space of time. Having tampered with an aircraft engine to dispose of Lester Nicholson, it was barely a challenge to swap Ralph's gout pills for something a little more lethal.

4. Death of Poll Doll

Now we know of Pat's mental instability, the case against the milk tanker should be reopened. The first Mrs Perks was just in the wrong place at the wrong time when Pat went into one of her schizoid rages. It was not helped by the fact that Poll Doll innocently began talking about sausages.

5. Death of Dan

While the records will always show that Dan was savaged by a sheep, the truth is that it was Elizabeth who forced him out of a car and made him confront the sheep. Despite the tendency of very old Archers to do very strenuous things, sheep-wrestling is no sport for a man in his nineties.

6. Death of Jack Archer

Peggoi has always been attracted to Jacks, but she became a bit of a killjoy with the late Jack. He was one of those people who liked a drink. Very much. Often. In large quantities. In other words, he was a very thirsty man. Peggoi drove him to a mental breakdown with her now legendary nagging. When he insisted on having the odd drink to be sociable, Peggoi had him incarcerated in a remote Scottish clinic where she had sold him for use as a guinea pig in germ warfare experiments. He was never seen again. Peggoi is now a wealthy woman.

7. Death of Walter

This was very straightforward. His habit of saying 'Me old pal, me old beauty' was so irritating, even to his friends, that Pru knocked up a batch of lethal scones, the very thing that was eventually to cause her own demise. What goes around comes around.

8. Death of Charlie Box

This was an interesting one. The whole village was suddenly plunged into mourning some years ago over the death of someone whose name had never been heard to pass anyone's lips. In fact he was a fictitious character invented to enable the burying of one of 'The Disappeared' to take place without suspicion. Anarchists demand an immediate exhumation.

9. Death of Guy Pemberton

A fine example of murder by telephone. The Village Bicycle nagged him over the phone, encouraging him to do the dirty on his hard-working son. Thus when he had his fatal heart attack, she was nowhere near the scene.

10. Death of Doris

Peacefully smothered with a pillow by Shulugh in order to expedite the transfer of Glebe Cottage to her greedy possession.

11. Death of Frank Bannerman

Murdered by Eddie so that he could buy his tractor off his widow.

12. Death of Hubert Weissman

Some years ago, this poor unfortunate was dug up in Ambridge. Fat Man Forrest was distinctly uncomfortable about it and it was hardly surprising. For poor old Hubert was simply following orders, flying a little errand for Adolf and when he landed it was quite clear that Fat Man gave a V-sign to the Geneva Convention. He should have pulled him from the burning wreck but instead he callously turned his back and went off to tend his marrers.

Horrible Hayley – Angel of Death
Friend of the Elderly and Imminently Dead

Hayley Jordan has rapidly turned into one of those nauseating goody-goody characters who put us off our suppers. Thankfully we are now building up a more realistic picture of the true character behind that whining Brum accent.

Animal lovers everywhere will have been deeply upset by the appalling episode in early 1999 where Horrible Hayley turned up at Nightingale Farm with Phallustair Blandvoice in tow and proceeded to bury Mrs Antrobus's beloved Afghan Portia. In their enthusiasm, they just about remembered to kill the poor animal first. That they were prepared to bury a perfectly good dog was nothing short of scandalous, but why did it happen? The answer is startlingly simple. Hayley cannot go for more than a few months without a death to enjoy, and poor Portia was by way of an interim sacrifice.

Her behaviour after the death of Jaaarn defied any kind of logic. Bereavement counsellors must have observed her with grim fascination to such an extent that next time some poor grieving city-dweller comes their way they can say, 'Ah, what you need to do is take up organic farming and sausage production. Never fails.'

Along the way, she must make a bob or two. To start with she got Jaaarn's engagement ring without having to marry him.

Frequent visits to Keeper's Cottage to see dear old murderer Uncle Tom must have been quite lucrative, as she pocketed the odd knick-knack while he rambled on about the length of his marrers.

Doubtless she has played a kind of Fagin role with HenrynBecky and the myriad of other people's children she farms, sending them to their posh homes with a little 'shopping list' of valuables. She will have got a good wedge from Foghorn for administering the poison to Tom and Pru, after which she has really gone into overdrive. Rent-free accommodation at Nightingale Farm, gradually milking poor old Mrs A for the late Teddy's remaining guineas and a whole lot of free furniture from all and sundry.

You have to hand it to her, she keeps plenty of irons in the fire and for a while was concurrently conspiring to make herself indispensable to Mrs A while making a major bid for a back-door 'partnership' in Bridge Farm. We saw the real Hayley when she was rumbled, thanks to Helen. Tony for once in his life made a firm intervention to make sure Hayley remained no more than a 'hired hand'.

Despite her claims to the contrary, Hayley was desperate to get back in with a chance of grabbing hold of Bridge Farm and she did it in the most underhand way. Realizing that Pat was away with the fairies, Hayley suddenly decided to pay her a visit. Pat was there surrounded by bottles of pills kindly donated by Smarmy Dr Dim, debating whether or not to take them. She was preparing to make her decision on sound medical grounds such as 'Ip dip sky blue', when she asked Hayley, 'Do you think I should take them?' Hayley, naturally delighted at being able to make a medical diagnosis, decided that, as Pat was not at that particular moment climbing the walls, it was unnecessary for her to take any medication. Luckily Helen came to the rescue, expressing surprise that Hayley had apparently become a doctor overnight and justly accusing her of 'worming her way back into the family when Mum's vulnerable'.

Whether or not she has any nannying qualifications is always open to question. No one will forget the time when she was heavily implicated in an attempt to disfigure young Peeep with toxic face paint. Until recently, her only official work seemed to be looking after HenrynBecky. While these are the kind of names you would expect children with nannies to have, there is something not quite kosher about this. Jose, their mother is described as 'a working mother' who works rather odd hours and likes to pop back and see her children during the day. This would imply that she works nearby, yet there is clearly no scope to work in Ambridge unless she is alongside Tugger and Carter fighting over 'tractor work'.

Whereas most people would regard nannying as being somewhat vocational, Horrible Hayley for a long time seemed to regard it as a fall-back for when she couldn't indulge her primary passion, making sausages. Her reluctance to look after the angelic Jamie Peacock-Perks and give him little runs from his cage occasionally was only overcome when she was told in no uncertain terms that she could sling her hook from Bridge Farm.

Horrible has sought to rationalize the death of Jaaarn and the thorny question of blame. She has come to the conclusion that the only person to blame is Jaaarn himself, which is quite convenient as the poor chap has little opportunity to defend himself and Hayley herself may otherwise bear some responsibility for the whole business.

More recently Hayley has lurched into childcare in a big way. 'The more the merrier' was her highly irresponsible attitude when offered Damien, BSE Josh, and little Peeep to look after as a job-lot due to the knee-capping of Foghorn. In Ambridge there appear to be no regulations about the child/carer ratio, and

Dickensian standards rule. Now she is installing herself in Lower Loxley where she is to preside over a whole menagerie of children without the slightest mention of child/carer ratios. Her main reason for taking up this opportunity is that she is to be provided with a 1981 model Ford Fiesta, maintaining the tradition amongst Ambridge proles for acquiring clapped-out company cars.

If Hayley is to get her come-uppance, it will probably be brought about not only by her all-consuming greed, but also her insatiable desire for publicity. We have all been forced to stand by helplessly while she has taken over at funerals, performed in the Red Nose Day debacle and thrust herself to the fore in any dreaded village production. We then had to suffer the embarrassment of her insisting upon talking to Radio Borsetshire on the subject of strawberries, edging out poor plodder Neil, who was trying in vain to broadcast some interesting facts. She then abandoned the children in her care in order to dress up as a strawberry for a cheap sales gimmick.

As she has become bolder, the sinister intent on the part of Horrible has become more apparent. There is no doubt that she sees her mission to take over the lives of all children and turn them against their parents. She has smothered poor Freebie, taught her common ways and done everything to sever the link with Kate. Just the slightest mention of Freebie visiting or even talking to her mother sets Horrible off in floods of invective. Indeed any time she doesn't get her own way she becomes violent in an almost pathological way. Her nose was clearly put out of joint when Loathsome Lizzie did the role of MC at Nelson's funeral. The fact that Horrible had hardly ever met him didn't stop her from thinking that she has the divine right to recite third-rate poems on these occasions.

She almost went into permanent depression when she couldn't find a hairdresser open on a Sunday to do her hair for her wedding. The Lord only knows what kind of a country she thinks this is. If she was that concerned, why didn't she give Sharon Richards a call? The whole business of her tacky wedding left Anarchists never more than three feet away from a bucket for some time. She showed herself in a snotty light from start to finish, turning up her stubby nose at the idea of a nice spread of chicken drumsticks and vol au vents for the wedding breakfast and she milked every last quid out of poor Mrs Antrobus.

There was one good sign that someone might have had enough of Horrible and decided to play a little trick on her. Most people being fitted for a wedding dress would have it taken in a bit if it was too big, but Horrible was told she would have to eat more. So we had the aural spectacle of Horrible stuffing herself with blocks of lard, cream cakes, etc. Ambridge is still waiting for its first bulimia or anorexia victim. Perhaps we need wait no longer.

Future Agenda

There is little evidence of forward planning in Ambridge, but Anarchists believe there are some extremely significant issues about the future to which it is essential that someone gives some proper thought NOW.

Who is going to be speaking in twenty to thirty years' time? There are many people who are unlikely to be with us, unless they are refrigerated like Walt Disney. Phil, Foghorn, Mrs Antrobus, Jeck and Peggoi, Great-great-great-great Auntie Chris, Joe Grundy, Boring George, Joan and Bert for starters. There are plenty of people around in Ambridge, but it's important that more of them chip in here and there and start to pull their vocal weight. Otherwise one day we'll tune in and there will be thirteen minutes of silence, broken only by the cuckoo and, if it's winter, the unceasing breaking of sticks. Is it too late for Trudy Porter to find a voice? Isn't it time the Carter kids put their vocal cords in gear and Alice emerges from purdah?

Archers Anarchists, willing to lend a hand with an almost Brownie-like zest, have considered a likely scenario for the future. We believe that when Jeck snuffs it, that will signal the end of Ambridge as we know it.

Look to the Fuchsia – The Woolley Empire
The death of Jeck Woolley in 2006 will see the arrival of a whole

string of pretenders to the throne at Grey Gables. Higgs will emerge from behind a wall of chrysanthemums to claim that Jeck had bequeathed the whole place to him many moons ago. Various 'sons' will turn up, pretending to be love children. Peggoi, if still alive, will be completely gaga and will spend every waking hour telling her children (who will be visiting her on a rotational basis three times a day) how no one ever visits her. Tony will have been given power of attorney over Peggoi's affairs, but to his utter chagrin he will discover that canny Jeck had made sure that none of his wonga was going the Archer way.

This will be particularly devastating news to all at Bridge Farm, who will have borrowed heavily in anticipation of copping most of Jeck's pile. Carolide, The Village Bicycle, will be sitting smugly with the certain expectation that Jeck will have rewarded her for her years of toil at Grey Gables. But Jeck will have decided that since she owns the Dower House and most of The Bull and is completely loaded anyway, she wants for nothing. He will therefore have left just two little keepsakes to her – the stuffed lynx and a CD of The Tommy Crocker Quartet's greatest hits.

Jeck will have given a surprising amount of consideration as to who should inherit his numerous interests and his decisions will rock the village. The Grey Gables side of things, including the country park and golf course and health club, will all go to Trudy Porter, someone who has never been heard to complain once in all her life and who was already working for Jeck before Carolide arrived on the scene. This will create the wonderful position where Trudy finally becomes the Bicycle's boss. Might she even be given a spanking new matching voice to accompany her new elevation?

But what of the village shop and the *Borchester Echo*? Hazel will get these and make a long overdue return to Ambridge. She will be furious that she hasn't inherited Grey Gables, but these two businesses will give her ample scope to cause local mayhem.

At fifty, Hazel will have lost none of her charm but will have developed a hard-nosed entrepreneurial streak. She will sell a half-share in the *Borchester Echo* to Matt Crawford and together they will relaunch the paper as a *Sunday Sport*-type publication. It will be full of stories of aliens landing on Lakey Hill and TFW indulging in three-in-a-bed sessions – in other words, business as usual.

The village shop will never be the same again. Villagers will have taken up the post office on the idea that they should 'Use it or lose it' and will have lost it. So far as the shop side is concerned, it will cease to be a general store and will become a kind of Ann Summers specializing in the occult. This will be greatly welcomed by the likes of TFW, Damien, Fallen, and Lynda. Jailbird Carter will be out on her ear, and Beddy Tugger is clearly not the right image for such a shop. Hazel will put the local dominatrix Sheyawn Haveitaway in day-to-day control as Manager.

Sadly, with the larger-than-life character of Jeck departed from the scene, Grey Gables will rapidly fail as a viable business. In a desperate effort to revitalize the place Trudy will enter into a disastrous experiment with Sean Myerson, who will have returned as suddenly and seamlessly as he arrived and departed before and it will be renamed Gay Gables. But despite the overwhelming enthusiasm for homosexuality in Ambridge, it will just continue to lose money.

It will be good old Matt Crawford who rides to the rescue. Matt, turning on the charm and his silver tongue, will make an offer to Trudy that she can hardly refuse. Matt will get the whole country park for a fraction of its true value, since no one will realize that he has already smoothed the way to ensure that he wins the necessary planning consent, even if it does have to be won on appeal. He's known as a very generous donor to party funds, which by now are much needed since trade unions were banned by the fifth Blair administration.

A whole new town is to be built, the planning envelope having gone jumbo size. But it's not bad news for everyone. Three broken figures can be seen beating a path to the prefab office where the hard-hatted Matt is in conversation with his forewoman (Debbie Aldridge-Crawford). It's none other than the One-eyed Monster, Neil Carter and Eddie Grundy. 'We hear there might be some bulldozer work going. . . '

GM Feud

In a village where every character appears to be genetically modified, it is perhaps unsurprising that the subject of GM food had been of so little interest many months after it was gripping the nation. The 'Ambridge Socialist', a North London-based movement that campaigns 'for a living wage in Ambridge: £7.00 an hour', actually approached Archers Anarchists seeking to find common cause in the perceived failure of the BBC to tackle the question of GM crops at Home Farm.

Their contention was that it was a Blairite conspiracy to silence any discussion on the matter. We duly considered the subject as carefully as we consider anything, which was rather half-heartedly, and came to the conclusion that while it was nice to know of the existence of 'Ambridge Socialist' we couldn't really go along with their philosophy. Not only do we consider that £7.00 per week would be far too much to pay the likes of Jailbird Carter and the Tuggers, but we rather like the idea of Brian Aldridge manufacturing triffids on a grand non-organic scale.

It would appear that we were worrying unnecessarily, for it was not long before the whole grisly business was being argued out among the great intelligentsia of Ambridge. The brains of such luminaries as Jailbird Carter and Beddy Tugger were soon going twelve rounds with those of Lancastrian 'Trasher' Tommy,

Neil and the One-eyed Monster.

But discussion over this issue has been sporadic even by the standards of Ambridge, where campaigns tend to blow themselves out like some kind of tropical storm. The first intimation that Brian was growing these crops came when Lynda Snell rumbled him. Brian managed to persuade her that what he was actually doing was trying to grow pollen-free crops so that her hay fever would become a thing of the past.

Poor Lynda swallowed this line for a while and unfortunately became the laughing stock of the nastier Ambridge folk. What was rather surprising was that for a time she most uncharacteristically ceased to raise any objection, whereas we would have expected one of her off-the-shelf (or trolley) campaigns to have emerged instantly.

Debbie, whose role in life is to take a contrary view to Brian and then be completely steam-rollered, has hardly expressed a view on the fact that Porton Down has come to Ambridge. Even Kate, who usually pauses between sponging off her parents just long enough to try to sever the hand that feeds her, barely broke sweat on the issue to begin with, although she is of course against it. Surely this is the kind of thing that would cause most of the alternative caravan club and dirty-plaited-hair brigade to turn up in force. Luther could have turned up to pay his maintenance for Freebie, and Morwena the Witch should have descended with her Kazoo and middle-class accent.

Tony objects to everything Brian does on principle because it is Brian who always ensures that the chip on Tony's shoulder is kept firmly in place. But even Tony had never spoken about Brian's GM experiments until That Fisher Woman accosted him and said she was writing an article for the parish rag about the issue and knew that Tony had 'strong views about it'. How she knew is something of a puzzle, because Tony had never previously mentioned the subject. However, he readily agreed that he was dead against it and exclaimed, 'I can't understand why I'm the only one who's saying anything about it.' The answer is probably quite simple – they were all indulging in a similarly strong silent protest and nobody had noticed.

One might ask what on earth TFW is doing writing about GM food in her parish magazine. It's typical of the woman, who will talk about anything except church matters. She should be writing about hassocks and cassocks, and God and Baby Jesus, and how many angels you can balance on a pinhead.

Tony formed a strange alliance with Robert Snell, who declared himself 'livid' that he found himself buying GM products in supermarkets without knowing about it. For someone who has always allowed his beloved 'Lyndybottom' to run all the village campaigns, it was rather strange that he should be so fired up by this.

A meeting in the village hall was convened to discuss Brian's crops. This was rather ambitious, since no one, bar Tony, TFW and Robert, apparently minded. Most people would have welcomed a few multiheaded animals and talking crops in Ambridge. But the antis knew what they were about as Lynda suddenly remembered that she was against it after all and Lancastrian 'Trasher' Tommy decided to back his father's line for once in his life.

Brian Monsanto Aldridge seemed to be allowed a massive amount of air time to tell us how wonderful his triffids were going to be and how beneficial they would be for the Third World. WD 40 manufacturers must have felt their noses being put well out of joint, since they had hitherto been under the impression that they were the official sponsors of *The Archers*. All credit to Brian, he did such a good job that most of us were positively drooling at the idea of GM food, all but manning the barricades at supermarkets to demand double GM rations. Not since mobile phones were discovered to enhance our memories had such an excellent PR campaign been mounted.

The public meeting was predictably biased against the wonders of GM crops, but then protest meetings do tend to be attended by protesters rather than the satisfied and enthusiastic majority. There was no sign of all the silent people from Glebelands and the council houses, who were doubtless sitting comfortably at home stuffing E numbers down their throats like there was no tomorrow.

Lancastrian 'Trasher' Tommy dismissed the few GM supporters at the meeting as 'wrinklies', a disparaging comment which must have caused great offence to the prune industry. Opinion diverged largely along class lines, the village riff-raff generally supporting Tony, as did a sprinkling of middle-class liberals such as Lynda and Robert.

A couple of exceptions were former trade unionist turned cyclops Mike Tugger, who seemed maniacally in favour of all things GM for reasons not totally unconnected, we suspect, with the large amount of 'tractor work' he was getting from Brian at the time. He reckoned it was 'the future of farming'. And Jailbird reckoned she would prefer to eat triffids than starve, on the basis that she couldn't afford poncy organic food.

Why did TFW chair the public meeting? It was very unclear under whose auspices the whole thing was being run – and where was George Barford, Chairman of the Parish Council and the obvious person to take the chair? At the meeting that we were privileged actually to hear rather than hear about, much talk was made of Kate's heckling of her father. Strangely we didn't hear a sound – perhaps the microphones were faulty. The only heckling we did hear came from the broad Lancastrian vocal cords of Tommy, who bellowed out 'too raaaaght' a couple of times while his father was speaking.

The village was, of course, on tenterhooks to hear on which side of the great debate would fall the weighty intellect of Sidney

Perks. Pub landlords generally hold a somewhat questionable place in society as the nation's opinion-formers. This despite the fact that their conversation is too often confined to a riveting account of the timed comings and goings of their regulars, coupled with an analysis of whether or not the male members would find themselves in the 'doghouse' as a penalty for their visit to their establishment. We were not disappointed when, shortly after the public meeting, Sid opined that most people 'couldn't give a monkey's'.

Things got rather lively when a group of helpful people kindly turned up to Home Farm to harvest Brian's GM crop. Brian, in whose mouth butter would not normally melt, got a bit annoyed because it wasn't quite ready for harvesting and he'd been saving it up to make sheaves of triffids for the harvest festival. He described the harvesters as a 'bunch of tree-hugging anarchists'. We assume he wasn't referring to us, because we don't like trees. We think they should all be cut down to make newspapers.

The good thing about the whole incident was that Deeevid weighed in and got a black eye for his busybodiness. The BBC managed to milk this story for weeks with the finger of suspicion being pointed firmly in the direction of spoilt wild-child Kate. The Radio 4 programme *Feedback* gave a lot of coverage to outraged people who felt that the protesters were being misrepresented as violent people who punch people like Deeevid.

As far as we are concerned, no one needs an excuse to punch Deeevid. Apparently, people who trash triffids are really nice people who, when not doing this public service, can be found helping old people across the road, a service they tend to provide without the cover of balaclavas.

It was obvious that the voluntary threshers were going to include people we knew, although, given their characters, it was rather incredible. When the Fuzz turned up at Bridge Farm the day after the Single Wicket Competition, to arrest Lancastrian 'Trasher' Tommy, the amazing truth of the whole affair suddenly dawned upon Anarchists throughout the nation.

As Tommy was being interviewed by his solicitor and the police, we were all beginning to regret the shortage of special-needs teachers in our schools. The poor bloke could hardly open his mouth without almost incriminating his co-conspirators. Those of us from outside Ambridge, with ready access to the media and national newspapers, realized the coincidence that Tommy had been pulled in at the same time as Prince Charles was launching a tirade against triffids.

From that point onwards it was quite obvious that, whoever else was made to carry the can for the Home Farm harvest, the other two miscreants were HRH and TFW. The latter had conveniently gone on her walking holiday until things had blown over. It is not the first time that royalty has turned up in Ambridge, but it was certainly game of our future king to throw himself into village matters with such enthusiasm.

The reactions to Tommy's deeds were fairly predictable. We had Mrs High and Mighty Aldridge going around on a horse that must have been well over 100 hands in height. In the same breath she would say that she was going to make Tony (whom she blamed for the whole thing) 'wish he'd never been born', and how keen she was not to divide the family.

This was rather unnecessary since, on the first point, Tony, knowing what his older sister is like, probably began wishing he'd never been born the moment he emerged from under the stork. On the other count, the Archer family is actually manufactured to divide, modelled on the traditional Kit-Kat style of breaking into two or four parts on demand. Jennifer got herself so wound up about the whole business that she told Pat that her family was barred from Home Farm.

Helen, who could doubtless see excellent marketing prospects for triffids, thought Tommy had behaved like an idiot – a statement on which she could have saved her breath had she added ontology as an option in her studies. She tried to equate the crime with the great sausage betrayal by describing it as a case of 'act now, think later, just like with Hayley and the sausages'.

Pat, who had gone from bonkers to Boadicea in the space of about a week, rather took Tommy's side, saying that 'at least he cares about something.' The possibility that this could excuse every criminal ever to have walked the earth seemed to have escaped her.

Kate was full of admiration for Tommy's daring and actually called round to say so. The prospect of those two cohabiting together would have been a delight. Since the average IQ level in the village would suggest that most of the inhabitants must have married their cousins fairly regularly throughout the ages, it wouldn't have been too much of a problem.

Tommy was bursting with Lancastrian pride at his principled stand. Described in the *Borchester Echo* as an 'Eco Warrior', he repeated his vow not to 'grass on my mates' – a rather over-familiar way of describing Prince Charles. Like all people with principles, he had great difficulty with the concept of a 'full and frank apology', the price demanded by Mrs High and Mighty. He could have taken a leaf from the book of the late Jaaarn, who was always rather adept at compromising his principles.

Peggoi weighed in with her two-penneth and, being a moral upstanding woman nowadays, was aghast to find that she had washed the overalls that Tommy had been wearing on the night of his daring deed, including traces of Deeevid's eye no doubt. She was all for grassing him up – an act which would have done wonders for family unity.

Peggoi has developed a unique and utterly futile solution to family conflict. This takes the form of organizing and enforcing a big family celebration just as people are at their most daggers drawn. Having tried it during the sausage business, she set about arranging a similar event to celebrate Jeck's eightieth birthday, bang in the middle of the GM conflict. Tommy, whose mental footwork is modelled on a tortoise, excelled himself for once by describing his nice old granny as 'The Gestapo'.

Tommy, with true Lancastrian grit, had no fear of going to prison but became rather concerned that the British justice system might include a fine that had to be paid in pigs. This was a notion that Mrs High and Mighty Aldridge rather cruelly sowed in his pedestrian mind. Once he'd had a taste of porridge when his bail was refused, Thomas felt somewhat different. He complained to Tony that he felt lonely in his cell, and then rather contradicted himself by saying that the occupant of the adjacent cell was being sick all night. As a qualified projectile vomiter, he ought to have felt he'd encountered a kindred spirit.

The trial of Tommy was destined to last for an age once the politically correct St Usha arrived to take up his defence. Seeing some fat fees on the horizon, she cheerfully encouraged him to claim that landing one on Deeevid could clearly be justified on the basis that the Bridge Farm pigs were in imminent danger of attack from Brian's triffids. Twelve good men and bonkers could surely be found in Borsetshire to go along with this line. St Usha was in her element, becoming an expert on GM issues overnight and wheeling out all manner of right-on loonies to slag off our beloved triffids.

One of the casualties of Lancastrian 'Trasher' Tommy's illegal exploits was that the 'y' at the end of his name mysteriously disappeared. Spontaneously, all kinds of people began calling him 'Tom'. We can only assume that the 'y' became detached while he was running away from the scene of the crime.

We were hopeful that Tommy would be deservedly convicted

but began to have some doubts about whether this result could be achieved when the prosecuting counsel came out with the devastating argument 'A hippopotamus remains a hippopotamus.' From that point on, it seemed clear that the jury were going to return a perverse verdict.

Perhaps the whole episode over GM crops gave a clue to the usually concealed politics of people in Ambridge. Anyone who was New Labour would agree with Tony Blair that triffids should be regarded as 'The people's triffids', and that having several heads is all part of 'New Britain'. The problem is that in Ambridge all the characters who seem to take that line are the most likely people to be Conservatives, such as Brian and Jennifer. Other pro-triffid people like Cyclops Tugger and Jailbird Carter would probably vote BNP because they think St Usha is taking their jobs. One can understand their point of view, as it is patently obvious that the only obstacle to Jailbird becoming a highly paid solicitor is the presence of Usha. But, above all, the whole GM business served to 'out' yet another Archer criminal in the form of Lancastrian 'Trasher' Tommy – thug and vandal.

The good thing about people in Ambridge is that once they have got something out of their system they let bygones be bygones. Ever since the trial, everyone has kissed and made up and although Brian presumably continues to farm triffids on a fair old scale, it is never mentioned.

That Fisher Woman
The Case Against

No one would ever accuse Archers Anarchists of being anything other than reasoned and balanced, so it may come as a surprise that we have not felt able to accord a Christian acceptance to 'The Reverend' Janet Fisher, despite her presence in Ambridge for a few years. It should be pointed out that the epithet 'That Fisher Woman', which we prefer to abbreviate to a more friendly 'TFW', was originally coined by Joe Grundy, who described her thus before she had so much as set a webbed foot in the village.

Some of the more right-on listeners doubtless think our objections to TFW are rooted in the fact that we are the kind of people who wish to prop up the bar at the MCC without hearing discussion of knitting patterns. Nothing could be further from the truth. The author has been known to create several woollen scarves and, having little more than a passing interest in cricket, would not be unduly concerned if the bar of the MCC took to admitting man-eating tigers. No, the letter columns of our newsletter are regularly peppered with reasoned arguments to suggest that TFW is a sham and an impostor, and this is the case that deserves examination.

No Suitcase
TFW is an androgynous creature who, in common with many

others, arrived in Ambridge totally devoid of any past. Ambridge arrivals are like escaped prisoners of war in that they turn up with just the rudimentary documentation that will suffice to get them into the community. In TFW's case, she came armed with nothing more than a dog collar and a middle-class accent.

Resistance is Futile

Before she arrived there was a healthy campaign waged by the neo-fascist section of the Church of England in Borsetshire. Peggoi Mitford-Woolley was one of the main driving forces behind the resistance to a beskirted vicar. She was ably supported by Derek Fletcher, a silent resident from Glebelands, who had never previously come so close to speaking. A less able couple of supporters were the late unlamented Fat Man Forrest and village idiot Bert Fry. You can add to that the completely useless support of Joe Grundy, who, as a devout Methodist, was rather disqualified from having an opinion. The fact that poor Joe doesn't get to the chapel as often as he ought should not be held against him and can be explained by the complete absence of a place of worship rather than any weakness of will on his part.

The key promoter of TFW was, needless to say, the awful Shulugh, who simpered on in her sanctimonious way and paved the way for her arrival. An extremely unholy alliance rapidly developed between Britain's most promiscuous church warden and the new vicarette. TFW was later to repay this loyalty in spades when Shulugh casually bedded the village doctor, cheated on her boyfriend, Phallustair, and one of her best friends, St Usha, and then coolly demanded a church wedding.

Once TFW arrived, resistance crumbled at an alarming pace. Most of the atheist villagers were pleased to see that organized religion in Ambridge had given way to a kind of pagan social work. It was clear that the only people who truly cared would be those who had a real involvement in the church. TFW cunningly picked these off one by one.

Phil Archer never gives a toss about who's in charge at St Stephen's as long as he can continue to be the organist. He's happily tickled the ivories through the reigns of numerous clergy. Music at the church has always been important to him. There is apparently a full-size cathedral organ in the church and a choir of King's College standards which seems to be comprised not only of silent characters but of non-mentioned ones. And all this is achieved without the expense of a choirmaster.

Derek Fletcher had fought a strong rearguard action against the ordination of women, but eventually even he had to accept that the impact he achieved by speaking out was greatly undermined by not having a voice. His continued silence should not, however, be taken as satisfaction with the new order and were he ever to be granted the power of speech things might be very different.

The most ridiculous capitulation to TFW acceptance was that of Bert Fry. He was wandering around the village telling anyone who would listen, which was generally nobody, of his great aversion to the imminent arrival of a vicarette. Then, on her arrival, she went up to him with a greeting along the lines of, 'Hello, you must be Bert Fry', and he never looked back. It says something for the state of the Church today that the village idiot is deemed to be churchwarden material but when his running mate is Shulugh that really says it all.

To her eternal credit, Peggoi Woolley has remained vaguely hostile to the whole TFW 'project', as modern commentators would describe it. She has to travel some distance for her Sunday worship, since TFW seems to have muscled in on most of the surrounding parishes, such as Penny Hassett and

Darrington. Thus All Saints', Borchester (mysteriously referred to as 'All Souls' by some people in the village) seems to have her custom for the time being. Peggoi has rather let herself down by attending some of the pagan rituals at St Stephens, such as the bizarre funerals of Jaaarn, Fat Man and Pru Forrest, presided over by TFW.

Fisher Fraud

As usual, it has fallen to Archers Anarchists to provide the most informed analysis of the scandals of TFW. We have the good fortune to boast at least three bona fide be-collared clergy among our ranks. Thanks to the diligent research by some of these experts, together with that of some lay God-botherers, we have been able to drive a coach and horses through the current regime at St Stephen's – about as close as Ambridge gets to public transport nowadays.

Several people have had the common sense to check in *Crockford's Clerical Directory*, only to find that there is no entry therein for a Janet Fisher. You might have thought that Bishop Cyril would have taken this basic step himself, rather than assuming that anyone who swans into his bishopric sporting a reversed collar and clutching the good book is a kosher cleric.

We have yet to discover why she is passing herself off as a proper vicarette. Is it to get easy access to the communion wine? Certainly she doesn't seem to be a frequent visitor to The Bull. She seems to have very little sense of duty when it comes to ministering to the sick, troubled or bereaved. This is hardly a full-time job in Ambridge, where illness has generally been something of a rarity, though she kept a low profile when Roooth had her attack of malignant Geordiness and was nowhere to be seen when Loathsome keeled over. There have also been a number of notable absences on the part of TFW when the grim reaper has been anywhere involved.

The late Mrs Barraclough, who was murdered by Dr Death, was not visited by TFW. Indeed TFW was heard to mutter something like, 'I must find time to get over and see her' shortly before Mrs B's death, only to miss the boat by a couple of lethal injections. When Jaaarn did his handbrake turns on the Fergie it was a long while before TFW showed up at Bridge Farm to comfort the bereaved, and the Health and Safety mob were several days ahead of her.

Mad 'n' Bad
TFW has done some very peculiar things that should really have resulted in her being sectioned indefinitely under the Mental Health Act. At the 1999 Palm Sunday Service she actually brought a donkey to the church. Her explanation that it was what Jesus was riding on Palm Sunday was completely unsustainable. By the same token she would have to flood the church to emulate the walking-on-water business, employ all the 'tractor work' whingers (workers in the vineyard parable), beat up a passer-by (good Samaritan) and buy up Borchester Cash and Carry (feeding of the 5K). And if she then got stuck in to the Old Testament it really doesn't bear thinking about – Mike Tugger would really have to be on his guard when she got to 'an eye for an eye'.

TFW is no lover of the country or its ways. She conspired with loony Bert Fry to drive out a bunch of bats from her belfry despite the fact that they are a protected species. It was a particularly un-Christian act to vilify bats who were happily living in belfries in times when the very idea of installing women vicars would have landed you in the Tower of London.

Fat Man Forrest was justifiably outraged by what they were doing, but unfortunately he had reached that age where the only words that would come out whenever he opened his mouth were, 'Oi, want to see moi Pru.' This was unfortunate because, instead of resulting in TFW being hauled before the courts, it just meant that some do-gooder would cart him off to the Laurels.

Keeping Christianity at Bay

One accusation that can never be levelled at the door of TFW is that of trying to spread Christianity around the village. She very rarely speaks of religion, lending weight to the notion that she is indeed a fraud. With typical modesty (TFW is the kind of woman who, if she were a nun, would wear a Day-Glo wimple), she defined 'the key to being a successful vicar' as 'knowing when not to interfere'. If ever there was a cop-out then this must be it, the perfect justification for perpetual indolence.

Good Friday 1999 was a bit of an eye-opener in Ambridge. TFW, with a rare bit of Christian symbolism, had bullied some of the Ambridge menfolk into carrying what she described as a 'replica wooden cross' from Darrington to Ambridge. One might ask what a wooden cross could possibly be a replica of? But it is also questionable whether there was much to be gained by asking people like Neil Carter, his back always bent with toil, to carry a heavy lump of wood around. People like Kathy Perks absolutely lapped it all up. 'She's so human for a vicar,' she drooled, and then by implication made the point that so many of us have felt for ages when she said, 'I'm glad she's making such a feature of Easter this year.' Easter does tend to be quite a big event in most Christian calendars.

Easter Day saw a typically off-the-wall sermon from TFW. She started off reasonably enough with the usual vicarly stuff about remembering the less fortunate rather than stuffing yourself with chocolate. Nothing wrong with that, unless you happen to be a Cadbury's employee. She seems to have a bit of a thing about chocolate because she gave it up for Lent, although she carefully avoided mentioning where her chocolate budget might have been reallocated.

Since thousands of British troops were engaged in NATO attacks on Serbia and the TV screens of our nation were full of harrowing footage of Kosovan refugees, we quite expected that TFW might encourage us to turn our thoughts in that direction. But not a bit of it. TFW wanted the people of Ambridge to cancel Third World debt and twin with an African village, and she had not a single word to say about the crisis facing Europe.

What exactly would be involved in this bizarre twinning practice was unclear. Presumably the main thing would be yet another place name in parenthesis on the 'Ambridge welcomes careful drivers' notice as you enter the village. As Ambridge doesn't really welcome anyone, it is already rather superfluous.

Also, would we have to endure the prospect of sanctimonious busy-bodies like Shulugh setting off for Africa armed to the teeth with Bibles and peace quilts? Or could we look forward to the already cosmopolitan village of Ambridge developing an African quarter and a source of cheap labour to lower further the employment chances of the Carters and Tuggers? It might be quite a good thing after all.

Having asked everyone to think about the Third World at a time when they should have been thinking about the second one, TFW then presided on Easter Monday at a pagan ceremony of the most vulgar nature. During this sinister ritual, children were told to stick two fingers up to the starving and were then forced to roll perfectly good free-range eggs down the slopes of Lakey Hill.

Holidays for the Hungry

TFW frequently displays a rather individual approach to the world's problems and in many cases her solutions are quite bizarre. Clearly eaten up by the problem of Third World debt, she suddenly had a brainwave that would solve the problem at a stroke. She decided to go on a walking holiday to Cologne. Such is her Svengali-like influence on some of her parishioners that she even managed to entice the Hindu St Usha to go with her.

Even the definitely non-cerebral Beddy Tugger felt moved to question is St Usha and TFW walking around would actually 'make any difference', a view echoed by the village elder, Phil Archer. This was obviously a naive question, as we all accepted that this selfless act of going on holiday would fill hundreds of thousands of empty bellies. Given all the pleasant walks that one could embark upon, however, the idea of walking from Birmingham to Cologne could have been considered a rather peculiar choice.

It does, moreover, open a whole new range of opportunities to solve other ills of the world in a similar manner. If we regard a 400-mile walking holiday as sufficient to write off Third World debt, we could confidently assume that an earthquake of say ten on the Richter scale could comfortably be compensated for by a couple of weeks in Butlins. An individual personal tragedy could, of course, require nothing more than a day off work on the part of some well-meaning third party. Even Armageddon could be seen off by a three-week cruise. Fat Clarrie was obviously thinking along the same lines when she commented that, if it would clear her own debts, she'd be perfectly happy to walk barefoot.

Not everyone is prepared to go along with TFW's schemes. Jailbird Carter has rapidly earned a reputation as the conscience of Ambridge ever since she was jailed for aiding and abetting an armed robber and absconding from prison. Remember it was Jailbird who let the rather scrawny cat out of the bag when she said at a public meeting, 'We all know why Dr Locke left the village, don't we?' So, too, it was Jailbird who said that she was not having any of the Jubilee Millennium Project because she didn't believe in ending Third World debt – people should pay their debts.

Such a politically incorrect view would obviously be given little quarter in the PC capital of the universe, but she was not entirely alone. Peggoi 'Call me old-fashioned if you will' (no, you're just a boring old trout, Peggoi) took the view that TFW should be looking after the needs of her parishioners. She described TFW's approach as 'short-sighted' and Jeck was certainly not prepared to support it. More significantly so did Bert Fry, adding 'quite a lot of people feel the same way'. Unfortunately they were the silent majority, a huge and largely impotent force in Ambridge. It might have been thought that Bert would carry some weight as a church warden, but he was clearly overridden by the ghastly Shulugh.

TFW took her holiday at a time when there were at least three people in Ambridge in dire need of succour. We had Pat with her sausage-induced breakdown, Joan Pargetter at risk of her life from El Ladbroke and Mrs Antrobus stumbling around the village asking to go to the bottom of the NHS waiting list.

So, once it became inevitable that TFW was going off on her holiday, that left the minor question of who was going to take church services during her absence? And here we enter the realms of something you just couldn't make up if you tried. Fornicator-in-Chief Shulugh Hebden-Blandvoice was given the job of leading a service. She has no qualifications to do so, unless going the distance with the village doctor behind the back of one of her best friends while supposedly going steady with someone else counts. Or maybe her qualification is simply her conviction – for taking and driving away?

There was a back-up to take the service in case Shulugh was rogering someone else that day, none other than pub quiz cheat Bert Fry. Was the Church of England safe in their hands? Apparently, if all else failed, Clive Horrobin would be let out on licence to do the honours.

The day the walking holiday began turned out to be one of

the most revolting PC exhibitions ever heard on *The Archers*. Half the village were, of course, only too keen to get up at 5.30 am on a Sunday morning and trundle off to Brum, where the walk was starting, to see off St Usha and TFW. All the usual suspects had turned up, including Shulugh and Roooth, who was nauseatingly sycophantic about the whole business.

We were then subjected to 'live sounds' from the march. Being worthy, alternative and protesting in nature, this included a lot of obligatory whistles. It is a very strange phenomenon that protests of this kind always include copious quantities of whistles and it has never been explained whether or not ends are more or less likely to be achieved if accompanied by whistling. To most of us it would never occur that our complaints might be addressed more readily if we refrained from washing for a few days and then began whistling. Come to think of it, if this system were to be used in restaurants, it would probably improve the service no end.

TFW's feigned interest in world poverty is frequently exposed as the sham it is. At harvest time in 1998 she put on the most grotesque display of gluttony when she attended two harvest suppers in the same evening. By the time she arrived in Ambridge from Penny Hassett she was still trying to cram food down her throat, but reached the point where she could eat no more. So did she then begin to gather together what was left in order to re-enact the feeding of the 5K, loading up Eddie's van and departing for Africa? Did she, hell! No, she hid food in the font, aided and abetted by the other phoney God-botherer Shulugh, causing an outbreak of insect infestation in the church.

Not content with using St Stephen's as a larder, TFW has turned it into a tourist office with brochures and advertising. The only person to speak out against this outrage was the reliable Peggoi, but having taken her custom to All Saints' in protest at the very existence of TFW, she is not really in a position to do much about it.

Book Burning

Undaunted and refreshed, TFW stormed back to Ambridge with the devastating news that she intended to replace the hymn books. This was bad news for the traditionalists, as it obviously heralded the introduction of heathen happy-clappy practices designed to drive the last vestiges of Christianity from a village that is desperately crying for release from the ever-growing forces of darkness.

It should be noted that TFW increasingly has an attitude of complete contempt towards poor Bert and any of his views that belies her claims to be an authentic holy Joe. When the poor man stood out against her insistence on introducing these politically correct hymn books, TFW's Christian response was, 'Bert will have to put up and shut up.' In fact there were quite a lot of rumblings about the new hymn books and there was a wonderful moment when she mentioned to someone that the whole business was making her wonder whether she should move on. Sadly, the obvious question 'Can I get your coat?' was never asked.

Tee Hee Hee

TFW has no genuine sense of humour. Her jokes are of the mirthless variety and she has the perpetual giveaway trait of the humourless, which is to tell people that she has got a sense of humour. This is a vital tool in the armoury of the mirthfully challenged since without being told we would never realize that our sides should by now be in danger of splitting.

Work-shy

The lack of effort TFW puts into matters religious is by now legendary but she really excelled herself at the appalling Tugger/Horrible wedding on Labour Day 2001. She had devised a kind of 'do it yourself' format whereby instead of reading out the vows for them to repeat, she simply left them to recite them from memory. This gave us the pathetic spectacle of dullard Roy desperately trying to remember the words, quite a challenge for a bloke who can hardly remember his own name.

Rampant Sex

For some reason that has never been properly explained TFW shares an office with Dr Dim and it soon became clear that she was leading him on like nobody's business. We can only assume she would parade around the surgery in her undies and of course she was always making vaguely suggestive comments. Dim being both a full-blooded male and dim, thought these signs meant that she wanted at least a tongue sandwich and was disappointed when she cried rape.

Luckily Jailbird had thoughtfully advised Bishop Cyril and he turned up to discuss the whole sordid business. You might have thought that there would be some spiritual dimension to this, but all that seemed to bother TFW was 'this could seriously affect my livelihood', yet another sign that she is not the real McCoy. Of course she discussed it all with Shulugh, herself an expert relationship wrecker, during the course of which she admitted that she 'really did fancy' Dim. Shulugh came out with what has to be the most hypocritical comment in 50 years of Ambridge life when she exclaimed 'What is it with these doctors!' Jailbird also appraised Sheyawn of the main details which ensured that the C of E would not be welcoming a convert from Catholicism in the near future. The reprehensible capacity of Ambridge citizens to forgive each other has come into play once again but it would be nice to think we have not heard the last of this one.

Mr Davies's Diary

Mr Davies is a regular visitor to Brookfield, where he and his family avail themselves of the rather spartan Rickyard Cottage. While it is a mystery to many of us why anyone would want to holiday in Ambridge, it does take all sorts and who are we to question them anyway? As luck would have it, Mr Davies was so fraught during one visit in 1999 that he inadvertently left his diary behind and, joy, oh joy, it fell into Anarchist hands. It is not altogether polite to reproduce someone's private diary without their permission, but we are Anarchists after all and are happy to live life on the edge. So here are just a few excerpts from that fateful week.

Saturday

Arrived in Ambridge, via Borchester. We stopped in Borchester to shop and pick up a few provisions. As usual shopping there was a joy. We wanted to go to the Cash and Carry but we didn't have a card so went into the only other shop – Underwoods – which was completely empty apart from Jennifer Aldridge. Parking was easy, as there were only a couple of cars in the multi-storey – both from Ambridge.

As soon as we reached Ambridge we were stopped by paramilitary types who fitted total silencers to the car. We filled in the usual paperwork with all the declarations, agreeing not to use the village shop, The Bull or Grey Gables, and above all not to speak while we were there.

It was nice to be welcomed on arrival by the excited silence of the Brookfield dogs and cats. Dished out cottonwool ear plugs to wife and kids as we had to knock at the door of Brookfield Farmhouse to get the key to the cottage. Even so, Mrs Foghorn caused a great deal of collateral damage to our eardrums as she force-fed scones down our throats without even a by your leave. We had been slightly taken aback when she first greeted us because she shouted, 'What are YOU doing here?' at us, but then we remembered that is the traditional Ambridge greeting – their equivalent of the Eskimos' rubbing noses.

Rickyard Cottage hasn't changed. It's still like Stalag Luft III. We set to work on the inventory. We've been turned over too many times before to get taken in by that one. Just as well we checked. There in black and white was listed a divided vegetable dish, but we searched high and low and it just wasn't there. Bloody typical! All the other crockery and utensils were down to the normal self-catering standard: tin openers that wouldn't be capable of opening a paper bag and unmatching cups and saucers with more chips than a large portion of McDonald's.

Sunday

Woken early by a strange Geordie whingeing sound that combined with an indignant mooing noise to make it impossible for us to sleep. The place was littered with dead hens and there seemed to be more foxes than cattle grazing in the fields. That Foghorn woman really seems to have let the place slide.

We looked at the timetable for buses, only to find it was about forty-eight years out of date. The last bus seen in Ambridge was apparently driven by Walter Gabriel.

One bit of good news, we were able to buy newspapers for the first time. Thanks to a silent but effective campaign by Robert Snell, the village is awash with newspapers. They're all the rage and the local children are silently making papier-mâché models like it's going out of fashion. Apparently there are one or two televisions in the village now and a couple of the children have discovered a new programme called Blue Peter. Mind you, getting the newspapers from the village shop is a rather strange procedure as no one works there on a Sunday. You have to enter via a skylight and leave the money in an honesty box, which seems a bit risky in a lawless place like Ambridge.

No one spoke to us all day. Just seen a mattress go past the window, followed by a strange small creature with horns and a tail. That Shulugh must be visiting Brookfield.

The only other excitement of the day was a trip to St Stephen's, where we were just in time for a special evensong to celebrate St Lucifer. Sacrifices were made, mainly consisting of diseased cattle and a whole string of interesting pagan rituals was enacted. Afterwards we played an exciting game of 'Find the Food' in which various buffet items had been hidden all over the church. The vicarette seems quite a good sort – she didn't mention God or Jesus once, which is so refreshing in a church service.

Monday

Managed to get a copy of Things to Do in Borsetshire, which turned out to be an A6 sheet. We went for a walk up Lakey Hill, but it was rather embarrassing as you just couldn't move for copulating couples. The litter was appalling and I've never seen so many syringes, even in a hospital. The wife just didn't know where to look.

We went on to Hayden Barrow, which was almost as bad. It was like Piccadilly Circus, with earnest couples saying things like, 'Remember when we first came up here?' and 'Do you know, I don't think we've been up here since ****.' In fact it seemed that amnesia had broken out in a big way up there. Desperate for some peace and quiet, we went over to Marneys, only to find Foghorn's husband sitting there trying to break the world record for Large Homely Pack Lunch Consumption.

Tuesday

Had a chat to Foghorn, who told me that she was very conscious of giving her guests the 'full Brookfield experience', but I can see through all that claptrap. It is quite obvious to me that the whole family regards us as a damn nuisance and that we are just there as a cash cow because they are such inefficient farmers. In fact a cash cow is about the only one they've got left.

We decided to go to Grey Gables and that was a strange business. Apparently it was Fornication Day and the manageress of the place was taking part in a Bonkathon. The under-manageress was there, Trudy Porter, but she couldn't speak, which made things a bit difficult. There was a strange sort of Brum/Jewish old man called Jeck, who made noises that sounded like a cow in calf. The food was French nouvelle cuisine so it was two parts of sweet FA served up on a plate the size of a satellite dish. We wanted to have a swim in the health club, but it seemed that ever since the woman from The Bull stopped running it, they had forgotten to replace her. The water in the pool was a funny colour and there seemed to be dogs swimming about in it.

Wednesday

Went to The Bull for lunch and if yesterday was a bit odd, you should just hear this. As we set foot in the door, a woman let out an anguished wail and said, 'Oh, not a couple of customers.' She then said 'I hope you don't want any food because I've got a child and I'm a teacher and I don't want to get my hands dirty cooking for scum like you.' Then a Brummie man who turned out to be her husband jogged in wearing a tracksuit and said, 'All part of the service we like to give in this traditional English village pub. Would you like a game of boules?'

What we actually wanted was a drink. The wife wanted half a lager, but Mr Perks said, 'What? Are you some kind of a homosexual or something? If you want lager you'd better go to the Cat and Fiddle. We don't want your sort here. It's Shires or nothing. All part of the service.' Eventually a silent woman called Freda rustled up a microwaved pie for us. There weren't many people in the pub, just a couple of blokes arguing about 'tractor work'.

Thursday

The wife's birthday. After the Grey Gables and Bull experiences I wasn't sure what to do but suddenly a strange woman called Peggoi appeared on the doorstep. Apparently she specializes in party enforcement. She can organize a *party including a whole crowd of reluctant guests and everyone turns up with a face like a wet weekend saying how much they're enjoying themselves. So we went along with it and Mrs Davies said afterwards she hadn't enjoyed herself so much since she had mumps as a child. You should have been there for the chorus of 'Happy Birthday' - you could have heard a pin drop.*

Friday

That's it, we're off. Today was the last straw. The cottage is just too poorly equipped to be able to cook proper meals, so we had asked if we could have breakfast with the people that the Brookfield crowd affectionately describe as 'The B&B scum'.

We went into Brookfield, where there were some ashen-faced guests, and it turned out that Foghorn had been knee-capped in some kind of demonic revenge attack. We weren't bothered about that, but we were less happy about the knock-on effect. It meant that Roooth was having to cook the breakfast.

Suddenly they announced that they'd had a cosy family meeting and had summarily decided to axe their B&B guests. An armed militia had been raised in the village and we were all escorted out, without even being allowed to take our possessions. Looting took place before our very eyes, with the village riff-raff, such as the Tuggers, Carters, Grundys and Horrobins, picking out what they wanted. Luckily we'd left anything valuable at home, but they were obviously delighted with all our dirty washing and flip-flops. As we left, we heard the sound of the eponymous bridge being blown up to keep out further visitors.

The Great Escape

The foot and mouth outbreak in the spring of 2001 caused great anguish in Ambridge when they finally heard about it. As a precaution, the inhabitants of Brookfield were all interned together with village idiot Bert Fry and a twenty foot high fence of razor wire was erected around the farm. This was supplemented with searchlights and look-out turrets. So the rest of the village should have been gobsmacked when, one Sunday during this period, Foghorn was seen coolly discussing cake outside the church with Horrible Hayley.

All members of the Archer clan accepted the need for the siege conditions. The ghastly Peeep had initially been evacuated to Glebe Cottage to enable her to continue going to school, but she was so alarmed by the evil influences of Damien Hebden-Blandvoice and his stick insects that she rapidly realized that she was in danger of becoming possessed.

After a thorough hosing down with undiluted Jeyes fluid, Peeep was allowed back into Brookfield where Foghorn was immediately appointed as governess. The idea that Foghorn, whose whole existence over seventy years has revolved around the production of scones, cakes and pastries could provide a balanced education according to the National Curriculum defies belief. Even by the unenviable standards of Ambridge, Peeep will clearly have no prospects at all of any profession beyond the oldest one.

Since Foghorn is permanently chained to the Aga except for a thirty-second recreation period each day, it should not have proved too difficult for her to obey the strictures to remain at Brookfield. Yet suddenly she found herself faced with the most awful of temptations. Horrible Hayley, who had enjoyed culinary collusions with Foghorn in the past (murder of Fat Man and Pru etc.), wanted to discuss her wedding cake and just how sickly it should be. Foghorn was desperate to get out of Brookfield for it is widely known that when discussing cake, you need to see the whites of the other person's eyes.

She immediately began to think how she could escape. The obvious solution was to strap herself to the underside of the milk tanker while no one was looking but this could be difficult because she would not know when it was going to stop and she couldn't rely on it conveniently running into Pat. And what if she found herself outside Borsetshire without a passport? She then considered disguise. It would be easy enough to pass herself off as one of Roooth's discarded pizza boxes and hide in the rubbish. Then she remembered that no one collects the rubbish even under normal circumstances.

So she then came up with the brilliant idea of becoming a tractor driver. The line she spun to Deeevid was that she wanted to learn to drive a tractor so that she could 'help'. Dim though he is, even Deeevid found it hard to see why they suddenly needed the services of a seventy-year-old lady as a farm labourer. But of course Foghorn's idea was that she could disappear over the fields and ram her way out of the farm. The one lesson she had was so hopeless that she had to return to the drawing board.

Naturally the final solution was to tunnel her way out. She obviously used Peeep as a lookout while she removed floorboards at Brookfield and dug a tunnel all the way under Jiggins Field, Marneys, etc., emerging surreptitiously somewhere in the churchyard. The whole plot worked like a dream, and Foghorn had correctly judged that when someone said of Horrible Hayley 'Oh she's over there discussing wedding cakes with Jill' this would be the one occasion in the last decade of Ambridge history when nobody would say 'And what are you doing here?'

Get Those Houses Built!

Archers Anarchists are never happier than when we're in sight of a pile of breeze blocks and there's a whiff of cement dust in the air. Over the years we've had our highs and lows as a series of philanthropic people have fought to provide a few more humble dwellings to house Ambridge's growing silent majority.

Many years ago now, Nelson built Hollowtree Flats, but although he lived there himself for a while, no one else apparently has taken up residence there since. It is possible that they have just disappeared to another part of the country, or abroad perhaps, in an Arkwright Hall sort of way.

In the late 1970s, Jeck Woolley, without a thought for himself, successfully fought to get a number of delightful fat cat executive starter homes built, now known as Glebelands. *The Book of The Archers* tells us that this development is near the Village Green and that all but one of the houses were sold before they were built. All the more strange therefore that the only known residents are the Fletchers. The most likely explanation is that all those who bought their homes in advance moved in immediately and as they were already inside and had no need to go out, the builders didn't bother to put any doors in. Obviously the

Fletchers bought the last house and it was necessary to provide a door so they could get in. Support for this theory came from a recent reference by Roooth to not wanting 'a strange girl from Glebelands' to babysit Peeep. If your formative years had been spent in a doorless house, you might be verging towards the odd.

Anarchists were spitting architrave at the failure of a later campaign to build houses at Sawyers Farm. On that occasion the Nimbys really got their act together and it ended in bitter disappointment for all worshippers of Blue Circle. It was obvious that Sawyers Farm itself was a bit cut up over the whole business because it went into a deep sulk and left the village in a huff.

But if we were to choose one man to lead us into battle, we could never have wished for a better, more committed developer than Mr Matthew Crawford. Matt is the most loveable character ever to have appeared in Ambridge. He works hard and gropes hard. And he has the foresight to realize that in a village where people have begun to breed like rabbits in recent years and where half the houses don't have doors, there is going to be a rather urgent need for somewhere to live.

Gem that he is, Matt managed to identify a site that would cause the renaming of Glebe Cottage to 'Wall View'. To inflict planning blight on an Archer is an act of true heroism. To set Archer against Archer and cosy villager against smug villager is even better.

The hypocrisy of so many Ambridge residents has been brilliantly encapsulated. The first objectors were Jeck and Peggoi, the same Jeck who had trousered a few quid when Glebelands was built. The dreadful Mrs Haveitaway who had thought nothing of sticking a tacky extension on her house without bothering with planning permission was immediately outspoken against Matt's little enterprise.

Most of the whingeing villagers leading the opposition to the closure of Loxley Barret School were too stupid to realize that their cause might be helped by having a few more brats to send there. And it needed Brain of Borsetshire, Moike Tugger, to bellow it out.

One or two of the younger people such as Horrible Hayley were impressed by the planning gain and assumed that she and Racist Roy would automatically be in line for one of the prole houses that Matt proposes to throw in, built to 1950s Soviet specifications with wall-to-wall low-grade asbestos. Jailbird Carter took a similar line, having an eye on these hovels for Elephant Man and Emmer in due course.

Bolstered by the good business sense of Doreen Rogers, Sid has been wise enough to give quiet encouragement to the development.

But when you are handing out prizes in recognition of severely induced nausea, the revolting Shulugh Hebden-Blandvoice is never far away. In this case her fat posterior was spread well and truly over the fence. Desperate to sell Glebe Cottage to her parents (a house she had acquired gratis, if you please, by murdering her grandmother) for as much dosh as possible, she tried to convince Foghorn that having a wall as your main view was a good thing. This is because she fancied the idea of a load of Tamaras and Phillipas moving in to Crawford Villas, all gagging for horse-riding lessons. As we recall from when she was screwing Dr Death, she doesn't like not being universally popular, so we have had to endure endless displays of equivocation as she won't dare come out fully in support of Matt.

At the time of writing we are still in the relatively early stages of the planning application, but if there is anything in our humble way that we can do to get those houses built, rest assured we'll strain every sinew. We want to see bribery, corruption, the lot — the whole due process of a normal planning application. Come on Matt, you know you can do it. We want to see those bulldozers roll.